Keep this book. You will
need it and use it throughout
your career.

HOSPITALITY SUPERVISION

Second Edition

Educational Institute Courses

Introductory

INTRODUCTION TO THE HOSPITALITY INDUSTRY
Fourth Edition
Gerald W. Lattin

AN INTRODUCTION TO HOSPITALITY TODAY
Third Edition
Rocco M. Angelo, Andrew N. Vladimir

TOURISM AND THE HOSPITALITY INDUSTRY
Joseph D. Fridgen

Rooms Division

FRONT OFFICE PROCEDURES
Fifth Edition
Michael L. Kasavana, Richard M. Brooks

HOUSEKEEPING MANAGEMENT
Second Edition
Margaret M. Kappa, Aleta Nitschke, Patricia B. Schappert

Human Resources

HOSPITALITY SUPERVISION
Second Edition
Raphael R. Kavanaugh, Jack D. Ninemeier

HOSPITALITY INDUSTRY TRAINING
Second Edition
Lewis C. Forrest, Jr.

HUMAN RESOURCES MANAGEMENT
Second Edition
Robert H. Woods

Marketing and Sales

MARKETING OF HOSPITALITY SERVICES
William Lazer, Roger Layton

HOSPITALITY SALES AND MARKETING
Third Edition
James R. Abbey

CONVENTION MANAGEMENT AND SERVICE
Fifth Edition
Milton T. Astroff, James R. Abbey

MARKETING IN THE HOSPITALITY INDUSTRY
Third Edition
Ronald A. Nykiel

Accounting

UNDERSTANDING HOSPITALITY ACCOUNTING I
Fourth Edition
Raymond Cote

UNDERSTANDING HOSPITALITY ACCOUNTING II
Third Edition
Raymond Cote

BASIC FINANCIAL ACCOUNTING FOR THE HOSPITALITY INDUSTRY
Raymond S. Schmidgall, James W. Damitio

MANAGERIAL ACCOUNTING FOR THE HOSPITALITY INDUSTRY
Fourth Edition
Raymond S. Schmidgall

Food and Beverage

FOOD AND BEVERAGE MANAGEMENT
Second Edition
Jack D. Ninemeier

QUALITY SANITATION MANAGEMENT
Ronald F. Cichy

FOOD PRODUCTION PRINCIPLES
Jerald W. Chesser

FOOD AND BEVERAGE SERVICE
Second Edition
Ronald F. Cichy, Paul E. Wise

HOSPITALITY PURCHASING MANAGEMENT
William P. Virts

BAR AND BEVERAGE MANAGEMENT
Lendal H. Kotschevar, Mary L. Tanke

FOOD AND BEVERAGE CONTROLS
Fourth Edition
Jack D. Ninemeier

General Hospitality Management

HOTEL/MOTEL SECURITY MANAGEMENT
Raymond C. Ellis, Jr., Security Committee of AH&MA

HOSPITALITY LAW
Third Edition
Jack P. Jefferies

RESORT MANAGEMENT
Second Edition
Chuck Y. Gee

INTERNATIONAL HOTEL MANAGEMENT
Chuck Y. Gee

HOSPITALITY INDUSTRY COMPUTER SYSTEMS
Third Edition
Michael L. Kasavana, John J. Cahill

MANAGING FOR QUALITY IN THE HOSPITALITY INDUSTRY
Robert H. Woods, Judy Z. King

CONTEMPORARY CLUB MANAGEMENT
Edited by Joe Perdue for the Club Managers Association of America

Engineering and Facilities Management

FACILITIES MANAGEMENT
David M. Stipanuk, Harold Roffman

HOSPITALITY INDUSTRY ENGINEERING SYSTEMS
Michael H. Redlin, David M. Stipanuk

HOSPITALITY ENERGY AND WATER MANAGEMENT
Robert E. Aulbach

HOSPITALITY SUPERVISION

Second Edition

Raphael R. Kavanaugh, Ed.D., CHA
Jack D. Ninemeier, Ph.D., CHA

EDUCATIONAL INSTITUTE
American Hotel & Motel Association

Disclaimer

This publication is designed to provide accurate and authoritative information in regard to the subject matter covered. It is sold with the understanding that the publisher is not engaged in rendering legal, accounting, or other professional service. If legal advice or other expert assistance is required, the services of a competent professional person should be sought.

—*From the Declaration of Principles jointly adopted by the American Bar Association and a Committee of Publishers and Associations*

The authors, Raphael R. Kavanaugh and Jack D. Ninemeier, are solely responsible for the contents of this publication. All views expressed herein are solely those of the authors and do not necessarily reflect the views of the Educational Institute of the American Hotel & Motel Association (the Institute) or the American Hotel & Motel Association (AH&MA).

Nothing contained in this publication shall constitute a standard, an endorsement, or a recommendation of the Institute or AH&MA. The Institute and AH&MA disclaim any liability with respect to the use of any information, procedure, or product, or reliance thereon by any member of the hospitality industry.

Project Editor: Priscilla J. Wood
Editor: Jim Purvis

Contents

Congratulations. . .

You have a running start on a fast-track career!

Developed through the input of industry and academic experts, this course gives you the know-how hospitality employers demand. Upon course completion, you will earn the respected American Hotel & Motel Association certificate that ensures instant recognition worldwide. It is your link with the global hospitality industry.

You can use your AH&MA certificate to show that your learning experiences have bridged the gap between industry and academia. You will have proof that you have met industry-driven learning objectives and that you know how to apply your knowledge to actual hospitality work situations.

By earning your course certificate, you also take a step toward completing the highly respected learning programs—Certificates of Specialization, the Hospitality Operations Certificate, and the Hospitality Management Diploma—that raise your professional development to a higher level. Certificates from these programs greatly enhance your credentials, and a permanent record of your course and program completion is maintained by the Educational Institute.

We commend you for taking this important step. Turn to the Educational Institute for additional resources that will help you stay ahead of your competition.

Preface

The hospitality industry has undergone many changes since the first edition of this book was released in 1984. Our industry will continue to be a dynamic one as it stretches to meet the expectations of an increasingly demanding consumer public. The constant changes to be implemented in the hospitality industry as we move toward the year 2000 will have tremendous implications for supervisors. All of those involved in supervising the activities of others will have higher-than-ever demands placed on them that will test their flexibility, increased technical competence, and ever-important human relations skills.

The hospitality industry remains labor-intensive. Staff members at all organizational levels are needed to produce the goods and services offered to guests by a lodging and food service operation. Most of these employees are entry-level personnel who interact constantly with guests. Their work is directed by supervisors who, in many cases, were promoted to their current positions based on their abilities to get results in positive ways. First-level supervisors and managers are essential to the ongoing success of any hospitality operation.

Hospitality Supervision is designed to explain the principles of supervision as they apply specifically to the hospitality industry. Supervisors are confronted daily with demands handed down to them from higher management levels, guests, and government agencies. At the same time, demands are pushing upward from the employees they supervise. This edition will help supervisors deal with these demands. In addition, this book has a number of unique features designed to meet the immediate, as well as long-term, career goals of hospitality supervisors.

The basic principles of management are clearly explained, as well as their practical applications in a day-to-day work setting. The text further provides relevant examples of proven ways to get maximum results through responsible supervision and management.

To ensure an accurate delivery of these management principles in real-life hospitality industry terms, a committee of distinguished hospitality industry executives provided us with guidance and technical assistance throughout the project. We owe a great deal of gratitude to Marc Clark, Director of Training, Opryland Hotel, Nashville, Tennessee, and to Patricia Dove, Vice President of Training, Red Roof Inns, Inc., Hilliard, Ohio. These individuals thoroughly reviewed chapters and provided us with quality feedback and excellent industry examples of supervision at work.

James E. Hart, Vice President of Operations, Mississippi Management, Inc., Jackson, Mississippi, and Michael B. Mallott, Manager, System Education, Hampton Inn Hotels Corporate Office, Memphis, Tennessee, served as reviewers for the first edition as well as for the second edition. They supplied direction and comments which enhanced the second edition.

In addition, we wish to thank the following committee members for their significant contributions to the text: Deb Steffes, Senior Management Development

Instructor, Best Western International, Inc., Phoenix, Arizona; John Bazemore, Management Development Specialist, Days Inns of America, Inc., Atlanta, Georgia; John Mayotte, Director of Training, Marriott Hotels and Resorts, Marriott Corporation, Washington, D.C.; Michael Norris, Area Supervisor, Red Lobster Restaurants, Farmington Hills, Michigan; and Wayne Romanowski, Personnel Director, Hyatt Regency—Dearborn, Dearborn, Michigan.

Study Tips for Users of
Educational Institute Courses

Learning is a skill, like many other activities. Although you may be familiar with many of the following study tips, we want to reinforce their usefulness.

Your Attitude Makes a Difference

If you want to learn, you will: it's as simple as that. Your attitude will go a long way in determining whether or not you do well in this course. We want to help you succeed.

Plan and Organize to Learn

- Set up a regular time and place for study. Make sure you won't be disturbed or distracted.

- Decide ahead of time how much you want to accomplish during each study session. Remember to keep your study sessions brief; don't try to do too much at one time.

Read the Course Text to Learn

- *Before* you read each chapter, read the chapter outline and the learning objectives. If there is a summary at the end of the chapter, you should read it to get a feel for what the chapter is about.

- Then, go back to the beginning of the chapter and *carefully* read, focusing on the material included in the learning objectives and asking yourself such questions as:

  —Do I understand the material?

  —How can I use this information now or in the future?

- Make notes in margins and highlight or underline important sections to help you as you study. Read a section first, then go back over it to mark important points.

- Keep a dictionary handy. If you come across an unfamiliar word that is not included in the textbook glossary, look it up in the dictionary.

- Read as much as you can. The more you read, the better you read.

Testing Your Knowledge

- Test questions developed by the Educational Institute for this course are designed to measure your knowledge of the material.

- End-of-the-chapter Review Quizzes help you find out how well you have studied the material. They indicate where additional study may be needed. Review Quizzes are also helpful in studying for other tests.

- Prepare for tests by reviewing:

  —learning objectives

  —notes

  —outlines

  —questions at the end of each assignment

- As you begin to take any test, read the test instructions *carefully* and look over the questions.

  We hope your experiences in this course will prompt you to undertake other training and educational activities in a planned, career-long program of professional growth and development.

Part I

A Framework for Supervision

Chapter Outline

Definition of Management
    Levels of Management
    Basic Management Principles
The Components of Management
    Planning
    Organizing
    Coordinating
    Staffing
    Directing
    Controlling
    Evaluating
Skills for Effective Supervision
    Technical
    Human Relations
    Conceptual
    Why Supervisors Fail
Supervisory Responsibilities
    Your Boss
    Employees
    Guests
    Other Professionals
    Yourself
Keys to Supervisory Success

Learning Objectives

1. Define management and identify three management levels.

2. Define authority, responsibility, and delegation.

3. List and describe the seven components of management.

4. Define planning, organizing, coordinating, staffing, directing, controlling, and evaluating.

5. Identify three skills necessary for effective supervision.

6. Describe the top three reasons supervisors fail.

7. Describe supervisory responsibilities.

8. Identify keys to supervisory success.

1

The Supervisor and the Management Process

IN THE HOSPITALITY INDUSTRY the term **supervisor** generally refers to someone who manages entry-level or other employees who do not have supervisory responsibilities. For example, a head cook supervises entry-level cooks; housekeeping supervisors are responsible for room attendants.

Supervisors have pressures placed on them by many groups (see Exhibit 1.1). Supervisors are confronted with demands not only from their employees, but from government agencies, higher management levels, guests, internal staff departments, and, if the property is unionized, union officials. "Demanding" can certainly be added to the description of a supervisor's job!

As a hospitality supervisor you must know and understand basic principles of **management** and apply them while managing the resources of a lodging or food service operation. The management process is essentially the same in any type of business and at all management levels in an organization, even if the organizational goals and the work environments of businesses differ. While this book will focus on directing the work of employees, you should understand that directing is only one of the management tasks supervisors perform.

As a supervisor you must have most technical skills, or at least be familiar with them. However, much of your time and effort will go toward managing the work of others, effectively dealing with your employees on a personal and professional level, and making decisions. This chapter will define management, outline basic management principles, and also discuss the components of management. It will discuss the technical, human relations, and conceptual aspects of your job and spell out your supervisory responsibilities. The top three reasons supervisors fail are given so that you may recognize and avoid them. After all, supervisors are made, not born.

Definition of Management

Management is the process of using what you have to do what you want to do. What you have are resources; what you want to do is meet organizational objectives.

Resources are the assets of lodging and food service operations. There are seven basic resource categories:

1. People
2. Money

3

Exhibit 1.1   Demands on the Supervisor

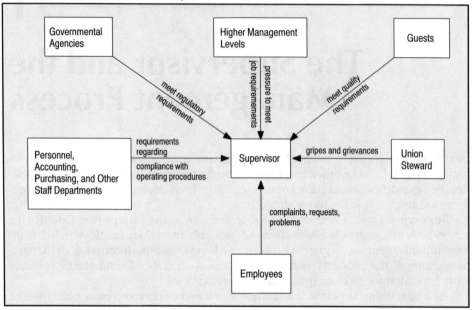

3. Time

4. Work procedures and methods

5. Energy

6. Materials (food and beverage products, room linens, etc.)

7. Equipment

All resources are in limited supply. No supervisor has all the resources he/she needs. Therefore, your job becomes one of determining the best way to use your limited resources to reach organizational goals.

Organizational goals ("what you want to do") outline what the hospitality operation wishes to accomplish and indicate why the business exists. Typical goals include:

- Increasing profits (for commercial operations) or lowering costs (for institutional operations)

- Defining and attaining quality standards for products and services

- Maintaining or creating a good public image

General organizational goals vary among properties. Even so, it's important at all properties that supervisors and managers at every level know what they are supposed to accomplish. Once they have a clear idea of what the organization's goals are, they can develop strategies to reach them.

Exhibit 1.2 Management Levels

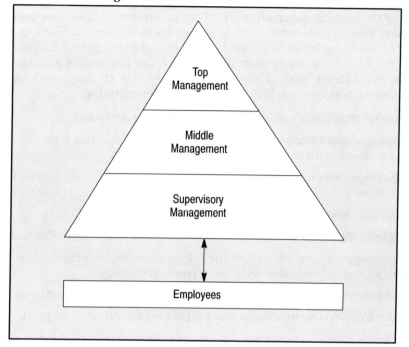

Levels of Management

There are three levels of management at most hospitality properties: top, middle, and supervisory (see Exhibit 1.2). Whether a management position is a top, middle, or supervisory position varies among properties. For example, in a privately owned hotel the general manager and perhaps the assistant or resident manager might be considered top managers. Department heads might be viewed as middle managers. Any other staff members whose duties, in part, involve directing employees could be classified as supervisors. But in a large company with many properties, there may be a Board of Directors, a Chief Executive Officer (CEO), and national and regional managers who would be considered top managers. General managers as well as department heads in individual properties might then be considered middle managers.

For our purposes we will consider management levels from the perspective of the property. At the property level, the general manager and assistant general manager are considered top managers. Department heads are classified as middle managers. All other staff members whose duties involve managing employees are classified as supervisors.

As a supervisor, you are critical to the success of the organization. You represent middle and top managers to your employees. Conversely, you also represent your employees to higher managers. As you can see, you are a linking pin, and to a large extent control the flow of communication up and down the organization.

Basic Management Principles

Many of the basic management principles that supervisors use have been known for many years. While some of these principles have been modified to meet the needs of changing business organizations, the underlying foundations of these principles have held steady over time. One of the pioneers of management research, Henri Fayol, studied management more than 60 years ago. Among his management principles are many that are still relevant today:

- *Concept of authority*—managers must be able to give orders.
- *Organizational hierarchy*—the line of authority should run from top management down to the lowest organizational levels.
- *Discipline*—employees must respect rules and policies that govern the organization.
- *Unity of command*—each employee should have only one boss.
- *Unity of direction*—only one plan should be used to attain an objective.
- *Common good*—the interests of the organization are more important than the interests of individual employees or employee groups.
- *Compensation*—fair wage and salary administration plans must be used.
- *Centralization*—many management processes should be centralized.
- *Division of labor*—employees should specialize in specific work tasks.
- *Matching*—employees should be placed in the positions most suitable for them.
- *Staff stability*—high employee turnover rates lead to inefficiency.
- *Employee initiative*—employees should be given some freedom to develop and implement plans.
- *Team spirit*—when employees work together as a team, a sense of unity can develop that will benefit the organization.[1]

The next sections will discuss three management principles—authority, delegation, and responsibility—more fully.

Authority. Authority is the power an organization gives to a supervisor to do something or to get something done. For example, a front desk supervisor has the authority to schedule and assign tasks to his/her employees; a supervisor in the purchasing department has the authority to buy products and services for the organization, within limits established by top managers.

There are two types of authority: formal and informal. **Formal authority** comes with the position a person holds in the organization. **Informal** or personal **authority** is the power you have because of your abilities and personal traits. If you are a supervisor with excellent technical skills, charisma, lots of excellent ideas, or other unusually good or attractive traits, then you may have personal authority to go along with your formal authority.

Exhibit 1.3 The Management Process

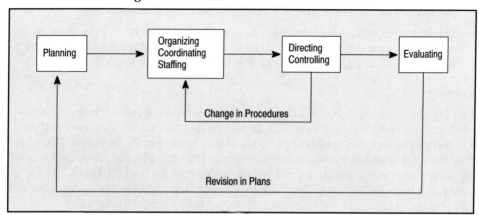

Delegation. Delegation is the act of assigning a task to another person. Sometimes authority is delegated also if the authority is necessary to get the work done. Since you can't personally perform all of the tasks that are assigned to your department or work area, delegating is obviously an important part of your job. Usually, tasks should be assigned to the lowest level at which employees have the ability and information necessary to complete them.

Responsibility. Those with formal authority are held accountable for the use of that authority. When you accepted your promotion to supervisor, you also accepted the responsibility that goes with the position. Supervisors are evaluated on how well they accomplish the tasks assigned to them. Some tasks you can accomplish alone; you need the help of your employees to accomplish the others. You can delegate a task or parts of a task to your employees. Even when you delegate a task, you are ultimately responsible for your employees' performances. If they fail to accomplish a task that you delegate to them, it will be your failure as well, since the task was not completed as required. Being responsible or held accountable for the actions of their employees is one of the hard facts of life for supervisors and managers.

The Components of Management

We'll discuss management by separating it into components. The basic management components are planning, organizing, coordinating, staffing, directing, controlling, and evaluating. Each component (sometimes called a function or activity) defines what a manager must be able to do. Exhibit 1.3 illustrates the sequential nature of these components. In practice, the components are interrelated. We will discuss these components individually. When you look at Exhibit 1.3, note the following:

- Planning leads to organizing, coordinating, and staffing.

- When planning, organizing, coordinating, and staffing tasks are completed, directing and controlling activities can begin. Sometimes changes in organizing, coordinating, and staffing procedures come about because of discoveries you make during the directing and controlling process.

- The last task, evaluating, assesses how well objectives have been met. After evaluation, you can make new plans to achieve new objectives or map out a different plan of attack if you did not achieve the first objective.

Planning

The **planning** process begins with top managers, who must create broad organizational goals to help managers and employees focus on what the property is trying to accomplish. Top and middle managers then create specific objectives that become the responsibility of various departments. For example, top managers working with department heads may develop an operating budget that calls for a substantial increase in sales. Revenue-producing departments such as rooms or food and beverage must then develop strategies for increasing their sales.

A second level of planning occurs when routine operating procedures are established. Such recurring situations as cleaning rooms or serving food and beverage products require standard plans that can be used frequently. These plans are often made by middle managers—department heads, for example—working with supervisors.

Daily activities require a third level of planning. For example, employee schedules must be written. Plans must also be generated for special events, new training programs, and other activities. Supervisors are responsible for much of this type of planning.

Effective planning incorporates the following principles:

- Goals must be established before plans can be developed.
- You must regularly set aside time to plan. It should be done as an important part of your job, not only when time permits.
- All the necessary information should be gathered before plans are developed.
- Planning should be done at the appropriate organizational level. It's not good use of a top manager's time to write employee schedules, for example. On the other hand, only top managers can develop strategic, long-range plans.
- You should be allowed to contribute to plans that affect your work. In turn, you should allow your employees to contribute to plans that affect their jobs.
- You should be flexible when planning. You should recognize that situations change and that other plans must be considered.
- Plans must be implemented. At the appropriate time, you must act with the best plan available.

Organizing

Organizing involves establishing the flow of authority and communication between people and organizational levels. Further, it specifies relationships between positions in the property. The sample organization chart in Exhibit 1.4 shows each position in a 350-room hotel and how it relates to the others.

Exhibit 1.4 Sample Organization Chart for a 350-Room Hotel

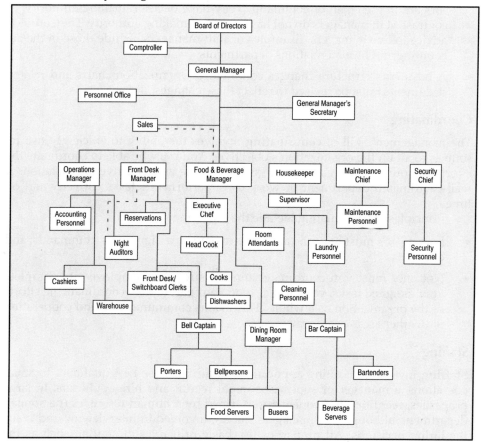

General organizing principles and responsibilities include the following:

- Authority should flow in an unbroken line from the top to the bottom of the organization.

- Each employee should have only one supervisor.

- Relationships between departments in the organization must be considered when managers organize. Events in one department often have an impact on other departments. All departments depend on other departments to some degree.

- Similar activities should be grouped together to structure departments within the property. For example, activities relating to rooms can be categorized into front desk and housekeeping departments.

- Similar tasks should be grouped together to create a position within a department. A position or job is a group of tasks to be performed by one person.

- Line managers such as the general manager, department heads, and supervisors are in the chain of command. They have decision-making authority. In contrast, staff managers do not have decision-making authority. They provide advice to line managers. Examples of staff managers include those in the accounting and human relations departments.

- A business's structure changes continually. Organization charts and related documents must be revised to reflect these changes.

Coordinating

The management skill of **coordinating** involves the ability to efficiently use resources to attain the organization's objectives. You must be able to coordinate the efforts of your employees through good planning and effective organization. A well-coordinated department or work crew performs its tasks correctly and on time.

Principles of coordinating include the following:

- Supervisors must have the authority to enforce assignments, commands, and decisions.

- Not only must you coordinate your resources and employees to complete your assigned tasks, you must also do your part to help coordinate the efforts of the organization as a whole. This means communicating and cooperating with other areas and departments.

Staffing

Staffing involves recruiting applicants and hiring those best qualified. In small operations, a manager or supervisor might recruit and hire applicants. In large properties, recruiting is frequently performed by a human resources (personnel) department, although line managers still are involved in interviewing and make the hiring decisions. All properties use basic principles of staffing such as the following:

- Jobs must be defined according to the specific tasks to be performed. Job tasks are listed in job descriptions.

- Personal qualities needed to adequately perform job tasks must also be considered. These are recorded in job specifications.

- All possible sources of job applicants should be considered.

- Job application forms should be used to collect information about applicants.

- Applicants should be screened. Tests can be used to assess the abilities of applicants. Preliminary interviews and reference checks will also help eliminate unqualified applicants.

- Employee orientation, training, and evaluation programs should be developed and implemented.

- Decisions about transfers, promotions, and demotions are part of the staffing process.

Directing

Directing includes all the activities necessary to oversee, motivate, train, evaluate, and discipline employees. Most of the remaining chapters in this book focus on some aspect of directing employees. Directing incorporates the following principles:

- The number of employees each supervisor directs should be carefully determined. There is no formula for calculating the optimum number of employees for each supervisor. The right number of employees depends on many variables, including the supervisor's experience, complexity of the work, and frequency with which problems are likely to occur. No supervisor should be given more people than he/she can handle.

- Employees must know what they are expected to do.

- Organizational goals are easier to attain when they mesh with some of the personal goals of employees.

- Delegation—the act of giving formal organizational authority to an employee—is a directing technique.

- Directing includes motivating your employees. Keep in mind that your attitude affects employee attitudes and performances.

- Procedures for employee discipline should include positive reinforcement as well as a variety of actions that you can use to help employees correct improper behavior. These actions range from informal counseling to termination.

- Don't relate to all employees the same way. Your leadership style should vary according to employee needs.

- It's important to gain employee cooperation. You should treat employees fairly and honestly.

- Solicit employee ideas and, whenever possible, use them.

- Show your appreciation to employees who perform their jobs well.

Controlling

Controlling helps to ensure that you are attaining your objectives. The control process begins with establishing performance standards, continues with assessing actual performance, and then involves making a comparison between performance standards and actual performance to determine whether—and to what extent—corrective action is necessary. Control is based on several principles:

- Operating budgets are the most important control tools.

- Preventive controls are more effective than controls imposed after things go wrong.

- Control cannot be accomplished until budget restrictions or performance standards have been set.

Exhibit 1.5 Relative Importance of Technical, Human Relations, and Conceptual Skills

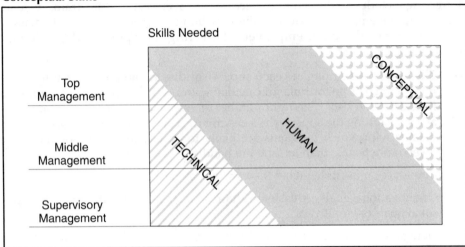

- Control depends on setting intermediate deadlines or goals to help you know whether you are on track. If you miss an intermediate deadline or goal, identify and resolve whatever problem or situation is hindering you.
- Corrective action is necessary when an employee's performance does not meet the organization's standards.
- The worst problems or obstacles to realizing your objectives should be handled first.

Evaluating

Evaluating means looking at how well you and your employees achieved your objectives. Many supervisors evaluate haphazardly or overlook this management task entirely. Evaluating principles include the following:

- Time to evaluate must be set aside regularly.
- Evaluation helps to establish new objectives.
- Input from guests and others outside the property is useful in the evaluation process.
- Evaluation helps in the assignment of organizational resources.

Skills for Effective Supervision

A supervisor needs three basic types of skills: technical, human relations, and conceptual. Exhibit 1.5 shows the amount of technical, human relations, and conceptual skills necessary for all levels of management. Note that, while supervisors need more technical skills and fewer conceptual skills than do middle or top managers, they need the same amount of human relations skills. That's because all levels of managers must meet their objectives through working effectively through others.

Technical

Technical skills are the skills you need to perform your job and effectively supervise the work of your employees. While technical skills are not the major factor in determining supervisory success, they are necessary. To train employees and direct them in their work, you must know how to do the work and be able to recognize when it's being done correctly.

Supervisors, however, may not be required to have the ability to perform employee jobs as fast or efficiently as their employees. It can be argued that supervisors must know only the basic components of their employees' jobs, understand job performance standards, and be able to recognize the extent to which their employees are meeting those standards. However, it is often easier to command employee respect if you are good at most of their jobs, if not all of them. As mentioned, such knowledge can add to your personal authority.

Human Relations

When one considers the list of **human relations skills** that a supervisor must possess, it's easy to understand why it's difficult to be a good supervisor. The art of dealing with employees begins with understanding your responsibility as a supervisor and continues with mastering the topics covered in the following chapters of this book. It's no wonder that many supervisors in the hospitality industry have more difficulty acquiring and applying human relations skills than they do technical skills. Human relations skills include communication, leadership, understanding of how people work in groups, and so on.

Conceptual

You must be able to understand all the management components and how they relate to and affect your work. You must be able to conceptualize problems as well as possible ways to solve them. To do this, you must be able to gather and study a great deal of information, relate one situation to another, and draw on personal experiences and those of others. Much of the supervisor's work, then, involves intellectual or **conceptual skills.**

Decision-Making. The ability to make a decision is one of a supervisor's most important conceptual skills. Some decisions are relatively easy to make. For example, if you have a staffing guide that tells you how many room attendants to schedule for a given occupancy rate, it's easy to decide how many attendants to schedule when, for example, an 80 percent occupancy rate is forecast. Other decisions are more difficult to make. For example, how can labor costs in your work section be reduced to meet a tough new operating budget? To comply with the budget, a great deal of research and thought, involving a re-evaluation of standard operating procedures, performance standards, scheduling practices, training programs, and other areas will be necessary.

When you are facing a decision, ask yourself several questions:

- *Is it my decision to make?* Generally, the closer to its origin that a problem is resolved, the better the decision is likely to be. A general rule is to pass as few decisions as possible upward and to pass as many decisions as possible downward.

- *Is this an easy decision to make?* Wise supervisors save time for more important matters by delegating the authority to make easy decisions to someone else. If you can't delegate, you should at least make the easy decisions quickly and move on.

- *What are the consequences of the decision?* Generally, the more important the consequences, the more resources you should commit to investigating the situation and making a decision.

- *Have I allowed a reasonable amount of time for making the decision?* Hasty decisions can lead to trouble. Taking time for careful study and analysis can often yield better alternatives.

- *Am I looking for the perfect solution?* Often, there are only satisfactory solutions to problems in the real world, not perfect solutions. Supervisors often waste a lot of time trying to find the elusive "perfect" solution when a satisfactory solution will do.

Supervisors can make decisions (and resolve problems) by using two different methods. The **programmed decision-making method** involves using procedure manuals, staffing guides, and job descriptions already developed to handle routine, repetitive situations or problems such as how many employees to schedule for a banquet, how to check in a walk-in guest, and so on. There are few options, if any, and there are guides to turn to, so these decisions are easy to make.

Non-programmed decision-making methods are used for non-routine types of decisions or problems. These methods call for the use of reasoning, judgment, creativity, intuition, and past experiences. New, tough, or unusual problems call for a non-programmed decision-making approach.

Why Supervisors Fail

You may be surprised to learn that an inability to perform technical aspects of the job is not among the top three reasons that supervisors fail. The primary reason supervisors fail is an inability to effectively manage and relate to their employees.[2] When a supervisor does not get along with his/her employees, low productivity, low morale, and high employee turnover are the likely results. In these circumstances, work probably is not completed on time, nor does it meet quality standards. This affects the supervisor's professional reputation and the relationship between the supervisor and his/her boss. If you are not performing to expectations, you will probably not be considered for promotion and eventually you may find yourself looking for another job.

Supervisors also fail because of character and personality shortcomings. Supervisors who are prejudiced, have low self-esteem, or have other personality problems may not be able to handle the responsibilities and pressures associated with the job.

Lastly, an inability to perform the basic management tasks—planning, organizing, coordinating, staffing, directing, controlling, and evaluating—can cause serious problems for supervisors. Again, the story is the same. If you fall short in any or all of these management tasks, your job performance will suffer, your relationship with your employees and boss will suffer, and the quantity and quality of your work and the work of your employees will suffer.

All supervisors can improve their skills. Supervisors are made, not born. You can learn how to manage employees and perform other management activities more effectively and efficiently by applying the basic principles of supervision and management described in this book. In addition, you can learn a great deal by copying the behavior of successful managers and leaders in your organization. As your competence grows, so will your confidence that you are helping your organization meet its goals.

Supervisory Responsibilities

Supervisors do not work in a vacuum. You are responsible to various individuals inside and outside the organization. The most important of these include your boss, employees, guests, other professionals, and yourself.

Your Boss

Everyone has a boss. Your boss reports to someone. Even the owner(s) of your property must answer to a large number of government agencies and, possibly, stockholders as well.

You are responsible to your boss for performing assigned work tasks. You help your boss and the organization fulfill objectives by meeting deadlines, quality standards, and other expectations; operating within budget limitations; following company policies; maintaining records; writing reports in a timely fashion; and so on.

You should be respectful to your boss and accept reasonable assignments without complaint. Think about how you would like your employees to treat you. You should treat your boss in much the same way.

Since you must implement the plans and procedures of your boss and other higher managers, you must be cooperative. The saying, "If you are not part of the solution, you are part of the problem," is one supervisors would do well to recall. If you constantly argue with your boss about his/her plans, resist necessary changes, or are otherwise uncooperative, you are not meeting your responsibility as a team player to get the job done.

Employees

You have responsibilities to your employees as well as your boss. First, you should recognize employees as individual human beings with differing backgrounds, interests, and needs. To the extent you do this, you help the organization, the employees, and yourself. Employees who are treated as individuals and not just "warm bodies" usually have higher morale and productivity. Other responsibilities to employees include:

- Providing a safe working environment.

- Adequately representing employees to higher managers.

- Disciplining in a positive and fair manner.

- Being consistent and fair in all decisions that affect your employees.

- Providing opportunities for career development. This includes whatever assistance is necessary to help a deserving employee get ahead.

Guests

You have an obligation to look at the organization as a whole, your work, and the work of your employees from your guests' perspectives. You should ask questions such as, "If I were a guest, what kind of products and services would I want? At what quality level?" To the extent that you can answer these questions and improve your own and your employees' performances, you will be fulfilling your responsibility to guests.

Other Professionals

Often, as supervisors work their way up the organizational ladder, they benefit from the experiences and assistance of others. There comes a time in the career of every supervisor when some of this assistance can be returned. When appropriate, you can assist others by coaching them or serving as a mentor. You can also become involved in professional associations and continuing education activities.

Yourself

Finally, you have a responsibility to yourself. Being a good supervisor not only helps the organization but helps you too. Most of us feel good about ourselves when we know we are doing the best possible job. When you do your job well, you also are more likely to be promoted. To be fair to yourself, you should have a career plan, make short- and long-range career goals, and develop strategies to reach them.

Keys to Supervisory Success

For many years management experts searched for common traits found among good supervisors. It was thought that, through research, the success factors in such areas as education, experience, intelligence, and personality could be identified. But, just as supervisors are different, so are the work environments within which they supervise. With so many variables, it was impossible to come up with any concrete conclusions. The principal finding was that each situation called for certain skills and abilities. As a result, skilled leaders also need to be able to adjust their approach to the unique needs of each situation and the available resources.

Can any keys to supervisory success be identified? There seem to be a few general traits that most good supervisors possess.

First and foremost, the successful supervisor is a good communicator. The importance of speaking, listening, and writing well cannot be overstated. Chapter 2 will discuss these skills in depth and help you become a better communicator.

Successful supervisors accept the duties and responsibilities of their jobs and put the good of the organization first. They not only withstand day-to-day pressures, they use them as motivators to do the job better. Part II of this text—Supervisory Responsibilities—can help you meet the demands of your job more effectively. It covers the supervisor's role in recruiting, selecting, orienting, training, managing, evaluating, coaching, and disciplining employees. Topics include how to interview applicants, types of training (including principles of adult learning), productivity standards, scheduling and forecasting, obstacles to effective performance evaluation, the myths of discipline, and the supervisor's relationship to employee unions.

Successful supervisors also have good self-images and positive personalities that help them shape the work environment. They are enthusiastic and they like to lead. These qualities help keep employee morale and motivation high and help transform a work crew from a collection of individuals into a team. Part III can help you become better at motivating employees and building team spirit. Topics include formal and informal groups, the supervisor as a team leader, leadership styles, getting to know your employees, identifying motivational problems, encouraging employee participation, types of personal conflicts, and tips for managing conflict.

Successful supervisors always seek to improve themselves. While the entire text is designed to help you become a better supervisor, Part IV—Improving Your Effectiveness as a Supervisor—provides information that can help you improve in two areas that frequently trouble supervisors: managing time and managing change.

Last but not least, a successful supervisor sets a career plan and sticks with it. As mentioned earlier, you should set career goals and create strategies to attain them. Chapter 14, "Professional Development and Future Trends," gives you some ideas on how to grow professionally. It provides some advice about what you can do now to climb the next rung on your career ladder, and also looks at future trends.

Endnotes

1. Henri Fayol, *Industrial and General Administration,* trans. J. A. Coubrough (Geneva, Switzerland: International Management Institute, 1930).
2. W. Richard Plunkett, *Supervision: The Direction of People at Work,* 2d ed. (Dubuque, Iowa: Brown, 1979), p. 131.

Key Terms

conceptual skills

controlling

coordinating

directing

evaluating

formal authority

human relations skills

informal authority

management

non-programmed decision-making
  methods

organizing

planning

programmed decision-making method

staffing   technical skills
supervisor

Discussion Questions

1. What is management?
2. What are the seven basic resource categories?
3. What are some of Henri Fayol's management principles?
4. Where does a supervisor get his/her authority?
5. How is planning done in an organization?
6. What are some basic principles of staffing?
7. What three basic skills must supervisors possess?
8. Why do supervisors fail?
9. What responsibilities do supervisors have to their employees?
10. What are some keys to supervisory success?

REVIEW QUIZ

When you feel you have covered all of the material in this chapter, answer these questions. Choose the *best* answer. Check your answers with the correct ones found on the Review Quiz Answer Key at the end of this book.

True (T) or False (F)

T   F   1. Department heads are classified as middle managers.

T   F   2. The basic components of management include staffing and evaluating.

T   F   3. The two types of authority are formal and informal.

T   F   4. Evaluating principles include all activities necessary to oversee, motivate, and train employees.

T   F   5. A supervisor must be able to understand all the management components and how they relate to his/her work.

T   F   6. The inability to perform technical aspects of the job is among the top three reasons supervisors fail.

T   F   7. The inability to perform basic management tasks can cause serious problems for supervisors.

T   F   8. A supervisor's responsibility to himself/herself is to climb the career ladder as fast as possible, no matter what it takes.

T   F   9. Basic keys to supervisory success *cannot* be identified.

T   F   10. It is considered selfish and unnecessary for supervisors to seek to improve themselves and further their careers.

Alternate/Multiple Choice

11.   The three levels of management are:

    a. top, middle, and supervisory.
    b. top, middle, and organizational.

12.   The general manager and assistant general managers are considered top managers at the:

    a. national or regional level.
    b. property level.

13.   The three management principles are:

    a. authority, delegation, and responsibility.
    b. delegation, authority, and organization.

14.   Which of the following statements about directing is true?

    a. Supervisors should supervise more employees than he/she can comfortably handle.
    b. The supervisor's attitude seldom affects employee attitudes and performance.
    c. It's important to ask for employee ideas and use them whenever possible.
    d. The supervisor should relate to all employees in the same way.

15.   Supervisors are responsible to:

    a. the boss, to themselves, and to employees.
    b. themselves, to employees, to guests, and to other professionals.
    c. guests, to themselves, to other professionals, to employees, and to the boss.
    d. employees, to themselves, to the organization, and to guests.

Chapter Outline

Learning Objectives

1. Describe commonly believed myths about communication and important aspects of them.

2. Identify when successful communication takes place, and discuss what Molly and Joe learned in the chapter's illustrative story.

3. Identify some barriers to effective communication.

4. Describe some of the barriers to specific supervisory situations.

5. Describe the three essential parts of organized speaking, both before a group and in face-to-face conversation.

6. Explain how to speak effectively on the job.

7. Explain the importance of improving your listening skills.

8. Identify factors which may prevent effective listening.

9. Describe techniques to use to improve your listening skills.

10. Identify the four stages of listening presented in the chapter, and discuss important aspects of each.

11. Describe how knowledge of non-verbal communication can help you on the job.

12. Explain the importance of good writing, and identify how you can make your business writing more effective.

2

Effective Communication

O N-THE-JOB COMMUNICATION may be formal or informal. Generally, there are three different kinds of business communication:

1. **Downward communication** refers to the passage of information from an organization's higher levels to its lower levels.

2. **Upward communication** refers to the passage of information from an organization's lower levels to its higher levels.

3. **Lateral communication** refers to the passage of information between peers, or members of the same level.

For communication purposes, it may be useful to envision various levels of management and employees joined together in a network of linking pins. The line employee, for instance, is linked to the department head through the supervisor, while the department head serves as a linking pin between the supervisor and the division head. Peers across the organization are linked to each other. As a supervisor, then, you play an important role which links line employees and upper management—and which links you to the organization's other supervisors. These links are strengthened through good communication, or weakened if communication is poor.

Clearly, the more effectively you communicate, the better you will perform your job. Your position as a hospitality industry supervisor requires good communication skills. If you wish to succeed as a supervisor, improve your communication skills to the greatest extent possible.

Successful communication is that which the speaker or writer sends and the listener or reader receives, and which both parties understand and act upon. Virtually all of us have communication habits that could use improving. This chapter will help you learn how. It begins by examining several communication myths, and points out particular barriers to communication, including personality differences and prejudices. The latter part of the chapter explores how to develop effective communication skills. These skills include speaking, listening, understanding non-verbal communication, and writing.

Some Myths About Communication

Before we discuss how the communication process works, we will examine several misunderstandings affecting communication. These misunderstandings may involve the following commonly believed communication myths.[1]

1. *We communicate only when we want to communicate.* This is not true. We communicate all day, everyday, often without realizing it. For instance, suppose you

listen to an employee discuss a report he has given you. Since your new baby kept you up for hours the night before, you are tired today. Without realizing it, you yawn and look at your watch several times, wondering if the workday will ever end. Since your employee does not know about your sleepless night, he concludes that you are uninterested in the report and in what he has to say. Inadvertently, you sent an incorrect message to him.

2. *Words mean the same to both speaker and listener.* In reality, words hold different meanings to different people based on their varying experiences and perceptions. For example, suppose you tell your employee that her work is "above average." To you, this means that she is a good employee with great potential, and you assume that she will view your words in the way you meant them. However, your employee has always been a high achiever, and to her, "above average" means barely acceptable. Thus, her morale and work may suffer if she thinks that she is not suited to the job.

3. *We communicate chiefly with words.* In reality, we communicate most of our messages non-verbally. We may say one thing but reveal our true feelings by our tone of voice, facial expressions, eye contact, gestures, or the way we sit or walk. For instance, imagine that you meet a co-worker in the employee lounge and ask her how she is. She responds, "Fine, thanks," but slumps in her chair, stares at the floor, and sounds and looks distressed. As you observe her, you believe her actions rather than her words. Indeed, all of us know that it is harder to lie with our bodies than it is to lie when we talk.

4. *Non-verbal communication is silent communication.* Some of us think that **non-verbal communication** can be seen but not heard. This is false, for we can hear certain types of non-verbal communication, such as laughter, weeping, or the tone of our voices. If you hear an employee whistling as he goes about his work, you probably assume that he is having a good day.

5. *Communication is a one-way street between the speaker and the listener.* This myth suggests that speakers talk *at* listeners rather than *with* them. In reality, though, effective communication is enhanced when both parties participate actively. They do this when the listener gives the speaker feedback. **Feedback** is a listener's reaction to the speaker's verbal and non-verbal communication. If you give an employee some instructions, you probably seek feedback to make sure that he/she understands you correctly. Examples of non-verbal feedback include shaking or tilting the head and furrowing the brow. Your employee may give verbal feedback by saying something like, "I see," "I get it," and "I don't understand."

6. *The message we communicate is the message that the listener will receive.* We all too often assume that our listener will receive our messages exactly as we intend them. Suppose that on Monday your boss asks you to write a report and states that it's due "soon." You look at your schedule and decide that you can work on it on Thursday afternoon. However, on Tuesday morning your boss asks for the completed report. You realize that you have miscommunicated: "soon" in your boss's experience means right away, while it means "this week" to you.

7. *There is no such thing as too much information.* Certainly too little information is not good, but neither is too much information. For example, problems can occur when employees are overwhelmed with too much paperwork. Further, you waste everybody's time if you tell your employees about matters that neither affect nor interest them. Few of us need to know every detail about every little thing. Even if all available information were accessible to us, we would simply not have the time to hear it, read it, or listen to it. Information overload is common in many organizations. It is important to concern ourselves with the quality of communication rather than the quantity of it. More is not necessarily better.

The Communication Process

Successful communication occurs when a speaker or writer sends a message and the listener or reader receives it, and the message is understood and acted upon by both parties. Exhibit 2.1 features a model of interpersonal communications. In the following section we use a story to explain each of the model's steps. Bear in mind that this is a slightly exaggerated story. Its very exaggerations, however, help to get across each step in the communication process, which is much more complex than most of us think. The exhibit and the story help to illustrate that.

An Illustrative Story

Joe is a busperson at the hotel restaurant. He knows that the restaurant is short of servers today because two of them called in sick just before the lunch rush began. He approaches Molly, the dining room supervisor, and volunteers to lend a hand.

Step 1

1. Molly begins by: Thinking about the message she is about to send

Molly considers Joe's offer and how she will respond to it.

Step 2

2. Molly sorts and selects from: Knowledge, experience, feelings, attitudes, emotions, perceptions

Molly is short two servers and the noon rush is about to begin. She knows that her staff will be busy with an extra banquet as well as the usual number of guests. She is lucky that Joe has offered to help in a pinch. Since he has bused tables for almost three months, he understands the importance of guest service.

Step 3

3. Molly puts the message into: Words, actions, signs, symbols

Molly arranges a message in her mind.

Step 4

4. Molly sends the message to Joe by: Speaking, acting, body language

Exhibit 2.1 A Model of Interpersonal Communications

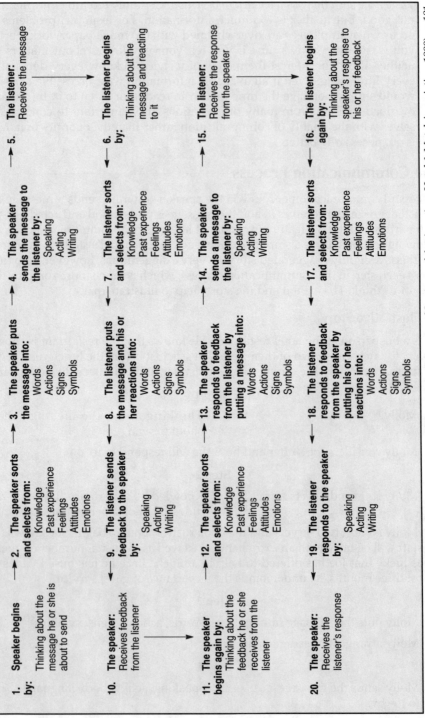

1. **Speaker begins by:** Thinking about the message he or she is about to send

2. **The speaker sorts and selects from:** Knowledge Past experience Feelings Attitudes Emotions

3. **The speaker puts the message into:** Words Actions Signs Symbols

4. **The speaker sends the message to the listener by:** Speaking Acting Writing

5. **The listener:** Receives the message

6. **The listener begins by:** Thinking about the message and reacting to it

7. **The listener sorts and selects from:** Knowledge Past experience Feelings Attitudes Emotions

8. **The listener puts the message and his or her reactions into:** Words Actions Signs Symbols

9. **The listener sends feedback to the speaker by:** Speaking Acting Writing

10. **The speaker:** Receives feedback from the listener

11. **The speaker begins again by:** Thinking about the feedback he or she receives from the listener

12. **The speaker sorts and selects from:** Knowledge Past experience Feelings Attitudes Emotions

13. **The speaker responds to feedback from the listener by putting a message into:** Words Actions Signs Symbols

14. **The speaker sends a message to the listener by:** Speaking Acting Writing

15. **The listener:** Receives the response from the speaker

16. **The listener begins again by:** Thinking about the speaker's response to his or her feedback

17. **The listener sorts and selects from:** Knowledge Past experience Feelings Attitudes Emotions

18. **The listener responds to feedback from the speaker by putting his or her reactions into:** Words Actions Signs Symbols

19. **The listener responds to the speaker by:** Speaking Acting Writing

20. **The speaker:** Receives the listener's response

Source: Stephen J. Shriver, *Managing Quality Services* (East Lansing, Mich.: Educational Institute of the American Hotel & Motel Association, 1988), p. 191.

Molly smiles, breathes a sigh of relief, and says, "We sure can use another pair of hands today. Why don't you take tables 11 and 12 to start with, and we'll see how you do?"

Step 5

5. Joe: Receives the message

Joe listens to Molly and nods to show he understands her.

Step 6

6. Joe begins by: Thinking about the message and reacting to it

He also starts thinking about what it means to serve guests.

Step 7

7. Joe sorts and selects from: Knowledge, experiences, feelings, attitudes, emotions

Joe has never waited tables, but has been watching the servers and thinks he can serve as well as they can. He figures that busing tables isn't much different from taking orders and serving food to guests. As a busperson, he has had a lot of contact with guests. He also thinks that all servers have to do is ask guests what they want and then bring it to them. "This will be a snap," he tells himself.

Step 8

8. Joe puts the message and   Words, actions, signs, symbols
   his reactions into:

Joe arranges a response in his mind.

Step 9

9. Joe sends feedback to Molly by: Speaking, acting, body language

Joe responds, "Sure thing, Molly. I'll get on it right away." Then he turns toward the kitchen.

Step 10

10. Molly: Receives feedback from Joe

Molly smiles. "Thanks," she says. "I really appreciate this."

Step 11

11. Molly begins again by: Thinking about the feedback she receives from Joe

Because Joe seems confident that he can handle the work, Molly thinks that he will do a good job. She doesn't have time to think for long, though, because the banquet guests have begun arriving. In addition, the main dining area is filling up quickly. Molly is busy with guests and other servers. When Joe said he'd "get on it right away," Molly turned her attention to other matters, relieved that the staffing shortage problem had seemed to improve itself.

Let's follow Joe and see how he handles his first time as a server.

First Joe joins an ongoing, heated discussion with the other busers about the basketball championships. He fails to bring his guests the restaurant's signature basket of freshly baked bread. When he finally remembers to take orders, his pen runs out of ink—but Joe thinks he can remember the orders anyway.

Joe fills out the guest checks once he returns to the kitchen and locates another pen. However, the orders Joe thinks he remembers are not the right ones. His guests are all in for an unwelcome surprise.

Joe makes other mistakes, including failing to make eye contact with his guests, not bothering to learn about the daily specials, and responding to questions by saying only, "I don't know." And he is much too slow—in waiting on the guests, in placing their orders, in bringing their bread and finally their meals, which are the wrong ones.

For the furious guests this is the last straw. They angrily get up to leave the restaurant and loudly demand to see the manager. Other guests turn to watch.

When Molly arrives, the guests tell her all about Joe's poor service. Molly tries to calm the guests, but they won't hear of it. They speak of horrible service and of never returning, and they stomp out.

Molly fumes. She angrily steps into the kitchen, where Joe is—once again—talking about basketball.

"Joe, I want to see you in my office. Now."

Step 12

12. Molly sorts and selects from: Knowledge, experience, feelings, attitudes, emotions, perceptions

Molly compares her knowledge of guest service and waiting tables to what she's heard about Joe's performance. She explodes, "That was the worst job of waiting tables that this restaurant's ever seen! I thought you knew about guest service!"

Her feelings, attitudes, and emotions are very apparent to Joe. He looks astonished.

Step 13

13. Molly responds to feedback   Words, actions, signs, symbols
from the guests by putting a
message into:

Molly arranges a message in her mind.

Step 14

14. Molly sends a message to Joe by: Speaking, acting

Molly, barely able to control herself, tells Joe that she is very angry. And she looks it. She jumps all over Joe for ignoring the guests, for getting their orders wrong, for not being courteous. She tells him that, because of him, some guests will never return. In addition, their reputation as a first-class hotel restaurant is ruined.

Step 15

15. Joe: Receives the response from Molly

Joe stands wide-eyed. He can't understand what the big deal is.

Step 16

16. Joe begins again by: Thinking about Molly's response to his feedback

Joe thinks that Molly is really out of control. He thinks also that everyone else can hear her, even though the door is shut.

Step 17

17. Joe sorts and selects from: Knowledge, experience, feelings, attitudes, emotions, perceptions

Joe compares his knowledge, experience, feelings, attitudes, and emotions about serving to what he thinks Molly's knowledge, experience, feelings, attitudes, and emotions must be. It's true that he messed up the orders, but he solved that problem by blaming the kitchen staff. But the way Molly's acting, you'd think it was the end of the world.

Step 18

18. Joe responds to feedback from   Words, actions, signs, symbols
    Molly by putting his reactions into:

Joe decides how he will respond to Molly.

Step 19

19. Joe responds to Molly by: Speaking, acting, body language

He flushes, looks surprised, and shrugs his shoulders. He decides that, in the future, he'd rather leave town than volunteer to help Molly again. He says bitterly, "OK, Molly, it'll never happen again."

Step 20

20. Molly: Receives Joe's response

Molly nods and pulls open her office door, making it clear that Joe is to leave. Then she slams the door shut as soon as he's gone. After pacing around her office for a minute or so, she begins to calm down. She feels bad about losing her cool with Joe. "He was only trying to help," she tells herself. Molly wonders what she could have been thinking when she allowed Joe to wait tables without any instructions, training, or direct supervision. She decides, "We need to talk."

At the end of the work shift, Molly asks Joe to return to her office. They talk about how her expectations for the job had differed from his. They also discuss the importance of guest relations and service, of paying attention to guests, of writing down orders, and of actually working instead of talking with friends.

Molly realizes that she should have made her expectations clear before Joe started serving. She also thinks that Joe might make a good server if he were given adequate training.

Molly and Joe talk for some time about how to avoid such misunderstandings in the future. They decide that the best way to communicate more effectively is to ensure that the entire message is received, understood, and acted upon by both the speaker and the listener.

As Molly and Joe found, it is easier to focus on our own messages and reactions rather than on someone else's. Both assumed that the other understood them completely. Because the communication process is so complex, it is easy to forget that others may not react to each part of our messages in the same way that we do. As Molly and Joe discovered, the entire communication process deserves more of our thought and attention.

Barriers to Effective Communication

Many barriers can decrease your ability to communicate effectively, including distractions, differences in background and experience, poor timing, emotions, personality differences, prejudice, and differences in knowledge and assumptions.

Distractions

Possible distractions in the workplace include too much noise, excessive heat or cold, interruptions, or physical discomfort. To aid the communication process, choose settings that are as distraction-free as possible for both the speaker and the listener.

Suppose that one of your best workers, Susan, approaches you about a personal problem she is having with a co-worker. Since you've often assured your employees that your door is always open to them, Susan feels free to talk with you. However, you leave your door open a crack, and a lot of outside noise filters into the room. In addition, you take two telephone calls, and a couple of your colleagues knock at your door and stay briefly to talk. Even when the two of you are alone, you shuffle your papers or drum your fingers on the desk. How do you suppose Susan will feel about confiding in you?

Differences in Background

Differences in background include the education, experience, and knowledge of the speaker and the listener. A new dishwasher may try to make friends with the chef, only to be rejected. A recent graduate of the hotel management school may try to tell an "old" manager how to run things. The speaker may send a message based upon personal knowledge, but it may do little good if the listener does not have similar knowledge.

For example, imagine that Shari, the newly hired assistant housekeeper, believes she knows all there is to know about increasing the number of rooms a room attendant can clean per day. She establishes a new procedure when Eve, the executive housekeeper, is on vacation for a week. When Eve returns, she learns what Shari has done. Eve angrily interprets Shari's action as a plot to take over the executive housekeeping position.

Poor Timing

Improper timing may cause both parties to say things that they do not truly mean. For example, someone may say something in anger and later regret it. Or the listener may be distracted or unwilling to listen. The best communication takes place when both the speaker and the listener are ready.

For example, you call in Ed, one of your employees, for a discussion about the convention beginning next Tuesday. You want to brief him about his role in assuring that the convention runs smoothly. However, Ed appears distracted. Usually an attentive listener, he seems lost in thought and doesn't give you the active feedback you've come to expect from him. He also quickly "forgets" things you told him just minutes earlier. Upon questioning him, you learn that he is preoccupied with a family problem. Therefore, you reschedule the discussion, allowing Ed sufficient time to work out his problem. Alternatively, you could discuss his problem first, and then get into the reason you've called your meeting.

Emotions

Either the sender's or the receiver's emotions can also create communication barriers. For example, suppose you call in a valued employee to discuss his recent performance, which has been deteriorating. The meeting, which you prefer to conduct in a businesslike manner, is intended to be informational. That is, you will objectively explain the problem from your viewpoint, and expect that the employee will accept your advice and begin to follow company policies and procedures. What you don't expect, though, is that the employee responds with anger. His anger makes you angry, and the meeting falls apart. The employee stomps out, leaving you alone to fume.

Personality Differences

The personalities of the speaker and listener can also bar communication. We are often so influenced by another's personality that we accept or reject his/her communication as soon as it begins. For instance, suppose you attend a day-long meeting at your property. You turn your full attention to a speaker who happens to be one of your favorite co-workers. However, if the next speaker is a co-worker whom you have never liked and with whom you have had serious disagreements, your attention almost certainly will waver. In fact, you may disregard the message completely.

Prejudice

We can be prejudiced both positively and negatively. If you use a certain cleaning method because that is the way you have always cleaned, you are positively prejudiced toward it. In addition, if you favor one employee and give her the choicest projects, you may be partial to her, and negatively biased toward your other employees. Finally, suppose you are a server at an upscale hotel restaurant. All of your friends are servers or bartenders. You shun dishwashers as a group because you think they represent a lower class of employee. In all of these cases, you may miss opportunities just because you don't consider them.

Either type of prejudice presents a communication barrier. To safeguard against prejudice, view everyone as an individual and give each person an opportunity to show you his/her strengths. In addition, keep your mind open to new people and opportunities, and consider all available evidence.

Differences in Knowledge and Assumptions

Communication may be hampered if your listener lacks the knowledge and experience to understand your message. This may happen, for instance, when you give only partial messages, such as might occur when you assume your listener has the same knowledge you have. To guard against this problem, question your listener to find out whether he/she understands your message completely, and allow ample time for questions.

Particular Barriers to Specific Supervisory Situations

Some of the major barriers to effective communication include these sender, or speaker, barriers:

- Allowing others to interrupt
- Interrupting others
- Talking too much
- Arguing
- Making statements that are too general or which exaggerate
- Blaming others
- Commenting or judging too soon
- Using excessive sarcasm
- Poor listening habits
- Poor speaking, listening, or writing skills
- Picking the wrong time, place, and method
- Sender is too busy to communicate well
- Negative attitude toward the listener or the message

Barriers may also occur on the receiver's end of the communication process. Such barriers include:

- Dislike of the sender
- Lack of interest in the message
- Thinking of what to say before the speaker finishes
- Being distracted by something else
- A disorganized and confusing message

- Poor listening skills

- Pretending to understand

- Not wanting to hear a message because it's unpleasant

- Emotions (fear, anger, tension)

- "Knowing" what the message will be and tuning out

There are additional barriers which interfere with effective communication in certain supervisory situations. These include biases resulting from relying heavily on stereotypes and first impressions, and sources of bias such as just-like-me, halo, contrast, and leniency errors.

First Impressions

When we first meet someone, we tend to make immediate judgments about him/her based on superficial factors like appearance, accent, age, and so forth. However, our first impressions may later prove incorrect. Seek more information, especially in interviewing applicants and orienting new hires.

Stereotypes

We may form general opinions about certain groups, and then apply our beliefs to individuals in those groups. If a group member behaves in a manner different from the norms we associate with the group, we may overlook the differences or assign unduly positive or negative values to them. Regard each employee as an individual, not just a member of a group, when coaching or evaluating him/her.

Just-Like-Me

We tend to like those who behave or think as we do, or who have similar backgrounds and characteristics. This may lead us to favor those who are similarly inclined and to disregard people who differ from us. Be especially careful to avoid this type of thinking when interviewing applicants or conducting employee evaluations.

Halo or Pitchfork Effect

Sometimes we may favor someone for one particularly valuable characteristic, and overlook all of the person's other traits (the halo effect). Or we may dislike someone because of one characteristic (the pitchfork effect). In either case, our entirely positive or negative views color our perceptions of the whole person. Avoid such all-or-nothing thinking, particularly when you are training employees or evaluating them.

Contrast Effect

We err when we compare individuals with others and rank them according to our perceptions of how they measure up. Whenever possible, judge every individual using the same absolute standards for the job. This is especially important in coaching and evaluating employees.

Leniency/Severity Effect

Some of us view the world positively, while others are clouded by pessimism. We may view others either too positively or too negatively, depending on our general outlook. If we see them too positively, we may be too lenient in our treatment of them. If we see them too negatively, our judgments of them may be too severe.

This effect can vary on a daily basis. When we are having a particularly good day, we may react less sternly to an employee's policy violation or failure to complete a task according to standards. We must work to evaluate performance consistently.

Strive to clearly see someone's strengths and weaknesses without bias. This is especially important when coaching, evaluating, and disciplining employees.

Developing Effective Communication Skills

If you watch other supervisors and managers at your property, you will realize that effective supervisors are also effective communicators. In fact, the most successful supervisors and managers are those who communicate well in every direction—up, down, and across the organization (laterally). The ability to communicate well may seem to come naturally to them. However, appearances are often deceiving. Most of us need to work at communicating well. Speaking, listening, understanding non-verbal communication, and writing are all skills that you can acquire.

Speaking

Effective speaking, whether before a group or in conversation with an individual, generally contains an *introduction,* the *main body,* and a *conclusion.* In this chapter, we are concerned primarily with communication between individuals. (Chapter 9 contains information on conducting effective meetings.)

The *introduction* of your informal talk or speech should:

1. get your listener's attention,
2. obtain the listener's interest, and
3. communicate your purpose for speaking.

Before beginning to speak, plan and organize what to say. This will involve identifying your main points and then making sure that you address them. Stick to your topic.

Get your listener's attention by announcing your intentions at the outset of your talk. Include what you want to talk about, why it is important, and what you expect to occur as a result. Obtain your listener's interest by explaining what your message means and how it affects him/her.

In the *main body* of your talk, present key points in a logical sequence. This will require planning and organization. Use spoken cues to tell your listener what's important. For example, you might say, "The main idea is ..." In addition, maintain eye contact with the listener, vary your tone of speech, and summarize/clarify at important points. Asking questions of the listener is one effective way to make sure he/she understands.

Summarize your message at appropriate times. One approach is to summarize at the end. Or you may wish to summarize key points during your discussion. This will keep your listener interested and also allow him/her to organize what you are saying. The final summary should repeat your talk's main ideas. You should also re-state what you expect your listener to do as a result of your talk.

Volume, Pitch, Tone, and Pace

If the *volume* of your voice is too high, listeners may decide that you are pushy or overbearing. Conversely, if you speak too quietly, people may not hear you. In addition, your quiet voice may tell others that you are shy, nervous, or unassertive, or perhaps that you want to speak confidentially. Strive to speak at medium volume, neither too loud nor too quiet.

The *pitch*, or sound level of your voice, is most effective when it comes naturally to you. In other words, use your normal voice. Trying to use a pitch that is higher or lower than your normal pitch will make you sound artificial.

You will probably vary the *tone* of your speech according to the situation at hand. For example, you might use a stern tone when disciplining an employee for the third time (for more on discipline, please see Chapter 7). You would probably speak gently to a nervous or frightened employee. In general, if you speak too warmly, you may sound insincere. People will be put off by your apparent phoniness. If you speak too coldly, you'll offend nearly everybody. Avoid either extreme.

The *pace* at which you speak may be revealing as well. For instance, if you speak too quickly, others may not understand what you are saying, or may think you are anxious, shy, or simply very busy. If you speak too slowly, others may decide that you think they are unable to follow your message, or that you are indecisive or uneasy.

Vary Your Speech

Vary your speech to fit the situation. Weigh each circumstance, considering several factors, including the listener's speech and mood, whether the setting is formal, and what the interchange will be. For example, if someone speaks softly because of a subject's confidentiality, you should respond in kind. Or if a guest seems reserved and shy, match his style by speaking quietly and warmly. Don't overwhelm him with a response that's inappropriately strong.

Speaking on the Job

Whether you speak in meetings or in any other context, you may wish to follow several general guidelines. First, plan and organize what to say. Stick to your main points without rambling or introducing unnecessary information. In addition, provide enough accurate information to support your position.

It is a good idea to gear your speaking toward your listener. That is, use language that the listener will understand, and make your message easy to follow. Pause occasionally to allow the listener to ask questions. Indeed, you may want to ask the listener for questions in order to check his/her comprehension. Whenever possible, maintain direct eye contact; this is crucial in groups and when speaking with just one other person. Furthermore, it is important to watch the listener's body language to see how he/she is receiving your message. It may be helpful to ask questions to confirm whether you are reading his/her body language correctly.

Learning to speak effectively will aid you in your supervisory duties. So will developing effective listening skills.

Listening

Every day we are bombarded by sounds of every kind coming from all directions. We can't help hearing them, although we hear selectively (that is, we notice some sounds while tuning others out). Hearing is largely a passive activity. In other words, we usually do not have to work at hearing something. We can just sit, stand, or lie idly by, and sounds come to us unasked for. We hear automatically. We hear even while we sleep.

Listening, however, is not the same as hearing. To listen well, we have to become involved. We also have to *decide* to listen. Listening, then, is something we can control. We can choose to become good listeners. If we are good listeners already, we can become even better. It is a skill we can develop, just as we can learn the skills of public speaking or writing. As a supervisor, you will need to exercise your listening skills in your everyday work. You will have to listen attentively to your manager, and to people outside your division and even your property. You will find, however, that you spend most of your listening time with your employees.

It would probably be safe to say that fully half of a hospitality employee's day is spent listening to others. For example, kitchen workers must listen to orders, instructions, and so forth all work shift long. If your employees have a lot of guest contact, they probably spend most of their time listening to guests and communicating with them. Since guest satisfaction is so important, it is necessary that hospitality workers learn to listen well.

Of listening, speaking, reading, and writing, listening may be the communication skill used most. When you were very young, you learned to speak. Later, when you were a small child in school, you learned to read and write. You may have reinforced your learning as you grew with further courses in writing, and, perhaps, public speaking. It is quite unlikely, however, that you ever studied listening. Elementary and high schools do not offer classes in listening. Colleges do not offer listening majors or even a basic course in listening.

Despite your lack of formal training in listening, you can take the time now to learn to listen effectively. This involves taking an active role when you're listening. This active role is completely different from the passive one you take when you hear something. You have to work at it, but the benefits gained will be well worth your time and effort.

For instance, your property will gain when you get information correctly the first time you hear it. Your manager will appreciate your efforts to listen to and carry out instructions. Your employees will appreciate the fact that you listen, really listen, to their concerns. With proper listening skills, you will become known as an effective employee, supervisor, and colleague. In short, learning to listen well will enhance your reputation as an effective communicator.

Exhibit 2.2 Causes of Poor Listening Habits

- Unsuitable listening environment: too much noise or too many distractions
- Allowing your mind to wander
- Thinking of something else
- Focusing on one word or idea at the expense of the whole message
- Negative reactions to speaker's mannerisms, appearance, dress, accent, and so on
- "Tuning out" because the message is difficult or dull
- Not paying attention
- Taking too many notes
- Talking to others in the group or audience
- Lack of desire or determination to listen

Obstacles to Listening

Obstacles to effective listening are created by many of the listener's own bad habits. For example, you may allow your mind to wander when your own thoughts and ideas seem more interesting than the speaker's. At meetings or lectures you may "tune out" because the information is boring or difficult. Sometimes your attention may wander when you would rather be elsewhere or you worry about the million other things you have to do. Perhaps you become distracted by one meaningful word or idea that grips your attention even when the speaker moves on. In addition, you might prejudge speakers or their topics, and form opinions before you've given them a fair hearing. It is also possible that you miss the message because you take too many detailed notes. Then again, your problem may be that you are too easily distracted by papers on your desk, by others talking, or by noises you hear in the hallway. (Some causes of poor listening habits are listed in Exhibit 2.2.)

Many of us are good at faking attention. Perhaps we learned in elementary school to look as though we were paying attention when we really were not. It is easy to fake attention by nodding our head, looking at the speaker, and saying "Uh huh" when it seems appropriate. However, others often catch on when we are not paying attention. Perhaps it has something to do with the vacant look in our eyes or the fact that we stifle yawns. If employees notice that you do not fully listen, they will think that you are not there for them. They will stop bringing their problems to you—and even their ideas and solutions.

Listening difficulties may also result from the difference between the rate at which we speak and the rate at which we listen and think/comprehend. The average speaker uses 125–150 words per minute. The average listener, however, can hear and understand more than twice as many words per minute.

Put this spare listening time to work for you. Rather than daydreaming, become actively involved in the message. Use extra moments to review what you

Exhibit 2.3 Tips for Effective Listening

- Relax.
- Let the speaker talk without interrupting.
- Show interest in the speaker.
- Maintain eye contact or look directly at the speaker.
- Observe non-verbal language.
- Maintain an active listening posture; lean forward, eyes on speaker.
- Use listening spare time to review and anticipate.
- Focus your attention on both the speaker and the message.
- Use self-discipline: concentrate on what the speaker is saying.
- Remove or ignore distractions.
- Avoid forming responses until the speaker has finished.
- Be patient; give the speaker plenty of time.
- Keep an open mind; don't prejudge.
- Listen to the entire message, not just single words or phrases.
- Empathize with the speaker. Put yourself in his/her position.
- Keep your emotions in check.
- Ask questions.

have heard. Anticipate what additional points the speaker will make. Do anything except let your mind wander off the topic.

Develop Effective Listening Skills

Most responsibility for effective listening rests squarely on the listener's shoulders. You have the power to decide how good your listening skills will be. Keep your mind open to any speaker or message. Decide from the start that you will listen. Judge a speaker on what he/she says, not on what you want him/her to say. Using non-verbal language, show that you are actively listening. Use your considerable powers of concentration.

This section suggests some active listening techniques you can adopt, such as mirroring, paraphrasing, summarizing, and questioning. In addition, Exhibit 2.3 lists some tips to improve your listening effectiveness. First, however, we turn to a discussion of four stages of active listening.

Model of Four Stages

In this listening model, the active listener moves through four stages of listening. They include focusing, interpreting, evaluating, and responding, in that order. The focusing stage is the most important, and a listener should devote most of his/her time and attention to it.

Focusing. Focusing involves turning all of your attention to the speaker, putting all other matters aside. It means concentrating on receiving the message. The four aspects of this stage include deciding to listen, creating the proper listening atmosphere, focusing on the speaker, and showing that you are attending to the message.

Decide to listen. Keep your attention focused and your mind from wandering. Set aside your own ideas. Concentrate on the speaker's words and message, not on his/her age, sex, position, image, or manner. Listen without becoming defensive. Be open to new ideas and concepts.

Create the proper atmosphere. Make it easy to listen by minimizing outside distractions. Choose a suitable location. Go into a private room or your office and close the door. Ask someone to take your phone calls and eliminate as many interruptions as possible.

Focus on the speaker. Establish and maintain eye contact with the speaker. Give him/her time to speak before you begin to question or comment. Concentrate. Listen to the content of the message. Avoid thinking about how you will answer once the speaker is finished. If you must take notes, keep them brief.

Show that you are paying attention. Use appropriate non-verbal communication—or body language—to show you are receiving the message and paying attention. Mirror the speaker's emotions. When necessary, ask questions to get more information. Ask the speaker to repeat parts of the message that you do not hear well or understand.

Interpreting. Essentially, the listener uses this stage to identify why the speaker is communicating. It is important to keep from judging. Then, determine the speaker's meaning, confirm that you understand, and show your understanding.

Keep from judging. Keep your personal biases out of the way. Don't judge the speaker by your personal standards or emotions.

Determine the speaker's meaning. Ask yourself what the speaker wants to get across. Determine the speaker's primary reason for talking with you. The speaker may be making casual conversation, expressing an idea, wanting to trade information, or hoping to persuade you about something. Try to figure out why the speaker is choosing to discuss this particular subject at this particular time.

Confirm that you understand the meaning. Find out whether the speaker really means what you think he/she means. Do this by asking questions or **paraphrasing** (re-stating or re-wording) the speaker's message. Continue questioning until you believe that you agree on what the message means.

Show that you understand. Use suitable words and body language (discussed later in this chapter) to communicate your understanding.

Reach a common understanding. Finally, the listener and speaker should reach a common understanding, which is the goal of the interpreting stage.

Evaluating. The goal of this stage is to verify that a common understanding is reached. You will evaluate the message as you try to discover whether the message is based on facts or on the speaker's opinion. To do this, you will gather more information, decide whether it is genuine, make your evaluation, and express your opinion.

Gather more information. Concentrate on the speaker's tone of voice and body language. Concentrate, also, on what the speaker does and doesn't say. "Read" between the lines. Ask for detail when you're given a lot of general information.

Decide whether the information is genuine. Try to separate facts from opinions and assumptions. Again, judge the message, not the messenger.

Evaluate the information. Decide what information you agree and disagree with as you listen. Form your own opinion based on what you have heard, not on beliefs or attitudes you bring to the conversation.

Communicate your evaluation. As you deliver your evaluation, support your words with body language. For example, if you agree with the speaker, you might lean toward him/her and look enthusiastic.

Responding. A listener responds to the speaker's message both while the speaker talks and after the speaker is finished. Once the speaker is finished, your response depends on learning what the speaker expects, considering your own time and energy, and deciding what to do.

Learn what the speaker expects. Ask questions to find out exactly what the speaker wants.

Consider your own time and energy. Decide whether your plans and schedule can or should accommodate the speaker's request. Remember to consider your own objectives, time pressures, and energy level.

Decide what to do. Weigh whether it is possible to meet the speaker's expectations. Determine how to respond. Then, communicate your plan to the speaker. Finally, end the discussion in an appropriate manner, consisting of a positive concluding statement that reviews any actions to be taken.

There may be times when the message you receive is a directive from your boss. When the directive is something you disagree with, you should take certain special steps. First, clarify your understanding of your boss's order. Second, clearly express your concerns and reservations about the directive. Be sure to provide accurate support for your beliefs. Third, seek feedback in the form of a response from your boss. If you succeed in persuading him/her toward a different action, explore new options together.

However, if your boss insists on the original course of action, demonstrate your support by positively following up on the action. If, though, you feel that the order is morally or ethically wrong or that it violates company regulations, take further action. In these cases, you should explain your concern again and inform your boss that you wish to speak to a higher-level manager about the issue.

Active Listening Techniques

The active listener uses a variety of techniques to aid the listening task. These include mirroring, paraphrasing, summarizing and self-disclosure, questioning or clarifying, and motivating the speaker to keep talking. Each of these is discussed further in the following sections.

Mirroring. Mirroring (or re-stating) involves exactly repeating some of the speaker's key words. For one thing, this shows the speaker just how a key word or phrase sounds to someone else. It also indicates that you are interested in the speaker's words and want to understand them. Furthermore, mirroring helps both you and the speaker determine the importance of any words the speaker uses. Identifying important words may help the speaker to examine other parts of the message. Some examples are listed below:

SPEAKER	I don't think I can finish this on time without help.
LISTENER	You don't think you can finish without help?
SPEAKER	This project is the most satisfying one I've ever been assigned.
LISTENER	This project is the most satisfying one you've ever had? That's great!
SPEAKER	I'm the only one on this crew who does any work.
LISTENER	You're the *only one* of your crew who works?

Be careful not to overuse mirroring, for it may become tedious or appear as if you're looking down on the speaker.

Paraphrasing. When paraphrasing, you use your own words to re-state what the speaker is feeling and trying to say. You tell the speaker what you think he/she means and feels. In paraphrasing, you work to reflect the content of the sender's message as well as the feeling behind the content. Paraphrasing is useful for various reasons. For instance, it helps you to clarify what the speaker is saying. It also helps the speaker, because your paraphrase reveals how his/her message sounds to others. Use it to communicate your honest desire to know what the speaker means.

Your use of this technique may help the speaker understand his/her feelings about the topic. It may also help the speaker reach a suitable solution.

SPEAKER	My deadline is next week, which means that I have a lot of overtime to work between now and then. And my baby-sitter just called and said she was sick, so she can't take the kids. I don't know what I'm going to do.
LISTENER	You're afraid you can't finish the job on time because there's no one to watch the kids.
SPEAKER	This job isn't any fun because everybody hates me. I try to be friendly, but they don't even notice I'm here. I just don't fit in.
LISTENER	You feel lonely here, and that makes you dislike your job. You wish everybody would be nicer.
SPEAKER	Cindy can be nice in a social setting, but she's hard to work with. She's always got a chip on her shoulder. She thinks she works harder than everybody else. She's always giving us dirty looks, and ignores us when we say hello. I hate even passing her in the hall, and now I'm assigned to work on a committee with her.

> **LISTENER**   You're uncomfortable around Cindy because she doesn't seem friendly at work, and that makes you nervous about working closely with her.

When paraphrasing, it is important to avoid using phrases which seem to "talk down" to the speaker, such as:

> "What you really mean is ..."

> "What you are trying to say is ..."

Avoid trying to put your own words in the speaker's mouth, or trying to force your view of things on the speaker.

Summarizing and Self-Disclosure. The listener uses summarizing or self-disclosure statements for several reasons. **Summarizing statements** condense parts of what the speaker said and stress important points. You may use them when you want to (1) focus attention on a certain topic; (2) show that you agree on specific points; (3) guide the speaker to another part of the subject; and (4) reach agreement on specific points, so that you may end the conversation.

The following are examples of summarizing statements:

> "If I hear you correctly, you want ..."

> "What we agree on is ..."

> "So you believe that what is happening is ..."

> "As I understand it, your main idea is ..."

Self-disclosure statements show the speaker how you feel about what he/she said. When you report experiences or feelings similar to the speaker's, it shows that the speaker is not the only one to think or feel a certain way. This helps the speaker to feel understood and less alone.

> "That reminds me of something that happened to me ..."

> "You're feeling the way I feel when ..."

> "Other employees have noticed the same thing ..."

Self-disclosure can also be used to communicate disagreement with the speaker's point or feelings. Communicating disagreement can help the speaker by underscoring sensitive areas and points at which discrepancy begins.

Questioning or Clarifying Statements. If you are listening actively, you may notice some statements that seem incomplete or do not tell the whole story. When this happens, ask questions to help the speaker clarify his/her thinking. Sometimes speakers leave out important points because they are caught up in the emotions of the moment. On such occasions, a speaker may use words or phrases that seem to come out of nowhere. Use questioning or clarifying statements to make the speaker's message clearer. You may choose either open-ended or specific questions.

Open-ended questions give speakers freedom to respond in any way they like. They also make the speaker respond with more than a simple "yes" or "no." Use open-ended questions when you want to (1) begin a discussion; (2) find out the speaker's ideas; (3) examine a touchy subject; or (4) avoid influencing the reply.

Open-ended questions often begin in these ways:

"What do you think about ..."

"How do you feel about ..."

"Can you tell me ..."

"Could you describe ..."

For example, you might ask the speaker, "How do you feel about the changes in the summer vacation schedule?"

Specific questions seek additional information about unclear statements. They ask for specific details when the speaker has provided only general information.

Specific questions begin with words like these:

"Who ..."

"Where ..."

"When ..."

"Why ..."

"Which ..."

"How many ..."

For example, you might ask the speaker a specific question, such as, "What do you think caused the guest's dissatisfaction?"

Motivating Speaker to Say More. The idea here is to encourage the speaker to continue talking. Use neutral words that communicate neither agreement nor disagreement. Your purpose is to show that you are interested and want the speaker to continue. The words you use are equal to positive nods of the head:

"That's interesting."

"I understand."

"Tell me more."

"Let's talk about it."

"I see."

"This seems very important to you."

"I'd like to hear your point of view."

"Really."

You can encourage the speaker further by using **empathy,** which is the ability to see circumstances from the other's viewpoint. Your empathy shows the speaker that you are a willing and understanding listener who can personally relate to his/her experiences and feelings. It also shows him/her that you are attentive and interested. Use empathy to show that you accept the speaker and want to establish a good relationship. In addition, use it when you want the speaker to continue talking. Encourage the speaker further by using words that avoid any kind of judgment. When you are empathizing, you may use phrases like the following. Note that they are very similar to the words you use when self-disclosing:

"I know just what you mean; I've had a similar experience …"

"This would be very difficult for me too …"

"It's very nice when something like this happens …"

"That would upset me also …"

"How wonderful for you …"

Non-Verbal Communication—Body Language

Non-verbal communication, or body language, is also important in day-to-day interactions.[2] As a supervisor, you will interpret the physical signals that employees, peers, and managers send when interacting with you or with others. While it is true that you will respond to messages people give you through their use of the language, you will also receive many messages through their facial expressions and physical actions. The spoken word is not the only means of human expression. Some people will argue that it's not even the most important one. The old saying, "Actions speak louder than words," supports this view.

Suppose you tell Lisa, a cook helper, that you are short a dishwasher for the lunch shift today. When you ask her to fill in, she smiles and says, "Sure. No problem." However, as she fills the dish machine, she bangs pots and pans around and slams them on the counter. She also breaks several plates and saucers.

What is Lisa trying to tell you?

If you are reading Lisa's body language correctly, you realize that she may be very upset about filling in for the dishwasher. Even though she told you she was glad to help you out, her actions give you quite a different message. Lisa is an excellent cook helper and you don't want to lose her. You also want to save as many dishes as you can. You know you must approach Lisa. Her angry actions may be related to something occurring outside of work, but she needs to know that her behavior is unacceptable. You must deal with her before the incident gets out of hand. You need to approach Lisa immediately and confront her with the inconsistency between what she said and how she is acting. For example, you might say, "Lisa, you said you'd have 'no problem' washing dishes. Now you seem upset. What's the matter?"

As this story illustrates, the words we use do not necessarily tell the whole story. We communicate with more than just our spoken language. Our non-verbal behavior, or body language, can betray our attitudes and feelings. Even though our words may say otherwise, our true feelings may be revealed by our facial expression, eyes, posture, gestures, and body movement.

Facial Expression

Facial expression is by far the most common non-verbal communication we use. The expressions on our faces reveal a lot about our attitudes. Most people look at their listener's face when they are conversing, especially at the listener's eyes and mouth, the most expressive features. Perhaps you have felt uncomfortable trying to talk to someone whose eyes are hidden by dark sunglasses. You may have felt that you were speaking to a wall. Think, in addition, how much easier it is to understand speakers when we can see their faces. By simply watching facial expressions we can know whether someone is happy or sad, angry or confused.

However, facial expressions are not always completely reliable. Most of us have learned to fake facial expressions when we think it is appropriate. Poker players, for instance, may wear a blank, so-called poker face even though they have never held a better hand and they are sure they will win the pot. And sometimes people "put on a happy face" to please parents, managers, or other authority figures, as Lisa did in the story that began this section.

While a smile often indicates happiness, it does not always do so. For example, it may communicate anger, nervousness, defensiveness, or embarrassment. Further, we may smile to express apology, such as when we accidentally step on someone's toes in a crowded room.

Eyes

The more people catch our eye and hold it, the more likely we are to pay attention to them. For example, a speaker who maintains eye contact with the audience is likely to be considered a good, friendly speaker. The reverse is also true. A speaker who looks at the floor or over the heads of the audience is likely to appear nervous, and possibly unreliable.

We generally suspect that people who avoid eye contact are uneasy or perhaps lying about something. Alternatively, they may be uninterested or nervous. An assertive, confident person is likely to meet our eyes, while a passive, unassertive person may avoid eye contact.

Posture

Someone's slumped shoulders will usually communicate depression or hopelessness, however temporary. An anxious person may move stiffly and tensely. In addition, he/she may wear a grim facial expression, with lips pressed tightly together, and a wrinkled brow. A tense person may avoid your eyes and may stand or sit with arms folded tightly across his/her chest. He/she may use sudden, rapid gestures. A relaxed person, on the other hand, sits and stands comfortably and gestures naturally.

Gestures

Although we may be quite unconscious of them, gestures often reveal a lot about our feelings and attitudes. For example, if an employee plays with her hair, chews her lips or fingernails, or repeatedly folds and unfolds a tissue, you may correctly conclude that she is uneasy. People may reveal their nervousness with repetitious

Our gestures often reveal a lot about our feelings and attitudes.

movements, including swinging their feet or drumming their fingers. People may also reveal tension when they smoke one cigarette after another. Repetitive gestures may indicate impatience or uncertainty as well as nervousness.

When someone is consciously or unconsciously keeping body language in check, it may be that he/she is trying to withhold verbal information as well. However, it is important to consider the entire context and the individual's personality and background.

Suppose you are arguing with a co-worker. As you begin to convince your colleague, you notice that he covers his mouth with his fingers. This is both a protective movement and an indication of your colleague's uncertainty. He may also rub the back of his neck with his palm, which is another common protective gesture. This gesture may signal that he realizes he is wrong, but he may not even be conscious of it or that he is using such a gesture.

Probably the most common body language signal is arms crossed in front of the chest. We may use this to close off the rest of the world, to form a shield between ourselves and a hostile environment. For example, you may find that an employee tightly folds his arms across his chest when you are scolding him. Crossed arms may also indicate anxiety, disagreement, or the desire to protect oneself. Again, though, it is important to consider the entire context; it would be unwise to make rash judgments. A person may simply be more comfortable sitting with his/her arms crossed.

Body Movement

Nodding usually indicates agreement, but we also nod to say, "I hear you" or "I'm paying attention" when we're listening to someone else. Again, it is important to judge the total context.

A person's walk can give clues to his/her general nature. For example, a determined person will walk firmly, while an impatient, aggressive, or busy person will walk quickly. A shy, uncertain person will walk hesitantly. Guests who are new to your property may enter the lobby uncertainly. Their hesitant steps will tell you that they could use your assistance.

When you're speaking before a group, such as in a meeting, walk *toward* the group to emphasize a particular issue. This will also increase tension. When you want to de-emphasize a point or decrease tension, walk *away* from the group.

Using Body Language on the Job

Your choice of body language also comes into play when visitors are in your office. For example, suppose you summon a troublesome employee to your office to discuss the employee's unacceptable behavior. To help underscore your position of authority, you may choose to sit in your chair behind your desk, while the employee sits in a chair in front of your desk. The desk will serve as a barrier between you. It will also show the employee that you are in charge. You would most likely choose this seating arrangement for a formal discussion or meeting.

However, if you want to establish a more informal atmosphere, you might consider moving the visitor's chair. For instance, you could place it along the side of your desk. This would decrease both the physical and psychological distances between you. It would also put you and your visitor on a more equal footing. If you want to establish an even warmer atmosphere, you might decide to sit with the employee in front of the desk. This would erase barriers, and would also put your visitor more at ease.

Employees may be somewhat intimidated when you call them to your office. It may be a good idea, then, to go to them, either to their offices or to their work stations, and conduct any informal business on their turf. They will be more at ease from the outset of any discussion.

No matter what your attitude, it will show through in your non-verbal behavior. If you resent a co-worker, for example, it may be difficult for you to hide it. Instead of trying to conceal it, you might be better off modifying your attitude. As much as possible, try to find something you can admire about the co-worker. Your genuine warmth will come through in your body language.

Put your knowledge of body language to work for you. It will help you to more easily understand others, including employees, co-workers, and guests. It can also assist you in your personal life. Your awareness of non-verbal communication will help you to learn to control the messages you send. If you understand how others perceive your actions and gestures, you can strengthen your communication with your conscious use of appropriate body language.

Writing

Writing represents one of the most difficult forms of communication for anyone to master. However, everyone in business—especially in supervisory or management roles—must spend time and effort writing. The importance of your writing skills will increase as you move to higher levels of responsibility. For example, if you are a new hospitality supervisor, you will have to learn to write memos to employees, co-workers, and managers. In addition, your boss may ask you to investigate a certain matter and then write a report summarizing your findings. Finally, you will need to write clear, concise comments when evaluating an employee's performance or when filling out discipline action forms.

It is very important to learn to express yourself effectively in writing. The messages or reports you write represent you and, to some extent, your supervisory ability. Clear, organized writing corresponds to—and symbolizes—the author's clear, organized thinking processes. The opposite is also true. A poorly written and disorganized communication will tell the world that you are a sloppy, disorganized thinker.

In fact, your written words may represent you for some time to come. Your memos in the general manager's files, for instance, can serve as lasting, concrete reminders of you and your abilities. Your strongly written reports may remind upper management that you are an efficient, organized, clear-thinking supervisor who is worth promoting. It is far better, then, to learn to write well and effectively from the beginning.

Business Writing Tips and Examples

Good writing clearly communicates information or ideas, as briefly as possible, to intended readers. At the same time, it obeys certain rules of grammar, spelling, sentence structure, and punctuation.

Before you begin to write, it is a good idea to plan your writing. It is not easy to write effectively, but you can simplify your task if you plan well. Planning also clarifies your thinking. You should (1) have a specific reader or audience in mind; (2) know your objective; (3) decide which essential information to include; and (4) determine how to present the information. These four points are discussed more thoroughly in the following section.

Have a specific reader or audience in mind. It is important to write with your intended audience firmly in mind. For example, a memo to your staff about summer vacation schedules would be far more informal than, say, a memo to your boss's boss about next quarter's forecast. Know whom you are writing to, and gear your tone, language, and level of writing to your audience.

Know your objective. Know your topic and stick to it. Determining a particular purpose for writing will keep both your thoughts and your writing clear.

Decide which essential information to include. This may involve some research. For instance, you may have to consult your files or speak to others in your department. However, you will do much of your writing without having to research. In this case, determining exactly what you want to say will make your job easier.

Decide how to present the information. The best way to do this is to make an **outline,** which is a list of significant points. To do this, write down each major point. Beneath each one list the minor points you wish to include. You might list them in this way:

1. Major point

    A. Minor point

        i. Sub point (if any)

        ii. Sub point (if any)

    B. Minor point

2. Major point

    A. Minor point

    B. Minor point

Finally, sort all points into a logical order.

You will find that using outlines actually makes your writing tasks easier. Outlines are valuable tools which will increase your writing effectiveness. They force you to organize your thoughts before you write them. In the process, they make business writing tasks faster to complete.

As your writing skills improve, your outlines may become briefer and easier to develop. You may modify them to your needs as you gain writing expertise, or you may modify them to fit each type of writing task. No matter how skilled you become at business writing, you should continue to prepare some sort of outline every time you start to write.

Use Specific, Active Language

Concrete nouns are specific rather than general. They express meaning more powerfully than general or abstract nouns. Non-specific nouns such as *area, aspect, factor, individual,* and *thing* are especially uninteresting. For example, it is livelier and more specific to say "The general manager met with four supervisors from our new Boise hotel" instead of "The general manager met with four individuals from Idaho." Note these additional examples:

GENERAL Last week, the executive housekeeper hired three individuals.

SPECIFIC Last week, the executive housekeeper hired two new room attendants and a valet.

GENERAL Chris, the new supervisor, is interested in many things.

SPECIFIC Chris, the new food supervisor, is interested in fishing, the martial arts, traveling, and camping.

Verbs in the **passive voice** are colorless because their subjects are acted upon; they do not act themselves. In the **active voice,** the subject of the sentence does the acting. Use active verbs whenever possible. They enliven every sentence, and therefore your entire piece of writing. Even though the passive voice is grammatically correct, the active voice is usually stronger because it is more direct. Furthermore, the passive voice often uses far too many words, and it may sound bureaucratic or self-important.

PASSIVE	The decision was made by George.
ACTIVE	George made the decision.
PASSIVE	The employee handbook was revised by the committee.
ACTIVE	The committee revised the employee handbook.
PASSIVE	The employee was praised by the supervisor.
ACTIVE	The supervisor praised the employee.

In some instances, the receiver of the action is more important than the doer of the action. In such cases, the passive voice is more appropriate:

Lee's managing style is copied by many new supervisors.

The new hotel was opened by the company in May.

How Hospitality Managers and Employees Read

Hospitality managers are busy people. Some managers, for example, may receive 20 or more memos, reports, and letters each day. Therefore, they do not have a lot of time to devote to every written message that comes their way. It is important, then, to write in as brief and clear a manner as you can. Readers will appreciate your efforts to simplify their work. You can do this by setting forth in clear, understandable language exactly what it is you want them to know.

Hospitality managers and employees read to gather information to help them do their jobs. As a hospitality operation prospers, written communication increases. With less time to read more and more material, hospitality employees find they must read more quickly. They have little time to figure out unclear, hard-to-understand writing.

A hospitality operation is not reader-oriented. Most hotels and restaurants are busy places. Every day, hospitality employees face unavoidable distractions. Frequent interruptions, telephone calls, and even conversation make concentration very difficult. Some hospitality managers may have privacy, but most supervisors and employees do not.

How, then, do hospitality managers and employees read? They read in the never-ending face of difficulty. Every time they start to read, they face interruptions which will probably lessen both their concentration and their grasp of the material. Make it as easy as possible for your readers to understand your messages. If you recognize the limitations the business atmosphere places on your readers, you can learn how to write for them.

Your good writing will allow easy reading and give your readers instant information. Writing for easy reading doesn't come easily. It's a skill you can learn if you follow the principles outlined in the next section.

Use Plain English and Shorter Sentences

Your readers are more likely to understand your writing if you use simple words and sentences. Make it a point to use words that are familiar to your readers. Make

The importance of reading and writing skills increases as you move to higher levels of professional responsibility.

sure *you* understand each word, too. If you have doubts about any word, choose another.

Some writers try to use complicated words in their efforts to impress others. Generally, it is a good idea to substitute plain words for fancy ones. When writing, use the same types of words you use when you speak. Concentrate on informing your readers, not impressing them. Examples of showy words are listed below, with plain English suggestions in parentheses.

ameliorate (help, improve)

ascertain (find out, learn)

commence (begin, start)

component (part)

endeavor (attempt, try)

facilitate (help)

impact on (affect)

optimal (best, finest)

peruse (read, study)

prior to (before)

utilize (use)

In addition, use short sentences. A piece of writing is easier to read and understand if most of its sentences are short. However, not all sentences should be short, because that could be dull. It is a good idea to alternate long sentences with short ones.

In general, limit your sentences to a *maximum* of three typed lines. Longer sentences contain more information than readers can easily absorb. How can you avoid long sentences? Begin by breaking the *and, but* habit. That is, break a single long sentence into smaller, stronger statements by removing the conjunctions *and* and *but.* Consider the following example:

Your readers are more likely to understand your writing if you use simple words and sentences. Make it a point to use words that are familiar to your readers, but make sure *you* clearly understand each word, too, and if you have doubts about any word, choose another.

If you have been reading carefully, the example is probably familiar. In fact, it is a long-winded version of the opening paragraph of this section. The fairly simple original sentences turned into complicated sentences with the addition of the words *and* and *but* in certain places. Take the time now to reread this section's opening paragraph. Then reread the long-winded, rewritten version. Do you find the original, simpler paragraph easier to understand?

Inverted Pyramid

Since your readers will probably have little time to devote to reading your communications, you may want to adopt the **inverted pyramid** style of writing. Newspaper reporters and writers use this method. They put their most important information at the beginning of reports, and leave less important detail for the final paragraphs. Reporters write with the knowledge that readers may skip closing paragraphs, or that editors may delete them entirely to fit available space.

Similarly, it will be useful for you to assume that your readers may be too busy to read your entire memo or report. It is important, then, to get to the point as soon as possible. Put your most important topics and paragraphs at the beginning.

Topic Sentence

Make sure every paragraph deals with a single topic. Begin each paragraph with a **topic sentence**—or main point—that shows what the paragraph is about. A short, simple topic sentence is stronger and easier to remember than a long one. In fact, a lengthy topic sentence may blur the intended message, and effectiveness may be lost. A one-idea topic sentence limited to $1\frac{1}{2}$ typed lines stays in readers' minds.

A short topic sentence helps both the writer and the reader. Using the topic sentence as a guideline, the writer logically develops the rest of the paragraph. For the reader, a briefly stated topic sentence delivers clear, instant information. It gets immediately to the point.

Once you have written your topic sentence, turn to the rest of the paragraph. The remaining sentences should relate to and support the point in the topic sentence. Usually, a topic sentence is more general than the sentences which support it. It may be helpful to think of the topic sentence as a generalization which needs supporting evidence. Other sentences in the paragraph will supply that evidence by providing detail or back-up material.

Each paragraph, then, will look something like this: Topic sentence. Detail. Detail. Detail. Detail.

Writing Memos

Generally, memos communicate information within an organization. They may contain information from the general manager to every employee, may summarize a supervisor's attendance at a convention, or may be an informal weekly report. A memo's length will vary according to its purpose. It is important, however, to keep the memo as short as possible. As with all writing, a memo should be as clear, concise, and to the point as possible. (Exhibit 2.4 presents a sample format to use for memos that you write.)

If the memo is long, you may choose to break it into sections highlighted with headings and subheadings. Your tone may be friendly, informal, and casual when you are writing to co-workers. You will probably use a more formal tone when writing a cover memo for an important report or when writing to your manager. (Refer to the checklist in Exhibit 2.5 to help you make your memos and letters the best they can be.)

Two Versions of One Memo

In the following section, we present two separate samples of one memo. Read Memo A first, and then read Memo B. As you read them, think of the principles you have read about in this section of the chapter. Decide which memo is better.

Memo A—Original

TO: All employees

FROM: Chris Greene

DATE: February 15, 1995

RE: Time sheets

In January the Accounting Department, because it met with difficulty processing employee paychecks on time, inaugurated an improved program devised to ameliorate the process and get the checks out on time. Many steps were taken by Accounting to get the process to the much-improved point at which it presently is. These steps included redesigning the time sheets, which were double-sided and designated Form T-300, and are now single-sided and designated Form T-310. As you know, the time sheets had to be turned in to yours truly by 3 p.m. Wednesdays, and then signed by me, and delivered to Accounting.

I am cognizant of the fact that myriad members of my staff are still utilizing the old time sheets, Form T-300, instead of the new time sheets, Form T-310. I have been apprised that your persistent use of the erroneous time sheets will have unfortunate repercussions. It will doubtlessly result in the misfortune of your hours not being processed and your paychecks not being dispensed in time.

Therefore, take judicious note of our company's revised time sheet, a copy of which is affixed to this memo. In the future, please see to it that you utilize the new, improved time sheet so that you will be paid in as propitious a manner as possible.

Memo B—Improved

TO: All employees
FROM: Chris Greene
DATE: February 15, 1995
RE: Time sheets

Please remember to use the new version of the time sheet (copy attached). In January, Accounting announced that the revised single-sided time sheet takes the place of the old, double-sided time sheet.

Using the new time sheet correctly will ensure your getting your paycheck on time every payday. Please fill out your weekly time sheet completely, sign it, and give it to me by 3 p.m. each Wednesday.

Exhibit 2.4 Sample Memo Format

You may want to use the following sample format for memos that you write.

MEMORANDUM

TO: Your Reader
FROM: You
DATE: Today's
RE: Subject

Paragraph 1: Contains a clear, direct topic sentence. This paragraph states why you are writing. It might also explain what you want readers to do when they finish reading.

Paragraph 2: Contains the most important proof or details supporting Paragraph 1. Alternatively, it may be about another subject entirely, presented with its own clear topic sentence.

Paragraph 3: Contains less important evidence or material, supported with less detail. Again, it may address a different subject.

Final Paragraph: Acknowledges the reader's time. Requests action or repeats an earlier request.

What is wrong with Memo A?

- It includes unnecessary history and detail.
- It uses too many "big" words, such as *inaugurated, ameliorate, cognizant, myriad, utilize, apprised, erroneous, dispensed, repercussions,* and *propitious.*
- It doesn't get right to the point.
- There is too much use of the passive voice.
- Its most important paragraph is the last one, not the first.
- It is too long.
- It sounds too formal and pretentious.

Exhibit 2.5 Checklist: Is Your Memo/Letter Well-Written?

1. *Is it organized well?*
   - Did I write with my readers in mind?
   - Did I determine my objective before beginning to write?
   - Did I decide which important information to include?
   - Did I make an outline first?
   - Do I sort my ideas in a logical order?
   - Will my reader immediately know what I am writing about?
   - Does each paragraph contain a topic sentence?
   - Do other sentences in each paragraph support the topic sentence?

2. *Is it clear?*
   - Does it clearly communicate my message?
   - Do I use plain English?
   - Are my words specific? Do they mean what I think they mean?
   - Do I use concrete nouns, rather than abstract nouns?

3. *Is it concise?*
   - Do I use active verbs?
   - Are my words strong and to the point?
   - Do I use words both my reader and I understand?
   - Do I include only what my reader needs to know?
   - Are my sentences limited to three typed lines?
   - Have I eliminated unnecessary instances of *and* and *but*?
   - Have I used the inverted pyramid style of writing?

4. *Is it accurate?*
   - Is all the information in the memo/letter correct?
   - Do I use proper grammar, spelling, and punctuation?
   - Do I refer to dictionaries and grammar texts when I am uncertain?

5. *Is it courteous and friendly?*
   - Do I use positive expressions?
   - Is my writing free of bureaucratic, pretentious, and legalistic language?
   - Do I use words like "please" and "thank you"?
   - Is my tone appropriate?

What is right about Memo B?

- The most important paragraph appears first.
- It gets to the point immediately.
- Its words and sentences are easy to understand.

- It is clear, direct, and compact.

- It tells busy employees exactly what to do.

- Its tone is appropriately informal, and still courteous.

- It uses language its writer probably uses when talking.

   Which memo would you rather receive: Memo A or Memo B?

Conclusion

It is a good idea to keep a dictionary and a grammar book at your desk. Feel free to refer to them often. In addition, you may want to attend writing conferences and seminars or enroll in writing courses. More effective writing skills likely will help you in your present position, and in any positions you have in the future.

   Finally, you will spend much of your time rewriting your memos, reports, and letters. The first draft of any communication will serve as the foundation for your finished product. You may go through a few revisions before you are satisfied with your message. This is normal; even the best writers spend much of their time revising. Your time will be well worth it.

Endnotes

1. This discussion is based on Richard C. Huseman, et al., *Business Communication: Strategies and Skills,* 2d ed. (Chicago, Ill.: Dryden Press, 1985), pp. 27–32.

2. Much of the material in this section is based on Julius Fast, *Body Language* (New York: M. Evans and Co., Inc., 1970), and *The Body Language of Sex, Power & Aggression* (New York: M. Evans and Co., Inc., 1977).

Key Terms

active voice
downward communication
empathy
feedback
inverted pyramid
lateral communication
mirroring
non-verbal communication
open-ended questions

outline
paraphrasing
passive voice
self-disclosure statements
specific questions
summarizing statements
topic sentence
upward communication

Discussion Questions

1. What are some of the commonly believed myths about communication?

2. According to the chapter, when does successful communication take place?

3. What did you learn from the illustrative story about Molly and Joe?

4. What are some barriers to effective communication?

5. What are some of the barriers to specific supervisory situations?

6. What are the three essential parts of effective speaking, both before a group and in face-to-face conversation?

7. What important points are contained in each of the three essential parts of effective speaking?

8. How can you use speech effectively on the job?

9. Why is it important to improve your listening skills?

10. What factors may get in the way of good listening?

11. What techniques can you use to listen more effectively?

12. What four steps of listening does the active listener move through? What are the important aspects of each stage?

13. How can knowledge of non-verbal communication (body language) help you on the job?

14. How are our true feelings revealed by our facial expressions, eyes, posture, gestures, and body movement?

15. How can you make your business writing more effective?

REVIEW QUIZ

When you feel you have covered all of the material in this chapter, answer these questions. Choose the *best* answer. Check your answers with the correct ones found on the Review Quiz Answer Key at the end of this book.

True (T) or False (F)

T   F   1. Successful communication occurs when a listener or reader receives it, and the message is understood and acted upon by both parties.

T   F   2. Timing has nothing to do with effective communication.

T   F   3. We should compare individuals with others and rank them according to our perceptions of how they measure up.

T   F   4. If you speak too quickly, others may decide that you think they are unable to follow your message, so they won't listen.

T   F   5. You have the innate power to decide how good your listening skill will be.

T   F   6. The goal of the evaluation stage of listening is to ensure that a common understanding is reached.

T   F   7. When paraphrasing, it is important to put your own words in the speaker's mouth in order to make sure the speaker accepts your views.

T   F   8. Making an outline before you start to write actually makes your writing tasks easier.

T   F   9. A topic sentence should come at the end of a paragraph.

T   F   10. Good writers don't need to refer to dictionaries or grammar books.

Alternate/Multiple Choice

11. When we dislike someone because of one particular characteristic, it is referred to as:

    a. the pitchfork effect.
    b. the halo effect.

12. The following sentence, "The apple pie was made by Owen," is written in the _____ voice.

    a. active
    b. passive

13. Which of the following is *not* a barrier to effective communication?

    a. distractions
    b. similarities in background and experience
    c. poor timing
    d. emotions

14. We can be _____ prejudiced in our communication:

    a. positively
    b. negatively
    c. both of the above
    d. none of the above

15. Which of the following is *not* one of the major sections of a formal talk?

    a. introduction
    b. topic
    c. main body
    d. conclusion

Part II

Supervisory Responsibilities

Chapter Outline

The Supervisor and the Human Resources
  Department
    Working with Human Resources
General Recruitment and Selection
  Procedures
Sources of Employees
    Promoting Current Employees
    Friends/Relatives of Current
      Employees
    Other Sources
The Supervisor's Role in Recruitment
    Internal Recruiting
    External Recruiting
    Making Jobs Easier to Fill
    Learning from Employee Turnover
Interviewing Applicants
    Analyzing Application Forms
    Beginning the Interview
    Conducting the Interview
    Questioning Techniques
    Closing the Interview
Selection—What's Next?
The Selection Decision
The Supervisor and Human Resources
  Planning
    Short-Range Approach
    Long-Range Approach
    Supervisor's Role
Human Resources Administration: A Key
  to Labor Control
Evaluating Recruiting and Selecting
  Procedures

Parts of this chapter are based on David Wheelhouse, CHRE, *Managing Human Resources in the Hospitality Industry* (East Lansing, Mich.: Educational Institute of the American Hotel & Motel Association, 1989).

Learning Objectives

1. Describe how line departments and the human resources department work together to recruit new employees.

2. Identify several possible sources of new employees.

3. Describe the supervisor's role in recruiting applicants.

4. Identify several internal recruiting techniques supervisors can use to staff their departments.

5. Describe several external recruiting techniques supervisors can use to staff their departments.

6. Explain what supervisors can do to make open positions easier to fill.

7. Describe the preparations supervisors should make before interviewing applicants.

8. Explain how to conduct an effective employment interview.

9. Describe questioning techniques to use during interviews.

10. Explain how to end interviews effectively.

11. Identify factors to consider when making selection decisions.

12. Describe human resources planning and the role the supervisor takes in it.

3

Recruitment and Selection Procedures

Large operations generally have **human resources** (personnel) **departments** which advise and assist the line departments. Among other tasks, human resources specialists can help you define, identify, and recruit the type of employee your department needs. Indeed, the human resources staff is involved in virtually all aspects of every employee's work history with your property. Through the human resources staff, you can learn about wage and salary compensation, benefits, employee relations, training programs, employee performance reviews, company policies and procedures, and employee motivation. Treat the human resources department as a valuable asset to your property, for that is what it is. Always remember that the human resources department performs a support function in company operations.

As a supervisor, you direct your employees' activities. You must select those applicants most qualified for particular positions, and give careful attention to the process through which individuals join your company. This may sound simple in theory, but in practice it is often difficult because of the many other daily demands on your time.

The Supervisor and the Human Resources Department

If members of the human resources department understand exactly what you need, it is easier for them to screen out those who do not qualify. This can happen when open lines of communication exist between your department and theirs. Human resources will then forward only the top applicants to you for follow-up interviewing. After you interview the top candidates, the human resources staff can help you make the final hiring decision. Your department, not human resources, should extend employment offers to a candidate. The employee-supervisor relationship begins here.

As a supervisor, you are in a **line department** position. Human resources personnel, on the other hand, perform a **staff department** function—that is, they are technical specialists who serve in an advisory role and provide direct support to you and other line employees.

You need to understand the basic policies and procedures which human resources personnel use when recruiting and selecting employment candidates. If you understand how the human resources department operates, you will more likely know how to work with it to meet your needs.

Attitudes toward human resources personnel, such as, "Why complain; they will send me who they want anyway!"; "What do I know? They're the specialists!"; and "They don't care about my problems!" are common in some operations. You play a very critical role: you must provide human resources personnel with pertinent details, such as the basic skills and abilities needed to perform the job effectively, and what you want the ideal candidate to be like. In addition to recruiting, human resources personnel can help screen all applicants, establish employee records, and provide general property orientation. Further, they can help you develop and implement appropriate training programs. You must work in cooperation with human resources in order to develop a fully productive department.

Working with Human Resources

The human resources department is responsible for helping you find the most qualified applicants. You, in turn, must provide information which will help the human resources department do its job. The final selection of an applicant should rest with you and your boss in the line department.

You can help human resources department staff members by providing current and accurate job descriptions and job specifications. Sometimes human resources employees use outdated job information when recruiting because the requesting department fails to submit current job descriptions. When this happens, there may be a big difference between how the job is described to applicants and what the work is actually like. Job specifications must likewise be accurate. As jobs, related duties, and necessary equipment change, so do the qualities needed to effectively perform the job. The human resources department must know about the changes in order to make the best possible placements.

The human resources department needs **lead time** to recruit applicants. While occasional emergencies occur, you will often have advance notice of expected vacancies. Give this information to the human resources department as soon as possible.

You may be able to suggest where and how to recruit possible employees. In working with employees, you learn a great deal about them. You may find that a lot of your good employees come from a particular school or vocational training program. Suggest these sources to human resources. In addition, tell current employees about position vacancies. They may know eligible individuals who would like to apply, and they may also have ideas about where else to look.

General Recruitment and Selection Procedures

Employee **recruitment** is the process by which qualified applicants are sought and screened to fill currently or soon-to-be vacant positions. The process involves announcing or advertising job vacancies and evaluating applicants to determine whom to hire. As noted earlier, you should be directly involved in recruiting and selecting your staff since you have first-hand knowledge about each job in your department. Moreover, you will have to work closely with new employees as you train and supervise them.

Sources of Employees

There are several possible sources from which to recruit employees for your operation. Consider promoting from within the property, hiring friends and relatives of current employees, and hiring applicants from other labor sources.

Promoting Current Employees

It may be possible to develop a career ladder program in the property (see Chapter 14). With this program, an employee who consistently meets or surpasses performance standards can train for progressively more responsible positions. Good employees are hard to find; encourage them to stay with the operation by offering advancement opportunities. **Lateral transfers** (from one section or department to another at the same level of responsibility) are also possible.

Advantages of internal promotion or transfer include improved employee morale and productivity. As employees see themselves and others being promoted to higher levels of responsibility and better pay, their feelings about themselves, their work, and their employer improve. As a result, employees may stay with the property longer.

Remember to train current employees as well, not just new ones. Training is most effective if it is offered continuously. Most positions are complicated, and requirements for positions may change. Use continuous employee development programs to improve the skills of employees who may deserve promotion. Moreover, employees promoted to new positions will probably need additional training to carry out their new responsibilities.

Friends/Relatives of Current Employees

There are both advantages and disadvantages in employing friends and relatives of current staff members. One advantage is that current employees already understand the job requirements and know what it is like to work for the property. If employees are favorably impressed with the workplace, they may recruit their friends. If your current employees are good, this may prove to be a bonus, because these employees may have friends and relatives of the same caliber.

One disadvantage is that, if several friends or family members work for the operation, what affects one may affect them all. For example, if one member of the group is suspended without pay, the entire group could react negatively.

Other Sources

Your property may routinely advertise vacant positions in newspapers. Public and private employment agencies can help locate applicants. Colleges, universities, vocational schools, and secondary schools with work study programs are other possible sources of new staff members.

You may also wish to contact groups which work with and train handicapped and disadvantaged people. Properties have reported success in hiring trainees from these sources, especially for entry-level positions.

The Supervisor's Role in Recruitment

You must define job tasks so that you and your employees know what to expect of each other. Everyone must know exactly what each job involves. The tool to use to define a job is called a **job description.** If you work for a large property, the human resources department will help you prepare job descriptions.

A **job specification** is a selection tool which lists the personal qualities employees need to perform a job adequately. For instance, if a cook must read and interpret recipes, the job specification should include those skills.

Find out what basic recruitment procedures your property uses. You will need to know how much lead time the property needs to fill a vacant position, for instance. By following all policies and procedures your property requires, you can make sure that your requests are handled completely and in an orderly manner.

If your property does not have a human resources department, you could be involved in initial interviewing and reference checking. If your property has a human resources department, you and, perhaps, your boss, should interview top candidates the department sends to you. It is extremely important to meet with applicants to discuss job-related matters and to answer any questions they might have about the workplace in general.

Internal Recruiting

Your property may use various recruiting techniques that enable it to fill jobs quickly with applicants from within the property. One of these techniques is internal recruiting. The benefits of **internal recruiting** include improved employee morale and motivation, and ready access to a skilled pool of applicants already familiar with the property. It provides you with an opportunity to reward good employees with new job responsibilities, while, at the same time, opening up entry-level positions to bring in new employees. Implementation of some of these techniques is within your reach.

Posting Job Openings. Posting job openings may reduce the property's turnover at some levels. Some employees may want to transfer to another department or into yours, or wish to step into higher positions. Employees applying for other jobs within your property or company deserve the same courtesy and respect you give outside applicants. If the job goes to someone else, truthfully explain your reasons to the applying employee. Try to understand and respond to your employees' needs. If employees do not qualify for open positions, help them develop skills which can prepare them for future openings.

There are two ways to post job openings. First, post all job openings for all employees to see, making information available to everyone. Choose a posting location visible to all employees, such as the department bulletin board or the property's employee dining area. This method increases employee awareness of opportunities. However, it could also result in unnecessary human resources paperwork if job requirements are not clearly stated, because unqualified employees may apply and will then need to be processed. Second, higher-level management could inform other supervisors about the open positions and ask them to provide the names of qualified employees to human resources or to the requesting department.

Internal recruiters should post open positions as soon as they learn about them. When practical, the property should maintain internal job postings for a certain time *before* advertising for outside applicants.

Cross-Training. Whenever possible, it is a good idea to train your employees to do more than one job in your department. Both your department and your employees will benefit from **cross-training.** You will have a supply of well-rounded employees who can substitute for others when you are short-handed, and the employees, in turn, can acquire valuable skills. This will increase their value to you and to the property. In addition, the employees will feel more challenged and valued as a result of their expanded skills and capabilities. With the shortage of qualified applicants, cross-training is becoming increasingly critical to the success of many properties.

Identify Employees' Other Skills. During evaluations, ask employees if they have skills which they are not using. Perhaps you could assign employees to jobs elsewhere in your department when opportunities to use their skills arise. If employees do not use their professional skills and are not truly interested in their jobs, they may leave the property. To avoid this, notify other departments if you think your employees would be better off in other positions within the property.

Develop a Call-Back List. To ease your ongoing recruiting efforts, develop a **call-back list** of all talented internal and external applicants who are interested in positions in your department. Keep another list of former employees who may be willing to help out on a temporary basis.

External Recruiting

Your property should also have strategies for recruiting outside applicants. New employees can contribute fresh ideas to your department. With different insights, they will help your property stay up-to-date, and may introduce creative, better ways of doing things.

Educational Work Programs. Most high schools offer work study programs, while many colleges offer **internship programs.** Such programs allow students to acquire practical work experience while earning school credit at the same time. Taking part in internship programs allows you to find good temporary employees who may permanently join your department later on. Many students would like to continue working for the same company once they've finished their studies. Moreover, if satisfied student interns report good experiences to their schools, your property may be able to choose from a larger, better pool of candidates in the future. It also shows your property's support for community involvement.

Networking. Networking can provide other sources of good candidates. Your network could include your friends, former teachers, professional contacts, and peers in civic and professional associations and at other companies. You may decide to cultivate relationships with others as well. For instance, high school and college teachers and advisers can recommend students who would enjoy working in your department. In addition, consult with vendors or service people who work with your property. They often know many skilled people who might make good employees. Many areas have trade, civic, or professional associations you could join to broaden your network.

Strengthening your network requires effort. For instance, it involves regular communication with your contacts. This may mean visiting them where they work or giving them a tour of your property. The important thing is to keep contacts aware of you and your property.

Exhibit 3.1 lists possible strategies your property can use to recruit applicants. In addition to the agencies named in the exhibit, your property may want to contact state employment services, single parent organizations, veterans' groups, and local associations that represent handicapped, elderly, and minority persons.

Making Jobs Easier to Fill

Your department will have an easier time locating qualified candidates if it makes working at the property as attractive as possible. There are certain steps supervisors can take to help, including setting up various forms of alternative work schedules. Such programs would have to meet the needs of both the department and the employees to be workable options for your property.

Alternative schedules differ from traditional eight-hour-day schedules. Options include flex-time, compressed schedules, and job sharing.

Flex-time. Flex-time allows employees to vary their times of arrival and departure. There is usually a period of time during each shift (core time) when all employees need to be present. The other hours can be flexible. For instance, if the hours between 10 A.M. and 2 P.M. are core time, flexible starting hours could be from 7 to 10 A.M. Flexible ending hours could be scheduled between 3:30 and 6:30 P.M., assuming your property requires an eight-hour workday with a 30-minute lunch period. With this arrangement, every employee's workday would end eight and one-half hours after it began.

Thus, one employee could start at 7 A.M. and leave for home at 3:30 P.M. Another could begin at 10 A.M. and finish at 6:30 P.M.

Such an arrangement can improve employee morale and performance. It could benefit the department as well, because the department is covered for nearly 12 hours a day without overtime pay. However, supervisors have to spend more time planning to make sure that each hour of the workday is covered.

Compressed Schedules. Compressed schedules allow employees to work the equivalent of a standard workweek in less than the usual five days. A typical adaptation is a workweek consisting of four ten-hour days. Unlike flex-time schedules, compressed work schedules do not change. However, many employees would rather take an extra day off on a compressed work schedule than work flexible hours. Benefits of compressed schedules include enhanced recruiting power, decreased absenteeism, and greater employee satisfaction.

Job Sharing. In job sharing, two or more part-time employees assume the responsibilities of one full-time job. The job-sharers can each be responsible for all duties of the job, or they might divide duties between themselves. The job-sharers usually

Exhibit 3.1 Recruitment Strategies

RECRUITMENT STRATEGIES

1. **Youth**
   Schools, Vo-Techs, Colleges
   — Meet with counselors
   — Speak to classes
   — Sponsor work study programs
   — Participate in career days
   — Invite classes to tour hotel

2. **Minorities**
   — Meet with representatives from minority community agencies and invite for lunch and tour of hotel
   — Advertise in minority newspapers
   — Visit schools in minority neighborhoods
   — Notices at churches in minority communities
   — Visit youth centers and place notices there

3. **Disabled Persons**
   — State Rehabilitation Agencies
   — National Alliance of Business
   — Private Industry Councils
   — National Association of Retarded Citizens
   — Goodwill Industries
   — Other local agencies

4. **Women**
   — Local organizations which assist women in transition
   — Community colleges, universities
   — Bulletin board notices in supermarkets, libraries, YWCAs, exercise centers
   — Flyers in parking lots
   — Displaced Homemakers organizations
   — Craft centers
   — Child care centers

5. **Older Workers**
   — AARP Senior Employment Services
   — Senior Citizen Centers
   — Synagogues and churches
   — Retirement communities and apartment complexes
   — Newspaper ads worded to attract
   — Retired military

6. **Individuals in Career Transition**
   — Newspaper ads
   — University evening programs
   — Referrals
   — Teachers
   — Unemployed actors
   — Laid off workers from other industries
   — Speak at community functions, i.e., Rotary, Toastmasters

7. **Lawfully Authorized Immigrants**
   — Ads in foreign language newspapers
   — Churches
   — English as a Second Language classes
   — Citizenship classes
   — Refugee resettlement centers
   — Employee referrals

Courtesy of Radisson Hotel Corporation, Minneapolis, Minnesota work different hours each day or on completely different days. Plan an overlap in work hours so that participants can confer when they need to.

Job sharing can reduce burnout, absenteeism, and turnover. In addition, it provides for job continuity. If one participant leaves, the other can pick up the slack and also train a newly hired staff member. Furthermore, the participants might be willing to fill in for each other on sick days or during vacations. Finally, both might work extra hours when your property is busiest.

Before you decide to adopt job sharing for your department, there are several preparations you'll need to make. These include assigning responsibility for specific tasks, deciding how to evaluate participating employees, and making sure that the job-sharers and their work standards are compatible.

Finally, while a job sharing program offers many advantages, the property must consider the program's effect on the costs of fringe benefits before adopting it.

Learning from Employee Turnover

Effective recruitment and selection procedures help bring the best applicants to the job, and the skillful use of basic supervisory principles helps retain these employees. However, given the high **turnover** rates at many properties, there will always be some staff members who terminate employment for a variety of reasons. In addition, the property itself may initiate separation, perhaps because of an employee's performance.

Follow consistent procedures when employees leave. Through **exit interviews** (also called employee separation interviews), you or others may be able to figure out why employees leave. When employees feel they have nothing to lose, they are much more likely to be honest about why they are resigning. The exit interview should be conducted by someone other than the employee's immediate supervisor. A resigning employee might be more honest with a third-party supervisor. (A sample format for an employee separation interview is shown in Exhibit 3.2.) You can often learn much that will improve the work conditions and reduce future turnover rates in the process. Conducted properly, exit interviews can help identify organizational problems. Information from these interviews can lead to major improvements in the way your organization deals with its employees.

Interviewing Applicants

The employment interview should give the applicant a good idea of what it would be like to work for your company. Once new employees are actually working, their general morale and productivity are affected by whether the job and the operation live up to their initial expectations. Therefore, it is very important that you give the applicant a reliable impression of both the position and the property. Here, as elsewhere, honesty is the best policy.

Analyzing Application Forms

If someone on the human resources staff has already interviewed the applicant, find out what questions he/she asked so you won't ask the same ones. Compare notes with the human resources department later.

Exhibit 3.2 Sample Form for Employee Separation Interview

EMPLOYEE SEPARATION INTERVIEW

Our company, like all businesses today, is concerned with the rate of employee turnover. When any employee is forced to make a job change, it represents an added expense to the employer plus a certain amount of confusion in the department from which the employee left. We are working toward making our organization an outstanding place to work and would sincerely appreciate your frank appraisal and honest answers to the following questions. This report is confidential and used for research purposes only.

Name

Supervisor   Department

I. Please indicate below the reason you decided to leave your employment with us.

1.	☐	Another job	8.	☐	Return to School
2.	☐	Dissatisfied with Supervisor	9.	☐	Dissatisfied with Company
3.	☐	Leaving City	10	☐	Salary
4.	☐	Pregnant	11.	☐	Transportation
5.	☐	Marriage	12.	☐	No chance for advancement
6.	☐	Released	13.	☐	Lack of Work (Boredom)
7.	☐	Short Timo Temporary	14.	☐	Other (Explain below)

II. 1. Was your job accurately explained to you at the time of your employment? ☐ Yes ☐ No
 2. Did you receive accurate job instruction? ☐ Yes ☐ No
 3. Was your pay adequate for the job you were doing? ☐ Yes ☐ No
 4. When difficult problems came up in your work, or things went wrong, how free did you feel about asking questions?

   ☐ Not Free At All   ☐ Reasonably Free
   ☐ Immediate Supervisor   ☐ Completely Free
        Hard To Approach

 5. What is your opinion of the Company's general working conditions?

   ☐   Good   ☐   Fair   ☐   Poor

 6. Did you understand the importance of your job? ☐ Yes ☐ No
 7. How long did you work with us? _____ Years _____ Months
 8. Did you feel a part of the Company? ☐ Yes ☐ No
 9. Would you tell us what you liked about your job?

 10. How would you rate your Supervisor?

   ☐ Does Excellent Job   ☐ Below Average
   ☐ Satisfactory   ☐ Poor

11. Is there anything the Company could have done, other than salary, to make your stay a more lasting one?

12. Is there anything else you would like to say?

Employee's Signature

Interviewer _____   Date _____

Exhibit 3.3 Previewing an Application: General Observations

- Is the application neat and clean—or messy, with erasures and misspellings?
- Did the applicant follow instructions?
- Is the handwriting acceptable for the job in question? Writing that goes above and below the lines may indicate poor dexterity or vision or limited education.
- Are there any omissions? These may indicate that the applicant has something to hide. They should be explored carefully.
- Does the signature match the handwriting? People who read and write poorly, or not at all, sometimes obtain an application, take it home, and have someone else fill it out for them.
- How long was the person employed in each previous job? If the length of employment gets shorter with each job, the applicant may have an intensifying problem.
- Do job responsibilities or pay rates indicate a career that is going up, staying at the same level, or going down?
- Do job choices indicate strong preferences for certain types of work?

Source: David Wheelhouse, *Managing Human Resources in the Hospitality Industry* (East Lansing, Mich.: Educational Institute of the American Hotel & Motel Association, 1989), p. 78.

Take time to review the employment application *before* meeting with the applicant. Look at the handwriting and neatness of the application. Also, look for normal career and salary advancements. Consider the application a record of the applicant's employment history, and pay special attention to unexplained gaps. Note which areas you wish to explore further (Exhibit 3.3 contains a list of questions to consider when looking over an employment application). Use a separate piece of paper to record your thoughts once the interview ends. Do not write on the application, because it is a legal document that may be reviewed by outside agencies.

Beginning the Interview

Although this section explains how to conduct employment interviews *per se*, you may be able to use this information in other types of one-on-one employee interviewing (such as in discipline procedures, performance evaluation, or exit interviews).

During the interview, be yourself and show your personality. This will help the applicant do the same. The interview itself should be relaxed and professional. It should also be private. Choose a setting where you will be neither distracted nor interrupted. If you conduct your interview in an office, put the applicant at ease by sitting on the same side of the desk; do not sit with the desk between you. However, it is a good idea to interview in an area which is close to the site where the new employee will be working. Give preferred applicants a tour before concluding the interview to provide them with a better understanding of the workplace.

Put the applicant at ease. Greet the applicant promptly; don't make him/her wait. Introduce yourself, smile, make eye contact, and shake hands. Begin the conversation by discussing something of interest to the applicant, perhaps a hobby listed on the application, which will help both of you relax. If the application lists the person's interests, talk about them. Alternatively, you might ask newcomers how they like the area. Once you have broken the ice, move on to the main body of the interview, which is discussing the job.

State the purpose of the interview. If you are conducting a ten-minute screening interview, say so at the beginning. Similarly, if you expect the interview to be 30 minutes long, say so. In addition, list the topics the interview will cover. For example, you might explain that you will begin the interview by taking a few minutes to get to know each other. Then you will review the application and discuss the job. Finally, you will provide an overview of the property, answer the applicant's questions, and describe the next step in the process.

Conducting the Interview

Use a conversational tone throughout the interview. Speak on the applicant's level without talking down to him/her. You should control both the topics discussed and the direction of the interview, but allow the applicant to set the pace. If the applicant is shy or if he/she speaks slowly, the pace will be slower.

If your property has no human resources department and you conduct the first interview, verify early in the conversation whether the applicant fulfills the job's primary requirements. Then, say that within the first three days of work, all new employees must prove that they have the legal right to work in the United States.[1] Mention any other qualifications that must be verified upon hiring, such as minimum age for serving alcohol.

Finally, make sure that the job meets the applicant's needs regarding pay and benefits, working hours and conditions, and kind of work desired. You can cover these topics quickly at the beginning of the interview or by reading the application beforehand. If the needs of the applicant and the property do not correspond, politely end the interview. Remember that an applicant desperate for a job may agree to anything to obtain it, even if it clearly is not suitable. Such an applicant, if hired, would probably quit as soon as something more suitable came along.

To begin questioning, ask about the applicant's job expectations. For instance, you might ask why the applicant applied at your property or what type of work he/she wants. Encourage the applicant with your own facial expressions and body language. Nod your head, maintain eye contact, lean toward the applicant.

Listen carefully as the individual responds. If the applicant hesitates before answering a question, he/she might be uncomfortable with the topic. Listen for vague responses or changes in subject, which could indicate the applicant's desire to hide something.

Listen to the applicant with sincerity and interest. If the applicant asks questions, be honest and direct when you reply. Otherwise, you risk alienating the applicant or losing credibility.

Ask questions in one major topic area at a time. Thoroughly discuss the applicant's work experience, for instance, before discussing education or personal history.

Questioning Techniques

One common questioning technique comprises two steps. The first step asks for specific information, and usually begins with the words who, what, where, which, or when. The second step follows the first, and addresses the same subject; it asks why or how. For example, you might ask, "Which position was your favorite?" After the applicant responds, ask, "Why was it your favorite?"

Alternatively, ask for a list instead of a single answer. This allows the applicant to be more spontaneous when responding. You might, for example, ask questions such as, "What are the best things about your restaurant job?" or "What are your three finest characteristics?" After hearing the list, ask which single characteristic is strongest.

A third questioning technique asks the applicant to make comparisons. For example, rather than asking what it was like to work with a certain chef, ask the applicant, "How did working with this chef compare with working with the chef at your previous job?"

Whatever techniques you use, it is important to listen to the applicant's answers. If they seem illogical or unreasonable, ask for more information. If answers are incomplete, encourage the applicant to go on by re-stating the answer as a question, such as, "You didn't really like your job, did you?" Use other responses to prod the applicant, such as "Really," or "I see." Commenting instead of asking questions will help maintain a conversational tone. Finally, you could simply say nothing when the applicant pauses. In all likelihood, the applicant will understand that you desire more information.

Alternatively, an applicant's unsatisfactory answer may be due to his/her uncertainty about what you're asking. In this case, you may wish to explain the question by suggesting some answers from which the applicant can choose. For instance, you could ask, "Did you leave that position because of the salary, the benefits, or because you had to work nights and weekends?"

Open-ended and Closed Questions. Open-ended, or indirect, questions permit the applicant to respond in a free and unstructured way. Such questions are broad and ask for responses of more than just a few words. Examples of open-ended questions include:

"What do you like and dislike about your present job?"

"Can you describe a typical day on your last job?"

"What do you look for in a position?"

Using open-ended questions offers several advantages. For instance, they enhance your opportunity to obtain meaningful information from the applicant. In addition, open-ended questions are easier to answer and are not threatening to the applicant. Finally, they communicate your interest in the applicant. However, open-ended questions take more time to answer.

Closed, or direct, questions, on the other hand, are restrictive and call for very brief responses. Use closed questions—which usually require yes or no answers—when you want to verify facts or quickly cover a lot of ground.

Learning to ask and analyze closed questions requires little training. Less time is needed for the question and response, and answers are often easy to jot down. Finally, you can more easily control the length of the interview. However, closed questions typically generate little information, and restrict the applicant's opportunity to provide additional information. Overdependence on closed questions results in interviews with little dialogue, gives you less information than you might need, and can lead to poor hiring decisions.

Specific Questions. Exhibit 3.4 lists many sample questions which may help you develop a complete interview format. Any question can give you insight into the applicant's character and abilities, depending on how the applicant responds. Make sure your questions are appropriate and relevant to both the applicant and the job.

Several categories of questions should be completely avoided, since they can violate the applicant's lawful rights. Exhibit 3.5 lists samples of lawful and unlawful pre-employment questions. Make sure you and your property know the current laws in your area, for these categories often vary according to state. Moreover, they may change from year to year.

Generally, avoid topics which will produce information which, by law, should not enter into employment decisions. These topics include the applicant's birthplace, age, religion or creed, race or color, height and weight, marital status, sex, national origin, citizenship, memberships in lodges and religious or ethnic clubs, and arrest records. However, in most states, it is legal to ask about conviction records or whether any felony charges are pending against the applicant.

It is illegal to ask questions specifically of one sex but not the other. For example, it is illegal to ask female applicants about child-care arrangements if you do not ask male applicants the same question. If a question is legitimately job-related, however, you must ask it of both male and female applicants.

Closing the Interview

Before ending interviews, ask applicants if they have anything they want to add. This allows them to ask questions about the property or to further explain their skills and experiences. What they say will give you further insight into their personalities, requirements, and concerns.

If you come across a good candidate whom you'd like to hire, you may be tempted to shorten the interview in order to save time. Instead, however, spend time talking about the goals of the property and your department. Talk about the company's successful products and services. Discuss the importance of the job for which the candidate is applying. Finally, represent your company as very selective about whom it hires. Everyone wants to hire into a successful operation, but no one values a job obtained too easily.

If you are seriously considering hiring an applicant, explain the job accurately and thoroughly. Explain what you expect of the employee and why. Mention any undesirable aspects of the position as well, such as swing shifts and weekend work. If you don't discuss negative aspects before hiring the applicant, you'll regret it later—and so will the applicant. If the applicant balks at what you say, don't make a job offer.

If you don't extend a job offer during the interview, let the applicant know when you will contact him/her. In first interviews or screening interviews, say that a hiring decision will be made within a few days. Once you decide, it's best to

Exhibit 3.4 Sample Interview Questions

Relevant to Job Background
- Did you regularly work 40 hours a week? How much overtime did you work?
- What were your gross and take-home wages?
- What benefits did you receive? How much did you pay for them?
- What salary/wage do you desire? What is the lowest amount you are likely to accept?
- Which days of the week are best for working?
- Have you ever worked weekends before? Where? How often?
- Which shift do you enjoy working the most? Which shift can't you work? Why?
- How many hours a week would you like to work?
- How will you get to work?
- Is your means of transportation reliable for the shifts you may be working?
- When you started your last job, what position did you hold? What position do you hold now or did you hold when you left?
- What was the starting salary of your present job or the last job you held?
- How often did you get pay increases on your present job or the last job you held?
- What three things do you want to avoid on your next job?
- What qualities do you expect in a supervisor?
- Why did you choose this line of work?
- Why are you interested in working at this hotel?
- Which work experience most influenced your career decisions?

Education and Intelligence
- When you were in school, what subjects did you like the most? Why?
- When you were in school, what subjects did you like the least? Why?
- Do you think your grades are a good indicator of your overall abilities?
- If you had to make the same educational decisions over again, would you make the same choices? Why or why not?
- What is the most important thing you have learned in the past six months?
- What good qualities did you find in your best teachers? Can these apply to work as well?

Personal Traits

Some of the following may be more suitable for people without much work background:
- What do you like to do in your spare time?
- How many times were you absent or late for your present or last job? Is that normal? What were the reasons?
- What does your family think of your working at this hotel?
- On your last job, were the policies concerning being absent without cause or late clearly explained to you? Were these policies fair?
- What was your first supervisor like?
- How did you get your first job? Your most recent job?

For the following questions about personal traits, job titles may be changed to meet the needs of the interview:
- Who has greater responsibilities—a front desk agent or a reservation sales agent? Why?
- Have you ever had to deal with an angry guest who complains about everything? If so, how did you work with the guest to resolve the issues?

- What do you consider the main reason people in the position you are applying for leave their jobs? What would you do to change this?
- What do you consider the most important responsibilities of a good front desk agent?
- Suppose your supervisor insisted you learn a task in a certain way, when you know there is a better way. What would you do?
- Have you ever had a supervisor show favoritism to certain employees? How did you feel about this?
- Of all your job experiences, what did you like the most? Why?
- Of all your job experiences, what did you like the least? Why?
- When you go to a store to purchase something, what qualities do you look for in the sales person?
- What was your biggest accomplishment on your last job?
- What would you have changed about your last job if you had the opportunity?
- If the opportunity was offered to you, would you return to your last employer? Why or why not?
- How much notice did you give your last employer when you decided to leave (or plan to give your current employer)?
- How would your former supervisor and fellow employees describe you?
- What strengths and weaknesses do you bring to this new position?
- What frustrates you on the job? How do you handle this frustration?
- On your last performance review, what areas did your former supervisor mention need to be improved? Why do you think the comment was made?
- What three areas would you most like to improve about yourself?
- What one thing have you done of which you are the proudest? Why?
- What is the funniest thing that has ever happened to you?
- What is important to you about the job you are applying for? Why?

Questions for Managerial Candidates

- What type of training program did you have for your employees? Who set it up and who implemented it?
- What have you done on your last job to improve the performance of the department you supervised? How was this measured?
- What are the most important attributes of a manager?
- What hotels were your biggest competitors? What were their strengths and weaknesses?
- How would your employees describe you as a supervisor?
- How many people did you have to discipline on your last job? Describe the circumstances. How do you feel about terminating employees?
- What did you do to motivate your employees?

notify every applicant, especially those who spent a lot of time or money applying or interviewing.

However, if you know during the interview that you will not hire the applicant, say so. It's kinder than stringing him/her along. Soften the blow by saying something like, "We're pleased so many qualified applicants have applied." Then, end the interview decisively. Explain why the applicant won't be considered. After you've ended the conversation, stand up, shake hands, and thank the applicant for his/her interest.

Exhibit 3.5 Pre-Employment Inquiry Guide

SUBJECT	LAWFUL PRE-EMPLOYMENT INQUIRIES	UNLAWFUL PRE-EMPLOYMENT INQUIRIES
NAME:	Applicant's full name. Have you ever worked for this company under a different name? Is any additional information relative to a different name necessary to check work record? If yes, explain.	Original name of an applicant whose name has been changed by court order or otherwise. Applicant's maiden name.
ADDRESS OR DURATION OF RESIDENCE:	How long a resident of this state or city?	
BIRTHPLACE:		Birthplace of applicant. Birthplace of applicant's parents, spouse or other close relatives. Requirement that applicant submit birth certificate, naturalization or baptismal record.
AGE:	*Are you 18 years old or older?	How old are you? What is your date of birth?
RELIGION OR CREED:		Inquiry into an applicant's religious denomination, religious affiliations, church, parish, pastor, or religious holidays observed. An applicant may not be told "This is a Catholic (Protestant or Jewish) organization."
RACE OR COLOR:		Complexion or color of skin.
PHOTOGRAPH:		Requirement that an applicant for employment affix a photograph to an employment application form. Request an applicant, at his or her option, to submit a photograph. Requirement for photograph after interview but before hiring.
HEIGHT:		Inquiry regarding applicant's height.
WEIGHT:		Inquiry regarding applicant's weight.
MARITAL STATUS:		Requirement that an applicant provide any information regarding marital status or children. Are you single or married? Do you have any children? Is your spouse employed? What is your spouse's name?
SEX:		Mr., Miss or Mrs. or an inquiry regarding sex. Inquiry as to the ability to reproduce or advocacy of any form of birth control.
CITIZENSHIP:	Are you a citizen of the United States? If not a citizen of the United States, does applicant intend to become a citizen of the United States? If you are not a United States citizen, have you the legal right to remain permanently in the United States? Do you intend to remain permanently in the United States?	Of what country are you a citizen? Whether an applicant is naturalized or a native-born citizen; the date when the applicant acquired citizenship. Requirement that an applicant produce naturalization papers or first papers. Whether applicant's parents or spouse are naturalized or native born citizens of the United States; the date when such parent or spouse acquired citizenship.
NATIONAL ORIGIN:	Inquiry into languages applicant speaks and writes fluently.	Inquiry into applicant's (a) lineage; (b) ancestry; (c) national origin; (d) descent; (e) parentage, or nationality. Nationality of applicant's parents or spouse. What is your mother tongue? Inquiry into how applicant acquired ability to read, write or speak a foreign language.
EDUCATION:	Inquiry into the academic vocational or professional education of an applicant and the public and private schools attended.	
EXPERIENCE:	Inquiry into work experience. Inquiry into countries applicant has visited.	
ARRESTS:	Have you ever been convicted of a crime? If so, when, where and nature of offense? Are there any felony charges pending against you?	Inquiry regarding arrests.
RELATIVES:	Name of applicant's relatives, other than a spouse, already employed by this company.	Address of any relative of applicant, other than address (within the United States) of applicant's father and mother, husband or wife and minor dependent children.

*This question may be asked only for the purpose of determining whether applicants are of legal age for employment.

SUBJECT	LAWFUL PRE-EMPLOYMENT INQUIRIES	UNLAWFUL PRE-EMPLOYMENT INQUIRIES
NOTICE IN CASE OF EMERGENCY:	Name and address of person to be notified in case of accident or emergency.	Name and address of nearest relative to be notified in case of accident or emergency.
MILITARY EXPERIENCE:	Inquiry into an applicant's military experience in the Armed Forces of the United States or in a State Militia. Inquiry into applicant's service in particular branch of United States Army, Navy, etc.	Inquiry into an applicant's general military experience.
ORGANIZATIONS:	Inquiry into the organizations of which an applicant is a member excluding organizations, the name or character of which indicates the race, color, religion, national origin or ancestry of its members.	List all clubs, societies and lodges to which you belong.
REFERENCES:	Who suggested that you apply for a position here?	

Source: Michigan Department of Civil Rights, Lansing, Michigan.

Selection—What's Next?

After recruiting candidates who seem especially promising, seek more information about them. For example, analyze information the candidates supplied on their job application forms and during preliminary interviews. It is always a good idea to check at least two references that candidates supply.

You may want to give the candidates appropriate selection tests. Some tests are controversial, such as those relating to honesty, aptitude, or psychological issues. They may or may not be relevant, and, in some cases, courts have ruled that such tests discriminate against minorities.

Other selection tests relate to skills necessary to perform specific jobs. For example, if you are looking for an experienced food server, you may ask applicants to demonstrate how to carry a loaded service tray or how to answer guest questions. Similarly, you might ask experienced room attendants to demonstrate how to properly clean bathrooms or make beds. First-level supervisors are often best qualified to observe and analyze the results of these and related selection tests.

Finally, your property may require applicants to take medical examinations before they are hired. If new employees will handle cash on the job, the property may wish to bond them (**bonding** is a type of insurance which will reimburse the company for thefts incurred by employees who misuse company funds).

You can perform other tasks helpful in the selection process. For example, you may conduct follow-up interviews. Sometimes supervisors claim they are too busy to interview a lot of applicants. They just want the human resources department to "send one or two of the best applicants." The entire selection process will work to your advantage if you make recruiting and interviewing the best candidates one of your highest priorities.

The Selection Decision

When deciding whom to hire, consider input from all concerned parties, including the human resources department. This assumes there is sufficient time to recruit several applicants for the vacancy. Providing enough time to interview many applicants will increase your chances of finding the right person for the job. This is much better than recruiting only one person and then modifying the selection process in a desperate attempt to fit the job to the applicant.

The labor shortage problem confronting properties throughout the industry will significantly affect the selection process. In fact, the process may become too easy by default. If unqualified applicants apply to high-turnover properties, many of them may be hired simply because no one else applies. As a consequence, orienting, training, and on-going supervision—which will last the entire time an employee is on the job—will become more difficult.

Many employees resign within the first months of employment. This could indicate that either the property's selection procedures or the orienting and training procedures are inferior. In extreme cases, both could be inadequate. However, it could simply mean that the candidate realized he/she did not like working in the service industry. Remember, though, it is part of every supervisor's job to make sure that all applicants and new employees form accurate impressions of the job and the organization.

The Supervisor and Human Resources Planning

Due to limited economic resources and failure to plan ahead, your property may not consider recruiting applicants until a vacancy occurs or another problem arises. Of course, there will be times when an employee quits without notice or when business increases unexpectedly. Until this happens, you probably have no idea that you need additional staff members. In emergencies, time pressures may prohibit use of the many effective personnel selection procedures. When a position opens under emergency circumstances, you might end up hiring literally the first "warm body" who applies for the job. This is not recommended, though, and should be used only as a last resort.

However, many of our industry's personnel-related problems—such as turnover, lack of training, and absenteeism—result from a lack of planning for human resources needs. If you are a first-line supervisor, you may have only a small role, if any, in determining personnel administration policies within your property. Nevertheless, you can help employees adjust to the job and perform efficiently in the shortest possible time if you organize the jobs well and design effective training programs.

Short-Range Approach

A simple, short-term approach for resolving emergency recruiting/selecting problems involves maintaining an active file of potentially eligible, pre-screened applicants. If individuals apply for jobs when none are available, ask them to fill out applications and participate in preliminary interviews. This practice builds an applicant file which forms the basis for recruitment efforts as vacancies occur. For example, if there is an urgent need for an experienced front desk clerk, contact those with applications on file to find out if they are still interested in the position.

Long-Range Approach

Top-level managers may prefer long-range approaches in planning for human resources needs. Long-range plans help ensure that an adequate number of qualified personnel are available when you need them. These approaches become important when key personnel leave, when the property undertakes an aggressive expansion program, or as the property takes steps to comply with affirmative action/equal opportunity programs.

Human resources planning should be ongoing. Your property should modify and update plans as changes occur. As the organization's personnel needs evolve, it should assess the number and type of positions required, and also review recruiting, selecting, training, and evaluating activities. When used effectively, long-range planning considers peak business times and periods of high turnover. With information like this, plans can be made to hire additional staff in anticipation of these predictable trends.[2]

Supervisor's Role

Supervisors can use basic procedures to undertake human resources planning within their own departments. It is important, first of all, to understand the departmental long- and short-range goals and the strategies designed to attain them. Then, match these with your present employees' skills. If you understand the organization's goals, you can assess future needs for employees. Ask yourself how many of your current employees will be available in the next six months, one year, etc., and how many new staff members you will need. Recognize that you will need to consult personnel in the human resources department for help in planning. Maintain effective communication channels with human resources staff. Also, you must understand and evaluate those procedures for which you are responsible. How well is your department meeting its performance goals? Have strategies to attain them changed? Do you need to take corrective action to bring your department more in line with established goals and plans?

Remember that your job starts long before employees are on the job and ready to work. Developing the groundwork for finding the best employees is difficult; it doesn't just happen. You must look beyond the current shift, month, and budget period and consider the time span the organization uses for long-range planning. What are your organization's goals? How do they affect you and your employees? Once you know the answers to these and similar questions, you are ready to help plan the department's strategies. This will prepare you to deal with routine aspects of the personnel administration process.

Human Resources Administration: A Key to Labor Control ———

This textbook focuses on one aspect of your job—the process by which employees are directed and controlled. The process begins with staffing for the hospitality operation.

Human resources problems probably would not be great if one employee, or a few, could do all the work. However, since there is too much work for the management staff or several assistants to do, it is necessary to divide the work. Few employees can be good at everything. Therefore, the operation must hire specialists, such as food and beverage servers, room attendants, front desk clerks, and others to perform small parts of all the necessary work. Once staffing begins, ask these questions:

- What work must be done?

- When must the work be done?

- Who must do it?
- How much can one specialist do?
- What is the relationship between the specialists?
- How many and what type of specialists do we need?
- What is reasonable compensation for their efforts?

When you can answer these and similar questions, you can begin to develop effective recruitment tools such as job descriptions and job specifications. In addition, you can build effective recruitment and selection techniques.

Evaluating Recruiting and Selecting Procedures

As one directly affected by the results of recruiting and selecting, you can help to periodically evaluate your property's recruiting and selecting procedures. Your ideas about the following issues may help those with selection responsibilities.

1. Does the property consistently use applicable policies and procedures for all candidates in every department?

2. What are the best and least helpful sources of job applicants?

3. Are current and accurate job descriptions, job specifications, and organization charts available?

4. Of the employees who are hired, how many are discharged during the probationary period? How many resign? Why?

5. What amount of employee turnover is due to poor selection decisions? How well do a supervisor's predictions of a new employee's success actually relate to turnover?

6. Do applications, interviews, and related selection tools provide a well-rounded picture of the applicants and provide all information necessary to make a sound selection decision?

Endnotes

1. For more information about the Immigration Reform and Control Act of 1986, see Jack P. Jefferies, *Understanding Hospitality Law,* 3d ed. (East Lansing, Mich.: Educational Institute of the American Hotel & Motel Association, 1995).

2. For more information on human resources planning, see David Wheelhouse, CHRE, *Managing Human Resources in the Hospitality Industry* (East Lansing, Mich.: Educational Institute of the American Hotel & Motel Association, 1989).

Key Terms

bonding

call-back list

closed (direct) questions

compressed schedules

cross-training

exit interview

flex-time

human resources department

internal recruiting
internship programs
job description
job sharing
job specification
lateral transfer
lead time

line department
networking
open-ended (indirect) questions
recruitment
staff department
turnover

Discussion Questions

1. How do line departments and human resources staff members work together to recruit new employees?

2. What sources of potential employees can you draw from to staff your department?

3. What role does the supervisor play in recruitment and selection?

4. What internal and external recruiting techniques can you use when staffing your department?

5. What can your property do to make open positions easier to fill?

6. How can supervisors learn from employee turnover?

7. What preparations should you make before interviewing job applicants?

8. What should you do to properly conduct an employment interview?

9. What questioning techniques can you use when interviewing job applicants?

10. How should you end a job interview?

11. What short- and long-range approaches can your property take in planning for human resources needs?

12. What is the supervisor's role in human resources planning?

REVIEW QUIZ

When you feel you have covered all of the material in this chapter, answer these questions. Choose the *best* answer. Check your answers with the correct ones found on the Review Quiz Answer Key at the end of this book.

True (T) or False (F)

T   F   1. The line department supervisor must provide human resources personnel with pertinent details such as the basic skills and abilities needed to perform the job effectively.

T   F   2. Training is most effective if it is offered continuously.

T   F   3. When practical, the property should maintain internal job postings during the same exact times it is advertising for outside applicants.

T   F   4. Teaching your employees to do more than one job in your department is called cross-training.

T   F   5. In job-sharing, two or more part-time employees assume the responsibilities of one full-time job.

T   F   6. During the interview, the interviewing supervisor should reveal his/her real personality.

T   F   7. Never mention the undesirable aspects of a job to an applicant you are seriously considering hiring.

T   F   8. In most cases, the applicant should be the one to end the interview.

T   F   9. Checking a candidate's references is generally a waste of time and should be avoided.

T   F   10. Human resources planning should happen as and when needed. Long-range plans are wasteful.

Alternate/Multiple Choice

11. Continuous employee development programs improve the skills of employees who:

    a. may deserve promotion.
    b. are being considered for termination.

12. A call-back list is a list of applicants who are:

    a. interested in positions in your department.
    b. former employees who may be willing to help out on a temporary basis.

13. An applicant's unsatisfactory answer during a job interview may be due to his/her:

    a. unwillingness to cooperate.
    b. uncertainty about what you're asking.

14. New employees are important to a property because they:

    a. contribute fresh ideas to the department.
    b. help the property stay up-to-date.
    c. bring in innovative ways to do things.
    d. do all of the above.

15. If an employment applicant's answers seem illogical or unreasonable:

    a. shake your head so he/she will stop lying.
    b. help him/her by providing some logical answers.
    c. ask for more information.
    d. prod the applicant by pretending to be angry.

Chapter Outline

General Property Orientation
Specific Job Orientation
    Orientation Checklist: A Helpful
      Planning Tool
Training
    Benefits of Training
    Types of Training
Principles of Adult Learning
    Ask Questions
    Job Lists and Job Breakdowns
    Training to Standards
    The Four-Step Training Method

Learning Objectives

1. Explain general property orientation and its benefits.

2. Explain the activities that may be involved in specific job orientation.

3. Describe the benefits of training to the employee, guest, property, and supervisor.

4. Identify and describe the different types of training discussed in the chapter.

5. Describe the important principles of adult learning presented in the chapter.

6. Explain why supervisors should ask questions when orienting and training employees.

7. Describe how to ask questions of trainees when you want to encourage participation.

8. Describe job lists and how to use them.

9. Describe job breakdowns and how to develop them.

10. Identify and explain the four steps used in the four-step training method.

4

Orientation and Training

THE MOST MEMORABLE DAY of an employee's time with an organization is often the first day. People can frequently remember what happened to them throughout that first day on a job. When employees first begin working they are often very enthusiastic and highly motivated. They want to do their jobs correctly and they want to meet your expectations. You should recognize this initial enthusiasm and help new employees to perform effectively on the job.

Despite their initial excitement, it is not unusual for some employees to find their first few days on the job awkward and somewhat distressing. Much of all turnover occurs within new employees' first few months on the job. High turnover during the early periods of employment often suggests that the recruiting process, the orientation process, the training process, or all three, may be inadequate. An inadequate orientation and training program may make new employees think that you do not care for them and that they have not chosen a good place to work. It is this negative perception, which can quickly overcome one's positive feelings about a new job, that a proper orientation and training program is designed to counter.

Even though you spend some time with each applicant during the selection process, your new employer-employee relationship seriously begins during orientation and training. This chapter begins with a discussion of general property orientation (known as new employee orientation in some properties) and continues with specific job orientation. Then, it addresses job training, including group, individual, and on-the-job training. The chapter also discusses the ways adults learn, and presents an in-depth discussion of the four-step training method, an on-the-job training method commonly used in the industry.

General Property Orientation

General property orientation in many large properties begins with a meeting conducted by the human resources department. New staff members meet as a group and are welcomed by the general manager or other property official. The property may show videotapes or slides to let new employees know about the organization's philosophy and the role each employee plays in meeting the property's mission and goals. Then, human resources staff may distribute employee handbooks and other materials, and review important policies and procedures. They may also discuss insurance and other benefits, guest and employee relations, and personnel forms. In addition, they may invite directors of major departments in to introduce themselves and say a few words. Human resources staff may give new employees a tour of the property.

Exhibit 4.1 Benefits of General Property Orientation

Benefits to the Company
- Consistent orientation: all employees receive the same overview
- Helps new employees feel they're working for a great company
- Keeps the organization on its toes; it must always remain competitive
- Allows senior management to become visible to line employees
- First impressions *are* lasting impressions; a good orientation program can build a strong foundation of company values and philosophy
- Improves employee understanding of the company's business goals and priorities
- Early start on building a strong "team" approach at all levels of the organization
- Lower turnover

Benefits to the Supervisor
- Ensures that all new employees are informed of policies and procedures
- Ensures that new employees understand their job duties, standards of conduct, etc.
- Orientation supports the supervisor's role
- Supervisors themselves can benefit by re-participating on an occasional basis
- A successful orientation program builds employee motivation
- Lower turnover

Benefits to the Employee
- A better understanding of the company's expectations of them and their performance
- Will help employees understand the value of their positions to the organization; builds self-esteem
- Employees realize that they are important to the operation, for not everyone can successfully work in the hospitality industry
- Gives an early, structured approach to learning about the company and the job
- Establishes early commitment to being a member of the team
- Builds an important foundation of employee motivation

Smaller properties with no human resources department may provide new employees with general information about the organization, its philosophy, and its mission. If practical, a tour of the entire property will help new employees see where they fit into the organization.

Exhibit 4.1 lists several benefits of general property orientation to the company, the supervisor, and the employee.

Specific Job Orientation

After your organization conducts its general property orientation, it is time to conduct **specific job orientation.** As supervisor, you must be mentally prepared to

Exhibit 4.2 Benefits of Specific Job Orientation

Benefits to the Department
- Consistency in employee training and development
- Resources must always be current
- Helps employees ensure quality service and meet guest expectations
- Ensures that required standards will be maintained

Benefits to the Supervisor
- Well-trained staff
- Consistency in staff performance
- Knowledge of staff capability
- Helps when evaluating employee performance
- Helps department run more smoothly

Benefits to the Employee
- Employee learns how to do the job correctly
- Builds self-esteem due to feeling of accomplishment
- Builds higher morale
- Creates team fellowship and cooperation
- Helps employee become productive more quickly

welcome and work with the new employee. It is critical that the new employee form a favorable impression of you, so be on time. One of your first duties should be to review the job with the new employee. Explain how it relates to other jobs. In addition, show the employee the location of all equipment he/she will need to do the job. Finally, discuss the type and duration of training the employee will receive. Several benefits of specific job orientation are presented in Exhibit 4.2.

This may be the time to review the contents of the property's **employee handbook** with each new employee (see Exhibit 4.3 for a list of subjects typically included in a property's employee handbook). Employee handbooks review important policies and procedures, and also discuss when breaks are taken, when employees receive paychecks, and whether employees can eat on the job. The handbook should be written specifically for your property so that it provides accurate, applicable information about actual policies, programs, and procedures. If possible, all areas in the handbook should be reviewed during orientation. This way, any questions new employees have can be answered immediately. Some properties include a tear-out page in the handbook which employees sign and return to human resources within the first weeks of employment.

Give new employees updated copies of their job descriptions so that they will understand the specific tasks of their jobs. Also, give them copies of the performance evaluation form your property uses. This will give new employees a better understanding of their job duties and how their performance will be measured. Tell them about promotional opportunities within the organization, and be sure to include success stories about employees who have been promoted to positions of higher

Exhibit 4.3 Sample Table of Contents for Employee Handbook

TABLE OF CONTENTS

Welcome to Our Company

About Our Company
    Our Philosophy
    What We Do
    Our Organizational Structure

About Your Earnings
    Your Salary
        Salary Grades
        Salary Review
        Cost of Living Increases
        Pay Periods and Pay Days
        Payroll Deductions

    Other Benefits
        Holidays
        Vacations
        Sick Leave
        Maternity Provisions
        Insurance Programs
        Educational Assistance
        Employee Honor Awards

Important Policies to Help You
    Probationary Period
    What to Do If You Cannot Come to Work
    Personal Appearance
    Overtime
    Job Problems
    Access to Personnel Records
    Recognition
    Use of Time Clock
    Rest Periods
    Before/After Work Requirements
    Employee Lockers
    Packages

Career Challenges
    Promotion from Within
    Equal Employment Opportunities
    Training Opportunities
    Employee Development Program
    Career Progression Paths
    Employee Appraisal Programs

We know you'll like us, welcome to the team!

---

responsibility in the property. Provide a copy of your property's organization chart so that they can understand the overall structure of the property and how they fit in. This is a good time to review planned career progression possibilities. (Professional development programs are covered more extensively in Chapter 14.)

Give new employees a tour of the department. Identify all work areas and take the time to introduce the new employees' co-workers as you encounter them. Before these introductions you must be sure to inform your current employees about each new employee and when he/she will begin work. For instance, you could tell your staff about the new employee at a department meeting. Let them know whether the newcomer is filling a vacancy. If the new employee is filling a newly created position, explain its purpose, requirements, and why it was created. Speak positively about the new employee. Note how the individual will add to the success of the department team. It is often effective to assign a "buddy" or "sponsor" to a new employee. This is an experienced employee chosen to show the new employee around, serve as an "answer-person," and act as a friendly face for the new employee.

An effective orientation program addresses each of the following issues. As you read through the list, think about how answers to each question would make new employees feel better about a new job:

- What exactly is the organization's mission? Why does the organization exist?

- What are the exact duties of the job?

- What are the employee's rights?

- What are the limits to what the employee can and cannot do without getting permission?

- To what positions can the employee advance within the organization?

- How does the employee fit into the organization?

- What performance standards must the employee meet to succeed in the job and organization?

- What are the general and specific benefits for which the employee is eligible?

- With whom will the employee work?

- How will the employee "fit in" with co-workers?

- What can the employee do to establish good relationships with all those with whom he/she must interact on the job?

- What type of training will the employee receive both immediately and later on to help him/her prepare for this and future jobs within the organization?

Exhibit 4.4 presents a general property, department, and position orientation and training schedule. The food and beverage department at Opryland Hotel (a property with 1,891 rooms) uses the schedule to train its servers. Note that the general property orientation lasts nearly two days, while the department and position orientation and training continues for eight more days.

Orientation Checklist: A Helpful Planning Tool

An orientation checklist, such as that found in Exhibit 4.5, itemizes orientation activities and information to review with new employees. Such a checklist offers several advantages. First, its adoption indicates that your organization is serious enough about planned orientation activities to commit them to writing. Further, it is a standard form used to orient all employees; its use helps ensure consistency throughout the property. The checklist also ensures that all orientation activities are carried out. Since both you and the employee must sign the checklist when

Exhibit 4.4 Server Training Schedule

FOOD AND BEVERAGE TRAINING PROFILE

Department: Beverage   Position: Server

Week 1

Mon	Tue	Wed	Thu	Fri
8:00 A.M.–4:00 P.M. Hotel Orientation	8:00 A.M.–4:00 P.M. Hotel Orientation	9:00 A.M.–4:00 P.M.	8:45 A.M.–3:30 P.M.	10:00 A.M.–5:00 P.M.
		9:00 A.M. Department Introduction	8:45 A.M. "Drink Presentation"	10:00 A.M. "Service Fundamentals Beverage Style"
	3:30 P.M. Training Manual Program Handout	1:00 P.M. Introduction to IBM	1:00 P.M. IBM Role Play	12:00 P.M. Floor Observation, All Outlets
4:00 P.M. Home	4:00 P.M. Home	4:00 P.M. Home	3:30 P.M. Home	5:00 P.M. Home

Off Saturday & Sunday

Week 2

Mon	Tue	Wed	Thu	Fri
5:00 P.M.–Closing	5:00 P.M.–Closing	2:00 P.M.–8:00 P.M.	10:30 A.M.–6:00 P.M.	10:30 A.M.–6:00 P.M.
Follow Seasoned Trainer Paperwork	Follow Seasoned Trainer Paperwork	Follow Trainer No Paperwork	Training Station Paperwork	Training Station Paperwork

Courtesy of Opryland Hotel, Nashville, Tennessee

orientation is completed, your signatures certify that you completed each activity. Finally, the signed orientation checklist formalizes the orientation process. It helps assure top management that orientation policies and practices are consistently followed.

The checklist should be updated as often as needed. Remind employees that, when they sign off on the checklist, they are saying, "I understand that I am accountable for knowledge of all items listed on the checklist."

Training

Providing employees with proper **training** is one of a supervisor's chief responsibilities. While you probably do some of the actual training yourself, you may often delegate training duties to regular department trainers or to talented employees (refer to Exhibit 4.6 to help you choose a suitable trainer).

Exhibit 4.5 New Employee Orientation Checklist

New Employee Orientation Checklist

Name of New Employee: —————————————————— Position: ——————————

Department: ———————————————————————— Supervisor: ——————————

Date Hired: ————————————————————————

Instructions—Initial and date when each of the following is completed.

Part I—Introduction

☐ ———— Welcome to new position (give your name, find out what name the employee prefers to be called, etc.)
☐ ———— Tour of resort
☐ ———— Tour of department work area
☐ ———— Introduction to fellow employees
☐ ———— Introduction to trainer
☐ ———— Explanation of training program
☐ ———— Review of job description
☐ ———— Explanation of department

Part II—Discussion of Daily Procedures

☐ ———— Beginning/ending time of workshift
☐ ———— Break and meal periods
☐ ———— Uniforms (responsibilities for, cleanliness of, etc.)
☐ ———— Assignment of locker
☐ ———— Employee meals (if any)
☐ ———— Parking requirements
☐ ———— First aid and accident reporting procedures
☐ ———— Time clock or "sign-in log" requirements
☐ ———— Other (specify)
☐

Part III—Information About Salary/Wages

☐ ———— Rate of pay
☐ ———— Deductions
☐ ———— Pay periods
☐ ———— Overtime policies
☐ ———— Complete all payroll withholding, insurance, and related forms
☐ ———— Other (specify)

Part IV—Review of Policies and Rules

☐ ———— Safety, fires, accidents
☐ ———— Maintenance and use of equipment
☐ ———— Punctuality
☐ ———— Absenteeism
☐ ———— Illness
☐ ———— Emergencies
☐ ———— Use of telephone
☐ ———— Leaving work station
☐ ———— Smoking/eating/drinking
☐ ———— Packages
☐ ———— Vacations
☐ ———— Other (specify)
☐

(continued)

Exhibit 4.5 *(continued)*

Part V—Employee Handbook/Related Information

☐ _____ Received and reviewed
☐ _____ Review of employee appraisal process
☐ _____ Review of organization chart
☐ _____ Review of job description
☐ _____ Review of department's responsibilities
☐ _____ Review of all benefit plans
☐ _____ Discuss performance standards/expectations
☐ _____ Discuss career path possibilities

Part VI—Miscellaneous Orientation Procedures (Review all other areas covered with the new employee)

_____

_____

_____

I certify that all the above activities were completed on the date indicated.

Employee _____   Date _____

Supervisor _____   Date _____

Benefits of Training

Training benefits everyone: the employee, the guest, the property, and the supervisor. It benefits the employee, who will suffer less stress because he/she knows how to do the job. In addition, it can prepare the employee for promotion within the property, thereby helping meet his/her personal and professional needs. It can help the employee realize his/her full potential. Training encourages self-development and enhances self-confidence. It can also help employees develop decision-making, problem-solving, and communication skills.

Training benefits guests, who expect to receive consistently good products and services which meet the property's quality and quantity standards. Well-trained employees ensure that a guest has an enjoyable experience at the property.

Training benefits the property by helping it to reduce costs, increase sales and profitability, and build a better image. Moreover, good training will encourage repeat business when satisfied guests return again and again. Good training also increases business through referral—satisfied guests tell others of their good experiences at your property. In the long run, the property realizes a return on its initial investment. A good training program offers employees future and career opportunities, not "just a job." Finally, a good training program shows that the property is people-oriented, a quality useful in recruiting efforts.

Training benefits the supervisor because it directly affects employee performance. Training improves employee morale, which in turn decreases turnover. Furthermore, training helps build trust and respect between you and your employees. It helps improve departmental and organizational communication. At the same time, your property will find that skilled, knowledgeable employees can offer guests

Exhibit 4.6 Are You a Good Trainer?

1. Do you consider preparation to be the first step in instructing an employee?
2. Do you spend at least as much time getting things ready for training as you do in the actual training session?
3. Do you use the performance standards from job breakdowns as your lesson plans?
4. Do you list key points around which you will build the instruction?
5. Do you devote time to explaining to the employee how he or she will benefit from the training session?
6. Do you determine what the employee already knows about the job before you start training?
7. Do you set up a timetable showing the amount of time you plan to spend training employees, and when you expect their training to be completed?
8. Do you expect that there will be periods in the course of the training during which no observable progress will be made?
9. Do you expect some employees to learn two or three times faster than others?
10. Do you both tell and show the employee how to do the skill involved?
11. When an employee performs incorrectly during training, do you acknowledge correct performance before pointing out areas that need improvement?
12. Do you give instructions so clearly that no one can misunderstand them?
13. Do you ask the employee to try out the skill and to tell you how to do it?
14. Do you praise correct performance frequently?
15. Do you expect 100% conformity to standards?

(All of the questions should be answered "Yes.")

Source: Stephen J. Shriver, *Managing Quality Services* (East Lansing, Mich.: Educational Institute of the American Hotel & Motel Association, 1988), p. 288.

higher-quality products and services. It can help you build a strong core of employees. And it offers you opportunities for your own professional development.

Types of Training

Hospitality operations may use various types of training methods. These include group training methods used to train many employees at one time. Your property may also wish to use training methods geared toward individual employees. These may include independent study or on-the-job training programs.

Group Training. Group training can be very useful when employers must provide the same information or skills training to many employees at once. Exhibit 4.7 reviews some of the more popular methods used in hospitality operations. Some methods, such as lecture and demonstration, are relatively straightforward to learn. While they may involve a significant amount of effort and practice to use correctly, they are methods with which most supervisors are familiar.

Other group training methods, such as those using role playing and case studies, involve significant planning efforts to inform trainees about the methods and

Exhibit 4.7 **Alternative Group Training Methods**

Popular Group Training Methods			
Method	**Overview of Procedures**	**Advantages**	**Disadvantages**
1. Lecture	Least effective method. One person does all the talking, may use handouts, visual aids, question/ answer to supplement lecture.	Less time needed for trainer preparation than other methods; provides a lot of information quickly when retention of details is not important.	Does not actively involve trainees in training process; trainees forget much information when it is only presented orally.
2. Demonstration	Very effective for basic skills training. Trainer shows trainees how to do something; can include opportunity for trainees to also perform the task(s) being demonstrated.	Emphasizes trainee involvement; several senses (seeing, hearing, feeling) can be involved.	Requires a great deal of trainer preparation and planning.
3. Seminar	Good for experienced employees. Can use several group methods (lectures, discussions, conference) which require group participation.	Group members are involved in the training; can use many group methods (role playing, case study, etc.) as part of the seminar activity.	Planning is time-consuming; trainer(s) must have skill in conducting a seminar; much time is required for training experience.
4. Conference	Good problem-solving approach. Group approach to considering a specific problem or issue—and reaching agreement on statements or solution.	Much trainee participation; obtains trainee consensus; can use several methods (lecture, panel, seminar) to keep sessions interesting.	Group may be hard to control; group opinions generated at the conference may differ from manager's ideas; conflict can result.
5. Panel	Good when using outside resource people. Provides several points of view on topic in order to seek alternatives to the situation. Panel members may have differing views but also must have objective concerns for the purpose of the training.	Interesting to hear different points of view; process invites employees' opinions; employees are challenged to consider alternatives.	Requires a great deal of preparation; results of the method can be difficult to evaluate.
6. Role Playing	Good for guest relations training. Trainees pretend to be selected people in specific situations and have an opportunity to experiment with different approaches to dealing with the situation.	Trainees can learn possible results of certain behaviors in a classroom situation; skills in dealing with people can be practiced; alternative approaches can be analyzed and considered.	Much time is spent getting points across; trainers must be skillful and creative in helping the class learn from the situation.

Method	Overview of Procedures	Advantages	Disadvantages
7. Case Studies	Good for teaching situational analysis. The case study is a description of a real or imagined situation which contains information that trainees can use to analyze what has occurred and why.	Can present a real-life situation which enables trainees to consider what they would do; can be used to teach a wide variety of skills in which application of information is important.	Cases are difficult to write and time-consuming to discuss; the trainer must be creative and skillful in leading discussions, making points, and keeping trainees on the track.
8. Simulations	Good for skill development. Trainees imitate actions required on the job (such as repeating the steps in a demonstration after it is presented).	Training becomes "real," trainees are actively involved in the learning process; training has direct applicability to jobs to be performed after training.	Simulations are time-consuming; they require a skillful and creative trainer.
9. Projects	Good for experienced employees. Projects require the trainees to do something on the job which improves the operation as well as helps them learn about the topic of the training.	Projects can be selected which help resolve problems or otherwise improve the operation; trainees get first-hand experience in the topic of the training; little time is needed up front of the training experience.	Without proper introduction to the project and its purpose, trainees may think they are doing somebody else's work. Also, if they do not have an interest in the project—for example, there is no immediate impact on their own jobs—it will be difficult to obtain and maintain their interest.

Adapted from Lewis C. Forrest, Jr., *Training for the Hospitality Industry,* 2d ed. (East Lansing, Mich.: Educational Institute of the American Hotel & Motel Association, 1990).

how to use them. You will likely need specialized training before you can use these methods to lead training activities.

The human resources department might use additional formats, such as seminars, conferences, and panel discussions, in its property-wide training efforts.

Independent Learning Courses. Individuals interested in self-improvement can take **independent learning courses** in many hospitality industry-related areas. Programs are available from the Educational Institute of the American Hotel & Motel Association[1] and from other sources.

Independent learning students read and study materials alone on their own time. Students complete examinations and submit them, to the organization offering the course, for feedback and final credit. These courses are appropriate for adult learners because they are self-paced, individualized, voluntary, and self-directed. An unlimited number of an organization's employees can enroll at once, yet each person proceeds at a self-determined pace. Since independent learning students complete the training on their own time, employers do not have to pay for training time, and study does not take employees away from their jobs. Employees can practice what they learn by applying new knowledge on the job. To encourage employees to become independent learners, employers may wish to fully or partially reimburse employees who complete courses successfully.

On-the-Job Training Programs. Training programs in the hospitality industry traditionally emphasize individualized **on-the-job training (OJT)** programs. With these programs, trainees work along with an experienced employee and learn procedures while watching, talking with, and helping the experienced employee. OJT works because it addresses the trainee's specific needs. Since it is conducted in the actual work place, OJT provides maximum realism. Moreover, employees receive immediate feedback. When they are positively reinforced, they gain incentive to continue doing well. And the trainer can correct problems immediately since the training involves only one trainee.

However, these training programs can often become ineffective when they are improperly planned and conducted. The supervisor may incorrectly reason that a trainee who follows a lead trainer for a sufficient period of time will be exposed to all aspects of the job. In practice, though, the trainee may be rushed through training because he/she must begin actual work. Another problem surfaces when the trainer is teaching unsatisfactorily. Further, the training method is time-consuming and therefore may be unsuitable to many fast-paced hospitality operations.

The OJT trainer must want to be a trainer and must possess the spirit of giving. Not all good employees are good trainers. Therefore, take time when selecting an OJT trainer.

One effective OJT approach, the four-step training method, is discussed more thoroughly later in this chapter.

Principles of Adult Learning

This section of the chapter discusses the ways adults learn. Adults reject many traditional methods used to teach children in our school systems. Indeed, not many adults are interested in all-day lectures or in homework consisting of repetitive exercises. Nor do they have the time to attend class five days a week for weeks at a time. Understanding the following principles of adult learning will help you train adult learners on the job.

The Desire to Learn. Adults learn most effectively when they are strongly motivated to do so, when they want to acquire additional knowledge or new "life skills." They must be ready and willing to learn. In addition, they want to know that the training will benefit them. If you explain what the employees will gain and make sure that the training itself is interesting and challenging, trainees are likely to be receptive.

The Need to Learn. Adults learn quickly when they need to learn. In addition, they learn best when they think they will gain immediate benefits and make prompt use of newly acquired knowledge or skills. Trainees expect results from each class, lecture, and homework assignment. They want direct, brief explanations, without unnecessary background or unusable information. They want the trainer to tell them precisely what to do, how and why to do it, and why it works. If adults think that training is not applicable or does not meet their needs, they will probably tune out—if they don't drop out entirely.

Learning by Doing. Adults learn best when they actively participate in learning. Adults retain more knowledge and information when they practice and use a new skill immediately. They learn best by practicing a skill themselves rather than watching a demonstration or simply listening to a series of lectures.

A Realistic Focus. Adult learning is enhanced when it is based on real problems, not imagined ones. The importance of realism in adult learning is very significant. Many adults resist working on a problem which is obviously developed just for training purposes. If a problem seems unrealistic, adult learners might assume that the trainer invented it, and that it would not occur in the real world.

Relating Learning to Experience. Adult learning must be related to, and integrated with, knowledge gained through a lifetime of learning. Adults will probably reject information which does not fit in with what they already know or think they know. In fact, adults' past experiences may prevent them from absorbing new information or even from perceiving it accurately.

This means that trainers must give adults every opportunity to become actively involved, to interrupt, ask questions, or disagree. This way, the trainer may grow to understand the trainees' experiences and attitudes. This may help the trainer to present new information in a way that acknowledges the adults' experience, thus making them more receptive to training.

An Informal Environment. Adults learn best if the training environment is relaxed and informal. It is best to present the material in a conversational way frequently asking for reactions from the participants. Grouping the participants in clusters of three to five instead of in the traditional classroom seating pattern adds to informality and encourages interaction. Adults will resist training if the trainer treats them like children or tries to manage the classroom. Trainers will have a more successful, pleasant teaching experience if they treat employees as professional colleagues instead of as subordinates. Indeed, employees often behave as they think their supervisors expect them to. If trainers treat employees like valued and responsible colleagues, employees will likely be more receptive to both the training and to meeting the organization's goals.

Guidance, Not Grades. Because they have been out of school for some time, adults may be unsure about their learning abilities. If their efforts are evaluated with tests and grades, adults may retreat from the learning experience rather than risk being humiliated with a bad grade. However, adult learners want to know how they are progressing and whether they are learning and performing correctly. Adults demand a lot of themselves; they lose patience and become discouraged when they make mistakes. Therefore, they need as much sincere praise as the trainer can give them. If you must criticize trainees, do it privately, in a constructive, pleasant manner. Most important, criticize learners' actions or performance, not the learners themselves.

Ask Questions

In orientation and training, it's important to involve the trainees as much as possible. Allowing trainees to ask questions and participate in discussions will enable them to learn more quickly and effectively and to retain what they've learned much longer. Obviously, then, it is very important that trainees actively participate in the training process. Encourage them to ask questions at any step in the process. To test comprehension, ask plenty of questions of your own. Most important, as trainees practice what you've taught them, ask them to explain what they're doing as they do it. This last point is crucial. People retain relatively little of what they read and hear. However, they remember much more if they become more actively involved in the learning process.

In a friendly way, ask trainees questions frequently to stimulate discussion and to test comprehension, but avoid putting trainees on the spot. Help them feel that their questions are important and relevant, and that no sincere question is a stupid one. Rephrase questions which get no response, and spend little time on unrelated questions.

When training groups of employees, use questions to stimulate and guide discussion. Call on various people, not just those who appear to know the answer. Call on them in an unpredictable order. When trainees ask you questions, turn the questions back to the group by asking something like, "Who can answer that?" or "Does anyone want to add anything?" Likewise, turn a question back to the one who asked it by saying: "What do you think the answer is?" or "What makes you say that?" Alternatively, turn a trainee's answer into an opportunity for discussion. When you receive a response, ask "Is the answer right?" or "Do you agree with the answer?"

Try to draw shy trainees into the discussion by addressing questions to them. Allow trainees plenty of time to respond. To encourage discussion, ask questions requiring responses that go beyond yes/no or brief answers. Avoid tricky questions unless you mention that you're challenging the trainees. Avoid long questions and ones which ask two things at once.

Job Lists and Job Breakdowns

Use job lists and job breakdowns for each position in your department to help you teach skills effectively, and to help you evaluate employee performance.[2] A **job list** is a list of tasks which an employee in a certain position must perform. A **job breakdown** details how to perform each task.

The job list should include every task for which the employee is responsible (see Exhibit 4.8 for a sample job list for a food server). When possible, the tasks should be listed in the order in which the employee will complete them. When you break each duty down and analyze it in the job breakdowns, include both knowledge and attitudes as necessary components of the duty.

As you draw up job lists, address the following questions:

- What specific duties will the employee perform?

- What units of work must the employee complete?

Exhibit 4.8 Sample Job List #1: Food Server

Job List*	
Position: Food Server	**Date Prepared:** 00/00/00
Duties: Employee must be able to:	J.B. Number**
1. Greet and seat restaurant guests	32
2. Serve water and light candles	33
3. Take beverage orders and serve drinks	34
4. Present the food menu and wine list	35
5. Assist guests in making food and beverage selections	36
6. Place orders in kitchen by using the call system	37
7. Serve food and clear table between courses	38
8. Serve wine and champagne	39
9. Serve desserts	40
10. Serve coffee and hot tea	41
11. Prepare the guest check and present to guest	15
12. Collect sales income; make change	16
13. Clear, clean, and reset tables for next party	26
14. Remove stains from dining room carpets	19
15. Provide booster seat or high chair for children	20
16. Clean side stations and serve pantry	27
17. Resolve guest complaints	45

* This is a partial job list. The list developed for a specific operation should include all duties to be performed.
** Job Breakdown Number. This refers to the specific job breakdown that breaks down the duty into its identifiable, specific steps. A given duty—and the appropriate job breakdown—can be applicable to and used in the job list of more than one position. For example, the host may also "Greet and seat restaurant guests." If so, the job breakdown number (32) for the food server position would also be applicable to the host position.

Source: Lewis C. Forrest, Jr., *Training for the Hospitality Industry,* 2d ed. (East Lansing, Mich.: Educational Institute of the American Hotel & Motel Association, 1990), p. 28.

- What materials must the employee handle?
- What equipment must the employee operate?
- What administrative tasks must the employee complete?
- What cleaning standards does the job entail?

The format of the job breakdown may vary according to your property's needs and requirements. Refer to Exhibit 4.9 for a sample of a job breakdown which serves both as a training guide and as a tool with which to judge employee performance. The first column in this exhibit lists a task taken from the job list

Exhibit 4.9 Sample Job Breakdown #1

	Job Breakdown	

Job Breakdown #36: The ability to assist guests in making food and beverage selections.
Equipment needed: Guest check, pen. (Guests will already have menus and wine list.)

Job List	How to Do It	Additional Information
1. Approach the table.	1. Stand erect. Look at the guests, smile, and greet them pleasantly. Introduce yourself. If you know their names, use them when you greet them. Be courteous.	1. You win the table with your first contact when you are pleasant and personable.
2. Take cocktail order.	2. Ask if guests would like a cocktail or appetizer wine. Be sure to get the complete details of the order, such as on-the-rocks, straight up, or extra olives. Remember which guest ordered each cocktail.	2. Most guests know which drinks they prefer. Be prepared to make suggestions, if appropriate. Do not push your personal preferences. Do not act surprised when a guest orders some non-standard drink.
3. Serve cocktails.	3. Place a cocktail napkin in front of each guest. Serve all beverages from the right with the right hand, when possible. Place cocktail glasses on napkins. Do not ask who ordered each drink. (You must remember.) As each drink is served, state what it is, such as Scotch and water, double martini, or Scotch-on-the-rocks.	3. Knowing who ordered what shows that you care about the order. Guests feel special when you repeat their order as you serve their drinks.
4. Check back for a second cocktail order.	4. Be courteous and bring the second round, if ordered, following the same procedure as the first round. Remove all first-round empty glasses and napkins. Put down new napkins and serve the drinks.	4. Check back when drinks are approximately two-thirds consumed.
5. Take the food order.	5. Ask the guests if they are ready to order. Explain the chef's specialty and answer any questions about the food. Take orders beginning with the women, when possible. Suggest appetizers, soup, or salads, as appropriate, to help them plan a complete meal. Proceed to the male guests. Be sure to inform the guests of the approximate cooking times of their selections. Communicate with the guest during this very important step. It is more than taking orders. It should be menu planning.	5. Guests expect you to know about the food. When you are asked a question and do not know the answer, do not bluff. Go to the kitchen or manager and find out the answer. Then go back and tell the guest. Suggesting menu items helps a hesitant guest make a decision he/she really wanted, especially if they may require some wait.

Job List	How to Do It	Additional Information
6. Take the wine order.	6. Ask, "Have you chosen a wine?" When you are asked to help, ask whether the guest prefers red or white, dry or semi-sweet, and other questions to get some idea of his/her preferences. Then point out two or three choices that fall within the characteristics described. The guest can choose according to price or other factors. Excuse yourself from the table and assure the guests that you will be right back with the first course.	6. Know the wine list. Always be careful to recognize the timid guest who is a novice at selecting wines. Be prepared to coach the guest through a selection process that will meet his/her needs. Experienced wine drinkers will usually know what they want to order and will not expect much assistance. This is not the time to feed your ego by demonstrating your technical wine knowledge and intimidating the guest. Be confident, but be courteous.

Source: Lewis C. Forrest, Jr., *Training for the Hospitality Industry,* 2d ed. (East Lansing, Mich.: Educational Institute of the American Hotel & Motel Association, 1990), pp. 32–33.

shown in Exhibit 4.8. The second column identifies the specific steps an employee must take to complete that task. These steps are written as performance standards.

Employees should be aware of the standards you use to measure job performance. Therefore, it is important to break down job tasks and document the standards, and make sure that employees understand them. If job breakdowns are to be effective, performance standards must be both *observable* and *measurable.* That is, a performance standard such as "Be pleasant" would be inappropriate because it is subject to interpretation. One manager may think an employee looks pleasant while another does not. This performance standard would be more appropriately written if it stated that employees should "Smile" when interacting with guests. A smile is both observable and measurable; an employee is either smiling or not, regardless of who is watching.

The third column presents further information which explains why each step is taken according to the standards listed in the second column. Use this "additional information" column to stress tips which may, for example, help the employee perform safely or treat guests courteously, while maintaining departmental standards.

You may wish to adapt this job breakdown format to include a fourth column which would allow you to simply check either "Yes" or "No" to indicate whether the employee performed correctly. Then, you could refer to this checklist when you write performance evaluations. A performance evaluation identifies an employee's strengths and areas which need improving. The latter indicate where an employee needs further specific training.

Developing Job Breakdowns. If your property is large, your department director may decide to form standards or task groups which will write all job breakdowns. Group members might include supervisors and experienced employees. In smaller properties, experienced employees, rather than a formal standards group, might write all department job breakdowns. Alternatively, your department may decide

Exhibit 4.10 Developing Job Breakdowns

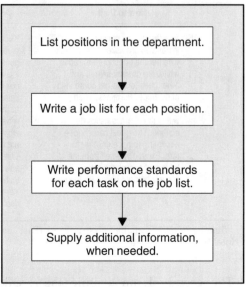

List positions in the department.

Write a job list for each position.

Write performance standards for each task on the job list.

Supply additional information, when needed.

Source: Margaret M. Kappa, et al., *Managing House-keeping Operations* (East Lansing, Mich.: Educational Institute of the American Hotel & Motel Association, 1990), p. 69.

to assign the writing job to employees who actually perform the tasks. Exhibit 4.10 shows the process of developing job breakdowns.

Many hospitality operations have a policy and procedures manual. Parts of it may help your department's standards group (or other appropriate personnel) write job breakdowns for each department position. For instance, the manual's procedures section may present job descriptions. The standards group can use them to write job lists and performance standards. The policy sections of the manual may yield further useful information.

Job breakdowns for tasks which involve equipment use may already be included in vendor-supplied operating manuals. If so, the standards group may refer to applicable pages.

Begin by breaking down each task on each job list by stating the specific observable and measurable steps an employee must take in order to complete the task. You and your boss might help the standards group begin writing performance standards for two or three department positions. As you write the standards, test each one by asking whether a supervisor or manager could evaluate an employee's performance by simply checking "Yes" or "No" in the "quarterly performance review" column.

After the standards group has practiced writing job breakdowns for a few tasks, your boss should assign the writing of job breakdowns for other tasks to individual group members. By a stated deadline, members should submit their completed work to your boss, who should have them assembled and typed in a

Exhibit 4.11 Training with Job Breakdowns

Training New Employees	Retraining Experienced Employees
Develop training plan from job list.	Identify training needs from performance evaluations.
↓	↓
Develop lesson plans from job breakdowns.	Develop lesson plans from job breakdowns.
↓	↓
Train according to performance standards.	Train according to performance standards.

Evaluate performance according to standards.

Source: Margaret M. Kappa, et al., *Managing Housekeeping Operations* (East Lansing, Mich.: Educational Institute of the American Hotel & Motel Association, 1990), p. 70.

standard format (perhaps similar to that shown in Exhibit 4.9) and distributed to all group members. The standards group can then meet a final time to carefully analyze each position's breakdown. After all job breakdowns are finalized, put them to immediate use to train current and newly employed staff.

Training to Standards

In addition to using job breakdowns to determine training needs of experienced employees, you may use them to train newly hired employees who have little or no hospitality experience (see Exhibit 4.11). Use job breakdowns to prepare thorough training plans. Base each session's lesson plans on the "performance standards" and "additional information" columns of the job breakdowns.

For instance, Exhibit 4.12 presents a sample three-day training plan based on the sample job list presented in Exhibit 4.8. The trainee thoroughly learns one group of related tasks—and demonstrates 100% conformity to performance standards—before beginning the next group. Note that the training plan follows the same order of tasks which appears on the sample job list. However, you may need to vary the sequence of tasks according to your department's needs.

The Four-Step Training Method

Trainers at your property might use a **four-step training method** to train both new and experienced employees. This method is essentially an OJT method based on

Exhibit 4.12 Sample Three-Day Training Plan

Position: Food Server

Date Prepared: XX/XX/XX

Employee: _____

Tasks: Employee must be able to:

Day 1

1. Greet and seat restaurant guests
2. Serve water; light candles
3. Take beverage orders; serve drinks
4. Present the food menu and wine list
5. Assist guests in making food and beverage selections
6. Place orders in kitchen by using the call system

Day 2

7. Serve food and clear table between courses
8. Serve wine and champagne
9. Serve desserts
10. Serve coffee and hot tea
11. Prepare the guest check and present it to guest
12. Collect sales income; make change

Day 3

13. Clear, clean, and reset tables for next party
14. Remove stains from dining room carpets
15. Provide booster seat or high chair for children
16. Clean side stations and serve pantry
17. Resolve guest complaints

the buddy system. The trainer, who may be a supervisor or a talented employee, works with the employee on a one-to-one basis. The trainer conducts training at the work station(s) the employee will actually use on the job.

This method offers several advantages. For example, it is inexpensive and requires no additional training equipment. Further, it is relevant to the job because it provides maximum realism. It gives the trainee immediate feedback on performance and allows the trainer to design and pace the training to meet the trainee's needs. It allows employees to cross-train. Finally, it provides direct, immediate benefits to the property.

The method's disadvantages include the fact that it takes trainer time. In addition, it may disregard job breakdowns, or rely on resource materials that are no longer current or accurate. Finally, an unqualified trainer may pass on bad work habits to the trainee.

Exhibit 4.13 Four-Step Training Method

STEP 1:	**PREPARE TO TRAIN**	
	WRITE	training objectives.
	DEVELOP	lesson plans.
	DECIDE	on training methods.
	ESTABLISH	a timetable for instruction.
	SELECT	the training location.
	ASSEMBLE	training materials/equipment.
	SET UP	the work station.
STEP 2:	**CONDUCT THE TRAINING**	
	PREPARE	the trainee.
	BEGIN	the training session.
	DEMONSTRATE	the procedures.
	AVOID	jargon.
	TAKE	adequate time.
	REPEAT	the sequence.
STEP 3:	**COACH TRIAL PERFORMANCES**	
	ALLOW	the trainee to practice.
	COACH	the trainee.
STEP 4:	**FOLLOW THROUGH**	
	COACH	a few tasks each day.
	CONTINUE	positive reinforcement.
	PROVIDE	constant feedback.
	EVALUATE	the trainee's progress.
	OBTAIN	employee feedback.

Adapted from Stephen J. Shriver, *Managing Quality Services* (East Lansing, Mich.: Educational Institute of the American Hotel & Motel Association, 1988), p. 282.

You can adapt this OJT method to meet your department's particular needs. Use it to train both individuals and groups. The four steps are: (1) Prepare to train; (2) Conduct the training; (3) Coach trial performances; and (4) Follow through. Refer to Exhibit 4.13, which summarizes the four-step training method at a glance.

The following sections briefly explain each step.

Prepare to Train. Although you may feel that you know your department's job skills well enough to teach them without preparation, it is a good idea to prepare a written format to guide you. This will help you to remember important details. This section shows how to prepare to train.

Write training objectives. Training objectives describe what trainees should know or be able to do after training. At the end of the training session, the trainees should be able to demonstrate each task (at the desired performance level), which should be listed in the job list column of the job breakdown. Explain what the training objectives are at the outset of the training session. Training objectives should explain that employees must demonstrate 100% conformity to standards.

Develop lesson plans. Write step-by-step lesson plans outlining the tasks which the employee will learn. Base lesson plans on the performance standards listed in the second column of the job breakdown.

Decide on training methods. Use the methods which will meet your training objectives. When possible, demonstrate the tasks and provide step-by-step visual aids. In fact, the more you involve a trainee's five senses—hearing, sight, touch, taste, and smell—the better the trainee learns.

Establish a timetable for instruction. Determine how long each training session will take. Schedule each session for a time when you will not be interrupted or distracted. For this reason, training sessions are usually scheduled during periods of low business volume. Finally, set realistic time frames.

Select the training location. When possible, train the employees at the work station(s) at which they will actually perform. Position the employees so that they can clearly watch the demonstration. Make sure that the employees are watching from the actual position they will take when completing the tasks. If the employees face a trainer who is correctly positioned, the employees' view of the task will be the reverse of what it actually should be. This may seem unimportant, but this can be very frustrating to new employees.

Assemble training materials and equipment. Set up all materials and necessary equipment in the training area before beginning the session. These may include appropriate job lists and job breakdowns, which are the most important training materials. The job breakdown should list the materials and equipment needed for each task. Ensure that all equipment is in working order.

Conduct the Training. This section describes how to conduct the training.

Prepare the trainee. Explain the session's training objectives. Tell employees exactly what you expect. Explain why the training is important, how it relates to the job and to the department, and how the employees will benefit. Spend as much time on the "why" as on the "how." Motivate employees to learn.

Begin the training session. Use job breakdowns to guide your training. Follow the sequence of steps in the performance standards columns of the job breakdowns. Explain each step and why it is important. Ask employees to examine the job breakdowns so that they will understand the standards by which you and the department will evaluate their performances.

Demonstrate the procedures. As you explain the steps, demonstrate them. Be sure to arrange the steps in a logical order. Trainees will understand and remember more if they can view the steps as well as hear about them. Encourage trainees to ask questions whenever they need points clarified.

Avoid jargon. Use words that employees new to the industry or property will understand. They can pick up on jargon later as they become more familiar with their jobs. If, during the training process, you use words or terms which may be unfamiliar to trainees, provide a list of the words along with definitions.

Take adequate time. Keep in mind that trainees may be hearing and seeing things for the first time. Therefore, go slowly and carefully. Explain and demonstrate each aspect of every step. Be patient when employees do not understand each step immediately. Gear the training to the employees' pace.

Repeat the sequence. Go over the entire step two times so that employees thoroughly understand the process. When demonstrating the step the second time, ask trainees questions to check their comprehension. Finally, repeat the steps as many times as necessary.

Coach Trial Performances. When trainees understand well enough to perform each step well, ask them to demonstrate and explain each step of the task. This practice allows you to check the trainees' comprehension. It also helps the employee develop good work habits. Your coaching helps employees learn to do the job with skill and confidence. Praise employees immediately when they perform properly, and correct them when they don't by reviewing the proper behaviors. Make sure that trainees understand and can explain each step and its purpose before moving on to the next step. (Coaching is discussed in more detail in Chapter 6.)

Follow Through. After the initial training period is completed, it is important to follow through to make sure that employees perform correctly. Do not wait until the employees' official performance evaluation to do so. Unfortunately, follow-through is often the most neglected area of OJT. It is important that trainees realize that they are accountable for their learning.

Follow-through consists of coaching, reinforcement, feedback, and evaluation.

Coach a few tasks each day. It's difficult for trainees to absorb more than a limited amount of new information at each training session. Limit information to what a trainee can reasonably understand and remember in one session. It is important to allow enough time for practice. Cover additional material in subsequent sessions until employees have learned all of the job responsibilities.

Continue positive reinforcement. Provide trainees with positive reinforcement when they perform well during and after training. This will help them remember what they have learned.

If new employees fail to meet performance standards indicated in the job breakdowns, correct the employees. First, compliment employees for the tasks they are doing correctly. Then, show them how to correct their bad habits, and explain why. This positive approach will help improve the employees' performances and also help them retain positive attitudes.

Provide constant feedback. Tell employees what they are doing correctly and what they are doing incorrectly. Encourage employees to ask questions about tasks they are learning to do. Discuss ways the employees can improve their efficiency and performance. Also, tell them where to seek help if you are not available.

Evaluate the trainees' progress. Determine whether trainees follow the correct procedures. Evaluate the training in terms of whether the trainees have met the training objectives. If not, provide further training and practice.

To help you keep track of trainee progress, use a checklist. Exhibit 4.14 presents the checklist that trainers at Opryland Hotel use when training beverage servers. When each step is satisfactorily completed, the supervisor notes the applicable date and also initials the form. For more information on employee evaluation, please see Chapter 6.

Exhibit 4.14 Beverage Server Training Checklist

Employee Development Profile—Beverage

Last: _____ First: _____ Position: _____

Address: _____ City: _____ Zip: _____

Department: _____ SS#: _____ Birth Date: _____ Hire Date: _____

	Date	Supvr Intls		Date	Supvr Intls
Orientation—Full			Jack Daniel's Introduction		
Orientation—Follow-Up			Cascades Introduction		
Reinstatement Orientation			Conservatory Introduction		
Spirit of Hospitality Part 1			Introduction to I.B.M.		
Spirit of Hospitality Part 2			Void Procedures		
Serving Alcohol With Care			I.B.M./Over/Short Procedure		
Drink Presentation			Credit Card Procedures		
Job Description			Safety		
Service Fundamentals Beverage Style					
Department Introduction					
Pickin' Parlor Introduction					
Stagedoor Introduction					

Trainer's Signature _____ Date _____

Manager's Signature _____ Date _____

Courtesy of Opryland Hotel, Nashville, Tennessee

Obtain employee feedback. Allowing the employees to evaluate their training is also a good idea. It can give you valuable insight and help you to improve your training program. For example, you could ask employees to fill out a training evaluation questionnaire which asks the following questions:

- Do you believe the training program was beneficial?
- What part was most helpful?
- How could we improve the program?
- Who were your trainers?
- How were they helpful?
- How could they have been more helpful to you?
- Were your supervisors available to you for questions?

- Do you feel you were ready when you were left alone on the job?
- Do you feel comfortable in your position?
- What is your opinion of the training program?
- On a scale of 1 (low) to 10 (high), how would you rate the training program?
- Do you have any additional comments to make about your training?

Such a questionnaire, which is based on the one Opryland Hotel's Food and Beverage Training Department asks new employees to fill out, serves several purposes. First, it measures the new employee's attitude toward the organization. Second, it helps the training supervisor evaluate the results of each employee's training program. Third, it encourages communication between the training supervisor, the trainee, and the on-the-job trainer. Finally, it provides insight into the performance of the supervisors who help prepare, deliver, and evaluate training efforts.

Endnotes

1. For information about Educational Institute courses and programs, please contact the Educational Institute of the American Hotel & Motel Association, P.O. Box 1240, East Lansing, MI 48826.

2. The training portions of this chapter are based on Margaret Kappa, et al., *Managing Housekeeping Operations* (East Lansing, Mich.: Educational Institute of the American Hotel & Motel Association, 1990), and Lewis C. Forrest, Jr., *Training for the Hospitality Industry*, 2d ed. (East Lansing, Mich.: Educational Institute of AH&MA, 1990).

Key Terms

employee handbook
four-step training method
general property orientation
group training
independent learning courses

job breakdown
job list
on-the-job training (OJT)
specific job orientation
training

Discussion Questions

1. How does general property orientation differ from specific job orientation?

2. What activities may be involved in a specific job orientation program?

3. How does training benefit the employee, the guest, the property, and the supervisor?

4. What are some of the benefits of independent learning courses?

5. How does on-the-job training work?

6. What are some of the advantages and disadvantages of on-the-job training?

7. What factors motivate adults to learn?

8. Why is it important to get trainees actively involved in learning?

9. How do you use job lists and job breakdowns?

10. What four steps make up the four-step training program?

REVIEW QUIZ

When you feel you have covered all of the material in this chapter, answer these questions. Choose the *best* answer. Check your answers with the correct ones found on the Review Quiz Answer Key at the end of this book.

True (T) or False (F)

T F 1. An important part of the general property orientation is a review of equipment and materials needed to do the job.

T F 2. Training benefits guests who visit a property.

T F 3. Repeat business is one benefit of proper job training.

T F 4. It is best to conduct on-the-job training in a quiet conference or meeting room which is free from interruptions.

T F 5. A lecture format is generally the best method to use to teach adult trainees.

T F 6. A job list details how to perform each task.

T F 7. Performance standards must be observable in order for job breakdowns to be effective.

T F 8. A job list should include a yes/no checklist which a supervisor can use to evaluate employee performance.

T F 9. Coaching trial performances is the final stage of the four-step training method.

T F 10. After carefully explaining each step of a specific job responsibility once, a trainer should coach a trial performance.

Alternate/Multiple Choice

11. Adults usually learn best when case studies are:

   a. highly theoretical.
   b. very realistic.

12. When conducting a training session, one should generally ask questions which require:

   a. a yes/no response.
   b. more than a brief answer.

13. A job breakdown:

   a. lists tasks an employee must perform.
   b. details how to perform each task.

14. It is useful to cover all of the following topics during the general property orientation, *except*:

    a. fringe benefits.
    b. guest relations.
    c. professional jargon.
    d. the organization's philosophy.

15. Which of the following training methods is *not* a group training method?

    a. role playing
    b. on-the-job training
    c. seminars
    d. case studies

Chapter Outline

Productivity Standards
    Determining Productivity Standards
    Balancing Quality and Quantity
Planning Staffing Requirements
    Fixed and Variable Labor
    Developing a Staffing Guide
Forecasting Business Volume
    The Nature of Forecasting
    Short-Term Forecasting
    Base Adjustment Forecasts
    Moving Average Forecasts
Developing Employee Work Schedules
    Evaluating the Scheduling Process
Monitoring and Evaluating Productivity
    Levels
    Increasing Productivity

Learning Objectives

1. Explain why productivity standards vary from property to property in the hospitality industry.

2. Explain how productivity standards are determined.

3. Distinguish between fixed staff and variable staff positions.

4. Explain how a staffing guide serves as a labor scheduling and control tool.

5. Identify the procedures that supervisors can follow in developing a staffing guide.

6. Explain the nature and limitations of forecasting business volume.

7. Distinguish the base adjustment forecasting method from the moving average forecasting method.

8. Describe several labor scheduling techniques available to supervisors.

9. Explain how a supervisor can use a weekly labor hour report to evaluate scheduling practices.

10. Identify procedures supervisors can follow to increase productivity by revising performance standards.

5

Managing Productivity and Controlling Labor Costs

In the labor-intensive hospitality industry, more than 30% of all sales revenue is typically used to meet payroll costs. This fact underscores the importance of the supervisor's role in managing productivity and controlling labor costs. No hospitality operation can afford unproductive employees or wasted labor hours. Consider the following example.

Let's assume that the profits earned by a hospitality operation are 8% of the revenue generated by sales. This means that for every dollar of sales, the operation earns a profit of eight cents. Let's assume that poor scheduling practices by supervisors in the operation result in overstaffing the departments and wasting $500 in unnecessary labor costs every week. How much must the operation generate in additional sales to pay for the wasted $500 in labor costs?

The answer is *not* $500 dollars. Sales revenue must also be used to pay for food costs, necessary labor costs, mortgage payments, taxes, and many other types of costs as well. The $500 in excessive labor costs must come out of the operation's profits. So, in order to maintain an 8% profit level, the operation must earn the $500 lost in profit by generating additional weekly sales of $6,250 ($500 divided by the .08 profit requirement).

The results of understaffing the department can be just as disastrous. While understaffing may decrease labor costs in the short run, over time it may increase turnover and decrease profits. The stress of constantly working short-handed may lead employees to quit. When performance standards are not consistently met, profits may decrease due to guest dissatisfaction and lost business.

This chapter focuses on the supervisor's responsibility to schedule the right number of employees to work each day. The chapter presents step-by-step procedures which can help hospitality supervisors to:

1. Develop productivity standards based on established performance standards.

2. Construct a staffing guide based on productivity standards.

3. Create employee work schedules by using the staffing guide with business forecasts.

4. Increase productivity by appropriately revising performance standards.

Productivity Standards

Productivity standards define the acceptable quantity of work to be done by trained employees who perform their work according to established **performance**

standards. For example, the productivity standard for room attendants in a housekeeping department establishes the time it should take a trained room attendant to clean one guestroom according to performance standards. The productivity standard for a food server might establish the number of guests a trained staff member can serve while meeting performance requirements.

Since performance requirements vary in relation to the unique needs and requirements of each hospitality operation, it is impossible to identify productivity standards that would apply throughout the industry. Supervisors must balance quality (performance standards) and quantity (productivity standards) in relation to the size and level of service of their departments. For example, the duties of room attendants vary widely among economy/limited-service, mid-range-service, and world-class-service hotels due to differences in room size and furnishings. Therefore, the productivity standards for room attendants will also vary among these types of properties. In fact, within the same hotel, the productivity standards for room attendants may vary with the different types of rooms that must be cleaned.

Determining Productivity Standards

A supervisor begins to establish productivity standards by answering the question: How long should it take for an employee to perform a specific task according to the department's performance standards?

Let's assume that, at a hotel offering mid-range service, the supervisor determines that a room attendant can meet performance standards by cleaning a guestroom in approximately 27 minutes. Exhibit 5.1 presents a sample productivity standard worksheet and shows how a productivity standard can then be established for room attendants working 8-hour shifts. Calculations within the exhibit take into account two 15-minute breaks and a half-hour unpaid lunch period. The exhibit shows that the productivity standard for room attendants is to clean 15 guestrooms per 8-hour shift. Similar observations and calculations would be made for other positions in the housekeeping department, such as for inspectors, housepersons, lobby attendants, etc.[1]

A dining room supervisor can also determine productivity standards by observing and tracking the time it takes for several trained employees to perform tasks according to performance standards. Just as the productivity standards for room attendants vary with the size of a guestroom and the types of furnishings that need to be cleaned, so productivity standards for dining room positions vary with the style of service and the specific menu items served during different meal periods.

Exhibit 5.2 presents a worksheet that a supervisor can use to determine a productivity standard for food servers. The worksheet provides columns for recording data and observations on the work of a single server over five lunch shifts. For each lunch shift, the supervisor records the following data:

- Number of guests served
- Number of hours the server worked
- Number of guests the server served per hour worked

Exhibit 5.1 Productivity Standard Worksheet—Room Attendants

Step 1
Determine how long it should take to clean one guestroom according to the department's performance standards.

Approximately 27 minutes*

Step 2
Determine the total shift time in minutes.

8 hours × 60 minutes = 480 minutes

Step 3
Determine the time available for guestroom cleaning.

Total Shift Time .... 480 minutes
Less:
    Beginning-of-Shift Duties .... 20 minutes
    Morning Break .... 15 minutes
    Afternoon Break .... 15 minutes
    End-of-Shift Duties .... 20 minutes

Time Available for Guestroom Cleaning .... 410 minutes

Step 4
Determine the productivity standard by dividing the result of Step 3 by the result of Step 1.

$$\frac{410 \text{ minutes}}{27 \text{ minutes}} = \frac{15.2 \text{ guestrooms}}{\text{per 8-hour shift}}$$

*Since performance standards vary from property to property, this figure is used for illustrative purposes only. It is not a suggested time figure for cleaning guestrooms.

Source: Margaret Kappa, et al., *Managing Housekeeping Operations* (East Lansing, Mich.: Educational Institute of the American Hotel & Motel Association, 1990), p. 26.

- Comments concerning how well the server performed according to performance standards

The exhibit shows that on April 14, Joyce served 38 guests during a 4-hour shift. This resulted in 9.5 guests served per hour worked (38 guests divided by 4 hours of work). Over a five-day period, the supervisor observed her work and then recorded comments relating to her efficiency.

Before calculating a productivity standard for this position, the supervisor would have completed worksheets for several trained servers who worked similar lunch shifts. In our example, the supervisor determined a productivity standard of 10 guests per labor hour. That is, in the supervisor's view, trained servers should be able to serve 10 guests for each hour worked without sacrificing established performance standards. Similar observations and calculations would be made for other dining room positions such as for hosts, buspersons, bartenders, and bar servers, etc.

Exhibit 5.2 Productivity Standard Worksheet—Food Servers

Position Performance Analysis

Position: _____ *Service* _____   Name of Employee: _____ *Joyce* _____

Shift: _____ A.M.—*Lunch* _____

	4/14	4/15	4/16	4/17	4/18
No. of Guests Served	38	60	25	45	50
No. Hours Worked	4	4	4	4	3.5
No. of Guests/Labor Hour	9.5	15	6.3	11.3	14.3
Review Comments	Even workflow; no problems	Was really rushed; could not provide adequate service	Too much "standing around"; very inefficient	No problems; handled everything well	Worked fast whole shift; better with fewer guests

General Comments

   Joyce is a better than average server; with all the tasks that service personnel must do in our restaurant, approximately 10 guests per labor hour can be served by one server. When the number of guests goes up, service quality decreases. When Joyce really had to rush, some guests waited longer than they should have had to. When the number of guests per labor hour dropped and Joyce was not busy, there was a lot of unproductive time.

Suggested Meals/Labor Hour
(for this position):   _____ *10* _____   Performance Review by: _____ *W. Brown* _____

Restaurant Manager

Source: Jack D. Ninemeier, *Planning and Control for Food and Beverage Operations,* 3d ed. (East Lansing, Mich.: Educational Institute of the American Hotel & Motel Association, 1991), p. 353.

With slight alterations, Exhibit 5.2 can be used to determine productivity standards for other hospitality positions, such as cooks, pantry workers, front desk agents, cashiers, and reservationists. For example, a productivity worksheet for a lunch cook would have space to record the number of meals prepared, the number of hours the cook worked, and the number of meals prepared per hour worked. Similarly, a worksheet for day-shift front desk agents would have space to record the number of check-ins and check-outs processed, the number of hours the agent worked, and the number of check-ins and check-outs processed per hour worked.

Balancing Quality and Quantity

Supervisors must effectively balance performance standards and productivity standards. For example, if quality expectations (performance standards) are set too high, the quantity of work that can be done accordingly (productivity standards) may be unacceptably low. Overtime pay for current employees and/or the scheduling of additional staff may be needed to ensure that all the work gets done. However, the increased labor expense of scheduling additional staff may be unacceptable in light of the department's budgeted labor expenses.

On the other hand, if quality expectations are set too low, the quantity of work that can be done may be unacceptably high. In this case, labor expense may be significantly below the amount planned for by the department's budget. However, low performance standards may not meet the expectations of guests. Complaints from guests about poor service and corresponding decreases in the volume of business can affect the operation's profits.

Balancing quality and quantity expectations results in realistic productivity standards. These productivity standards should form the basis for budgeting the department's labor expense and for planning staffing requirements.

Planning Staffing Requirements

The first step in planning staffing requirements is to determine which positions within the department are fixed and which are variable in relation to changes in business volume. Once this is determined, productivity standards can be used to develop a staffing guide for variable staff positions.

Fixed and Variable Labor

Fixed staff positions are those that must be filled regardless of the volume of business. Many of these positions are salaried and managerial in nature, and may include department managers, assistant managers, and some supervisors. Fixed staff positions also generally include a limited number of hourly positions. The actual number and type of fixed staff positions will vary from property to property.

Since fixed labor is the minimum amount of labor needed to operate the lodging or food service facility regardless of business volume, it represents the minimum labor expense. During slow business periods, labor expense should be kept as low as possible. Therefore, several times during the year, top managers should review the amount of fixed labor needed in each department. During this review managers may consider the following temporary actions to reduce labor expense during slow business periods:

- Eliminate or curtail a particular service. For example, reduce the hours of dining room, concierge, or valet parking service.

- Assign salaried staff duties normally performed by hourly employees. For example, an assistant restaurant manager might be stationed at the host stand, seating guests and taking reservations.

- Adjust tasks performed by hourly fixed staff. For example, given the proper cross-training, a front desk agent may be able to function as a cashier and/or reservationist.

The number of **variable staff positions** to be filled on any given day will depend on the expected volume of business. For example, the number of front desk agents scheduled to work will increase as the expected number of morning checkouts and afternoon/evening check-ins increases. In the housekeeping department, the number of room attendants, housepersons, and inspectors needed will depend primarily on the number of rooms occupied during the previous night. Similarly, the number of kitchen and dining room staff members scheduled to work will depend on the number of guests expected for breakfast, lunch, and dinner.

Developing a Staffing Guide

A **staffing guide** is an important labor scheduling and control tool used by supervisors. With a well-developed staffing guide, a supervisor can properly schedule the correct number of employees to work each day and, at the same time, help to ensure that the department's labor expense remains within boundaries set by the operation's budget.

Exhibit 5.3 presents a partial staffing guide for variable staff positions in the housekeeping department at the fictional King James Hotel. The following sections explain in detail how the number of labor hours, the number of full-time employees (often referred to as "full-time equivalents"), and the amount of labor expense was calculated for day-shift room attendants. The explanation also serves as a step-by-step procedure that supervisors can follow in developing a staffing guide for their own departments.

Step 1—Determine Total Labor Hours. The first step in developing a staffing guide is to use previously established productivity standards to determine the total labor hours for positions that must be scheduled when the hotel is at specific occupancy levels. Let's assume that the productivity standard for day-shift room attendants is 30 minutes (.5 hour) to clean one guestroom. Let's further assume that all rooms are of the same size and contain the same types of furnishings. Given this information, the supervisor can calculate the total number of labor hours required at various hotel occupancy levels.

For example, if the hotel is at 90% occupancy, there will be 225 rooms to clean the next day (250 rooms × .9 = 225 rooms). It will take a total of 113 labor hours to clean them (225 rooms × .5 hour = 112.5 labor hours, rounded to 113). At 80% occupancy, there will be 200 rooms to clean (250 rooms × .8 = 200 rooms). It will take 100 labor hours to clean them (200 rooms × .5 hour = 100 labor hours).

Step 2—Determine the Required Number of Employees. At the King James Hotel, full-time room attendants work an 8-hour shift and take a half-hour unpaid lunch period. Taking into account a morning and an afternoon break (15 minutes each, or 30 total minutes a day) and the time needed for performing tasks at the beginning and end of the shift (15 minutes each, or 30 minutes total), 7 hours of the total shift are spent cleaning guestrooms. Since the productivity standard is .5 hour to clean one guestroom, a day-shift room attendant is expected to clean 14 guestrooms during an 8-hour shift (7 hours ÷ .5 = 14).

Given this information, the number of full-time, day-shift room attendants that must be scheduled at different occupancy levels can be determined by dividing the number of occupied rooms by 14. For example, when the hotel is at 90% occupancy, there will be 225 rooms to clean the next day. Dividing 225 rooms by 14 indicates that it will take 16 full-time, day-shift room attendants to clean those rooms (225 rooms ÷ 14 = 16.07, rounded to 16). When the hotel is at 80% occupancy, there will be 200 rooms to clean. It will take 14 room attendants to clean them (200 rooms ÷ 14 = 14.29 room attendants, rounded to 14).

Exhibit 5.3 Sample Variable Staffing Guide

					King James Hotel						
Occupancy %	100%	95%	90%	85%	80%	75%	70%	65%	60%	55%	50%
Rooms Occupied	250	238	225	213	200	188	175	163	150	138	125
Room Attendants (A.M.) (Productivity STD = .5)											
Labor Hours	125	119	113	107	100	94	88	82	75	69	63
Employees	18	17	16	15	14	13	12	12	11	10	9
Expense	$625	$595	$565	$535	$500	$470	$440	$410	$375	$345	$315
Housepersons (A.M.) (Productivity STD = .08)											
Labor Hours	20	19	18	17	16	15	14	13	12	11	10
Employees	3	3	3	2	2	2	2	2	2	2	1
Expense	$100	$95	$90	$85	$80	$75	$70	$65	$60	$55	$50
Lobby Attendants (Productivity STD = .07)											
Labor Hours	18	17	16	15	14	13	12	11	11	10	9
Employees	3	2	2	2	2	2	2	2	2	1	1
Expense	$90	$85	$80	$75	$70	$65	$60	$55	$55	$50	$45
Inspectors (Productivity STD = .09)											
Labor Hours	23	21	20	19	18	17	16	15	14	12	11
Employees	3	3	3	3	3	2	2	2	2	2	2
Expense	$115	$105	$100	$95	$90	$85	$80	$75	$70	$60	$55
Room Attendants (P.M.) (Productivity STD = .14)											
Labor Hours	35	33	32	30	28	26	25	23	21	19	18
Employees	5	5	5	4	4	4	4	3	3	3	3
Expense	$175	$165	$160	$150	$140	$130	$125	$115	$105	$95	$90
Housepersons (P.M.) (Productivity STD = .07)											
Labor Hours	18	17	16	15	14	13	12	11	11	10	9
Employees	3	2	2	2	2	2	2	2	2	1	1
Expense	$90	$85	$80	$75	$70	$65	$60	$55	$55	$50	$45
Total Labor Hours	239	226	215	203	190	178	167	155	144	131	120
Total Expense	$1,195	$1,130	$1,075	$1,015	$950	$890	$835	$775	$720	$655	$600

Source: Margaret Kappa, et al., *Managing Housekeeping Operations* (East Lansing, Mich.: Educational Institute of the American Hotel & Motel Association, 1990), p. 75.

The actual number of room attendants scheduled to work on any given day will vary depending on the number of full-time and part-time employees the supervisor schedules to work. For example, when the hotel is at 90% occupancy, the supervisor could schedule 16 full-time room attendants, or 12 full-time room attendants (each working 8 hours) and 8 part-time room attendants (each working 4 hours). Either scheduling technique would approximate the required total of 113 labor hours.

Step 3—Estimate Labor Expense. This step of developing a staffing guide requires the supervisor to calculate the estimated labor expense needed to operate the department at specific occupancy levels. This can be done for day-shift room attendants at the King James Hotel simply by multiplying the total labor hours by the average hourly rate for room attendants.

To illustrate, let's assume that the average hourly rate is $5.00. When the hotel is at 90% occupancy, the next day's estimated labor expense for day-shift room attendants is $565 (113 total labor hours × $5.00/hour = $565). Regardless of the combination of full-time and part-time employees that are eventually scheduled to work, the total labor expense for day-shift room attendants should not exceed $565, when the hotel is at 90% occupancy.

In order to complete the staffing guide, the supervisor must make similar calculations for other variable staff positions in the department. Let's assume that the executive housekeeper and the department supervisor at the King James Hotel have reviewed the productivity standards for other positions in the department and have determined the following:

- One inspector is needed for every 80 occupied rooms, yielding a productivity standard of .09 (7 hours ÷ 80 occupied rooms = .09).

- One day-shift lobby attendant is needed to service public areas when 100 rooms are occupied, yielding a productivity standard of .07 (7 hours ÷ 100 occupied rooms = .07).

- One day-shift houseperson is needed for every 85 occupied rooms, yielding a productivity standard of .08 (7 hours ÷ 85 occupied rooms = .08).

- One afternoon-shift room attendant is needed for every 50 occupied rooms, yielding a productivity standard of .14 (7 hours ÷ 50 occupied rooms = .14).

- One afternoon-shift houseperson is needed for every 100 occupied rooms, yielding a productivity standard of .07 (7 hours ÷ 100 occupied rooms = .07).

These productivity standards are multiplied by the number of occupied rooms to determine the total labor hours required for each position when the hotel is at specific occupancy levels. Dividing the total labor hours for each position by 7 determines the number of full-time employees that must be scheduled to clean the hotel. Multiplying the required labor hours by an average hourly rate determines the estimated labor expense for each position.

A more fully developed staffing guide than the one shown in Exhibit 5.3 would indicate total labor hours, required full-time employees, and expense amounts for additional occupancy levels. With such a tool and with reliable occupancy forecasts, the supervisor can effectively and efficiently schedule the correct number of employees to work each day. In addition, if the budgeted labor expense for the department is based on the same productivity standards as the staffing guide, the supervisor is assured of keeping labor costs in line with management's expectations.

Forecasting Business Volume

No matter how precise the department's staffing guide, accurate labor scheduling depends on the reliability of forecasts which predict the volume of business for a particular month, week, day, or meal period.[2] Most hospitality organizations

Exhibit 5.4 Sample Ten-Day Volume Forecast—Rooms

TEN-DAY VOLUME FORECAST—ROOMS

Motor-Hotel _____
(LOCATION)

Date Prepared _____
Week Ending _____

	DATE											
	DAY	THUR.	FRI.	SAT.	SUN.	MON.	TUES.	WED.	THUR.	FRI.	SAT.	Totals
		Previous Week										
ROOMS DEPARTMENT		F A	F A	F A	F A	F A	F A	F A	F A	F A	F A	F A
Rooms occupied—Indv.												
Groups												
Arrivals—Ind. Resv.												
Group Resv.												
Estimated walk-ins												
Sub-Total												
Departures—scheduled												
estimated												
Sub-Total												
TOTAL ROOMS OCCUPIED												
House Count												
In House												
Arrivals												
Walk-ins												
Sub-Total												
Departures												
TOTAL HOUSE COUNT												

SPECIAL COMMENTS
(i.e., types of groups—V.I.P., etc.)

F = Forecast
A = Actual

Source: David L. Balangue, "Payroll Productivity (Part IV: Staff Planning)," *Lodging*, November 1978, p. 39.

develop monthly, ten-day, and three-day forecasts of business volume. The supervisor uses the monthly forecast to generate work schedules for employees in the department. The ten-day and three-day forecasts are used to fine-tune the work schedules in light of anticipated increases or decreases in business.

Exhibit 5.4 presents a sample form that can be used by rooms division managers to develop a ten-day forecast. Note that the form includes space to record house counts (the number of occupied rooms) for each day of the previous week. Also, the form enables managers to evaluate their forecasts by comparing the forecasted house count with the actual number of occupied rooms. Exhibit 5.5 presents a similar ten-day forecast form that can be used by food service operations. Exhibit 5.6 presents a sample three-day forecast form that can be used to revise predictions made on the ten-day forecast.

Forecasting in large hospitality properties is often the responsibility of a committee made up of representatives from key departments. In small properties,

Exhibit 5.5 Sample Ten-Day Volume Forecast—Food

TEN-DAY VOLUME FORECAST—FOOD

Motor-Hotel _____
(LOCATION)

Date Prepared _____
Week Ending _____

FOOD DEPARTMENT	DATE																						
	DAY	THUR.		FRI.		SAT.		SUN.		MON.		TUES.		WED.		THUR.		FRI.		SAT.		Totals	
		Previous Week																					
		F	A	F	A	F	A	F	A	F	A	F	A	F	A	F	A	F	A	F	A	F	A
Dining Room																							
Breakfast																							
Lunch																							
Dinner																							
Total D.R. Covers																							
Coffee Shop																							
Breakfast																							
Lunch																							
Total C.S. Covers																							
Banquet																							
Breakfast																							
Lunch																							
Dinner																							
Total Banquet Covers																							
Room Service																							
Total R.S. Covers																							
TOTAL FOOD COVERS																							

SPECIAL COMMENTS
(i.e., types of groups—V.I.P., etc.)

F = Forecast
A = Actual

Source: David L. Balangue, "Payroll Productivity (Part IV: Staff Planning)," *Lodging,* November 1978, p. 39.

the general manager and/or designated supervisors may prepare the necessary forecasts.

Exhibit 5.7 shows the number of people involved in making short-term (3- to 10-day) forecasts. Across all properties surveyed, the range of the number of personnel involved was 1-6 people. The larger the property, the greater the number of personnel involved in the forecast. For example, the mega-hotels (1,000 or more rooms) that responded use six people in developing their rooms forecast, while hotels with fewer than 150 rooms involve an average of two people.

The Nature of Forecasting

In order to use forecasts as effective labor scheduling tools, supervisors need to understand the nature and limitations of forecasting. First, forecasting deals with the future. A forecast made today is for activity during a future period, whether it is

Exhibit 5.6 Sample Three-Day Revised Forecast—Rooms

THREE-DAY REVISED FORECAST—ROOMS			
	Yesterday	Today	Tomorrow
Day			
Date			
Guest Count			
Room Arrivals			
Room Departures			
Room Count			
Room Vacancies			
% of Occupancy			
Forecasted % of Occupancy			
Condition			

Exhibit 5.7 Personnel Involved in Making Short-Term Forecasts

	Rooms Forecast	Food & Beverage Forecast	Catering Forecast
Average number of personnel involved	3 people	3 people	2 people
Person responsible for final forecast	General manager (GM) and to a lesser extent the front office manager	Food and beverage director and to a lesser extent the GM	Director of catering and to a lesser extent the food and beverage director

Source: Raymond S. Schmidgall, "While Forecasts Hit Targets, GMs Still Seek Better Guns," *Lodging*, November 1989.

tonight's dinner sales or next year's rooms sales. The time period involved is significant. A forecast today for tomorrow's sales is generally much easier (and likely to be more accurate) than an estimate today of next year's sales. The more removed the forecast period is from the date the forecast is made, the greater the difficulty in making the forecast and the greater the risk that the actual results will differ from the forecast. Long-range forecasts are periodically reviewed and revised on the basis of new information obtained after the forecasts were made.

Second, forecasting involves uncertainty. If management were certain about what circumstances would exist during the forecasted period, preparing the forecast would be a trivial matter. Virtually all situations managers face involve uncertainty; therefore, judgments must be made and information gathered on which to base the forecast. For example, assume that rooms sales for a major hotel are forecast one year in advance. The manager (forecaster) may be uncertain about competition, guest demand, room rates, and so forth. Nevertheless, using the best information available and his/her best judgment, a forecast must be made.

Third, forecasting generally relies on information contained in historical data. Historical activity (for example, past sales) may not be a strong indicator of future activity, but it is considered a reasonable starting point. When historical data appear to be irrelevant to the future time period, the forecasts should be modified appropriately. For example, a successful World's Fair might have a major impact on hotel occupancies for several months. However, in projecting future hotel occupancies after the fair ends, the recent historical information may well be much less relevant.

Fourth, by their nature, forecasts are generally less accurate than desired. However, rather than discarding forecasts due to their inaccuracy, management should consider using more sophisticated forecasting models when their cost is justified. Forecasts should be revised as soon as there is a change in the circumstances on which the forecasts were based. For example, an enhanced food and beverage reputation due to favorable publicity may call for reforecasting next month's food and beverage sales. The revised forecast should reflect an anticipated increase in sales due to the favorable publicity.

Short-Term Forecasting

Exhibit 5.8 is a summary of lodging industry short-term sales forecasting approaches by three profit centers: rooms, food (restaurants), and catering (banquets). Short-term forecasts in this research refer to forecasts covering from 3 to 10 days.

The major purpose of each short-term forecast is to allow for staffing and, in food and catering, for ordering the food supplies to service the dining guests. Another purpose is the motivation of personnel, that is, using the short-term sales forecast as a target or goal for the team to meet.

The methods used by the majority of respondents differ by profit center. Most hotels, especially those with reservation systems, forecast room sales using the room reservations at the time of the forecast plus an estimate for walk-ins. For example, a hotel may show 100 rooms reserved for the following Monday and add the average of walk-ins for the past four Mondays of 15 to equal a rooms sales forecast of 115 rooms.

Exhibit 5.8 Short-Term Forecasting Methods

	Rooms	Food	Catering
Major purposes of forecast:	Staffing (98%) Motivating personnel (25%)	Staffing (100%) Order food (72%) Motivating personnel (19%)	Staffing (82%) Order food (72%) Motivating personnel (16%)
Methodology:	Room reservations plus estimated walk-ins (93%) Prior period sales adjusted based on intuition (7%)	Prior period sales adjusted based on intuition (46%) Meal reservations and estimate for walk-ins (28%) Capture ratios related to the rooms forecast (26%)	Booked catered events plus esti- mate of additional sales (90%) Prior period sales adjusted based on intuition (10%)
Expression of short-term forecast:	Daily number of rooms sold (80%) Daily sales dollars (55%) Daily number of rooms by type (35%) Daily sales dollars by type of room (20%)	Total covers (79%) Total sales dollars (61%) Food covers by meal period (60%) Sales dollars by meal period (44%)	Total sales dollars (70%) Total covers (67%) Sales dollars by catered event (47%) Covers by catered event (47%)

Source: Raymond S. Schmidgall, *Hospitality Industry Managerial Accounting*, 3d ed. (East Lansing, Mich.: Educational Institute of the American Hotel & Motel Association, 1995), p. 331.

A second approach is adjusting the previous period's sales based on intuitive expectations for the forecast period. Only 7% of the lodging establishments reported using this approach, and the majority of these users (60%) were establishments with fewer than 150 rooms.

The most common approach used to forecast short-term food sales by hoteliers (46%) is using the previous period's sales figure and adjusting it for expected differences for the forecast period. For example, if 100 covers were served at the previous Monday evening dinner, the hotel's forecast for the coming Monday evening would be 100 plus or minus an adjustment for expected differences. These differences could be based on house guests, local events, weather forecasts, and other similar factors.

Twenty-eight percent of the hotels rely in part on meal reservations and estimated walk-ins, while 26% use capture ratios—that is, ratios based on hotel guests or some variation of hotel guests. An example of a capture ratio is a hotel which estimates its dinner covers to be 40 plus one quarter of the estimated house guests for the night. If the estimated house guests total 200, the dinner covers forecasted equal 90. This is determined as follows:

$$
\begin{aligned}
\text{Forecasted dinner covers} &= a + bx \\
\text{where } a &= \text{estimated covers for walk-ins} \\
&\quad \text{(non-hotel guests)} \\
b &= \text{percentage of hotel guests} \\
&\quad \text{expected to eat dinner} \\
x &= \text{hotel guest count for evening} \\
\text{Forecasted dinner covers} &= 40 + .25(200) \\
&= \underline{\underline{90}}
\end{aligned}
$$

The sales forecasting methods reported for catered events include two alternatives:

- Ninety percent use the number booked for the catered events plus an estimate for additional sales not booked when the forecast is made.

- Ten percent use previous period catered sales adjusted for expected differences.

As Exhibit 5.8 shows, the short-term sales forecast is expressed in a variety of ways. For rooms, the most common way is rooms sold (80%); for food sales, the most common is total covers (79%); and for catering sales, the most common is the total forecasted catering sales dollars (70%), followed closely by total covers (67%). Many hotels express the sales forecasts in more than one way.

Most hoteliers compare their actual results to their short-term sales forecasts in order to determine their forecasting accuracy. Then, in the future, they can refine their forecasting method and allow for forecasting error in staffing and ordering supplies. The following sections present two forecasting methods widely used in the hospitality industry.[3]

Base Adjustment Forecasts

One of the simplest forecasting methods is to use the most recently collected data as the basis for the forecast. For example, a food service manager's sales projections of $50,000 for the current month may be based upon the $50,000 sales of the previous month. To take seasonality into account, a forecaster might use sales from the same month of the previous year as a base and either add or subtract a certain percentage.

For example, assume that a hotel's January 19X1 rooms sales totaled $150,000. The projection for January 19X2, using an anticipated 10% increase due to expected increased rooms sales and prices, would be $165,000, computed as follows:

$$
\begin{aligned}
\text{Base}(1 + 10\%) &= \text{Forecast for January 19X2} \\
150,000(1.1) &= \underline{\$165,000}
\end{aligned}
$$

Although this method is very simple, it may provide reasonably accurate forecasts, especially for estimates of up to one year.

Moving Average Forecasts

In some cases, the major cause of variations among data used in making forecasts is randomness. Since managers do not make business decisions based on randomness that may never again happen, they attempt to remove the random effect by

Exhibit 5.9 Weekly Meals Served

Week	Actual Meals Served
1	1,000
2	900
3	950
4	1,050
5	1,025
6	1,000
7	975
8	1,000
9	950
10	1,025
11	1,000
12	1,050

Source: Raymond S. Schmidgall, *Hospitality Industry Managerial Accounting*, 3d ed. (East Lansing, Mich.: Educational Institute of the American Hotel & Motel Association, 1995), p. 325.

averaging or "smoothing" the data from specified time periods. One such approach to forecasting is the moving average, which is expressed mathematically as follows:

$$\text{Moving Average} \ = \ \frac{\text{Activity in Previous } n \text{ Periods}}{n}$$

where n is the number of periods in the moving average

Exhibit 5.9 reveals weekly sales for weeks 1–12. Using a three-week moving average, the estimate for the number of meals to be served during the thirteenth week is 1,025, determined as follows:

$$\text{3-Week Moving Average} \ = \ \frac{1,025 \ + \ 1,000 \ + \ 1,050}{3}$$

$$= \ \underline{\underline{1,025}} \text{ meals}$$

As new weekly results become available, they are used in calculating the average by adding the most recent week and dropping the earliest week. In this way, the calculated average is a "moving" one because it is continually updated to include only the most recent observations for the specified number of time periods. It should be noted that the more periods averaged, the less effect the random variations will have on the forecast.

Developing Employee Work Schedules

Forecasts are used in conjunction with the staffing guide to determine the "right" number of labor hours to schedule each day for every position in the department.

Supervisors have found the following tips helpful when developing work schedules:

- A schedule should cover a full work week.

- The work schedule should be approved by appropriate managers before it is posted or distributed to employees.

- Schedules should be posted at least three days before the beginning of the next work week.

- Schedules should be posted in the same location and at the same time each week.

- Days off, vacation time, and requested days off should be planned as far in advance as possible and indicated on the posted work schedule.

- The work schedule for the current week should be reviewed daily in relation to forecast data. If necessary, changes to the schedule should be made.

- Any scheduling changes should be noted directly on the posted work schedule.

- A copy of the posted work schedule can be used to monitor the daily attendance of employees. This copy should be retained as part of the department's permanent records.

Whenever possible, work schedules should be developed to meet the day-to-day (and even hour-by-hour) demands of business volume. For example, if a large convention group is expected to check in between 2 P.M. and 4 P.M. on a particular day, additional front desk agents may need to be scheduled during those hours. Also, additional room attendants may need to be scheduled to work earlier in the day to ensure that clean rooms will be available for the large number of expected arrivals. If the dining room attracts local business people during the lunch period, more cooks and servers may need to be scheduled during the rush time than are scheduled for other hours during the shift.

Some supervisors use a schedule worksheet to determine when employees are needed to work. Let's review how the supervisor might have completed the schedule worksheet shown in Exhibit 5.10. After receiving the forecast of 250 estimated guests, the supervisor checked the staffing guide and found that 18 labor hours should be scheduled for the position of assistant cook. Knowing that the peak hours during the dinner period are between 7:30 P.M. and 9:30 P.M., the supervisor staggered the work schedule of three assistant cooks to cover these peak hours. Joe was scheduled to work earlier to perform duties at the beginning of the shift, and Phyllis was scheduled to work later to perform duties at the end of the shift.

Not every supervisor would need to complete a schedule worksheet for each position during every workshift. In many departments, business volume stabilizes, creating a pattern of labor demands. However, all supervisors must develop work schedules that meet the particular business demands of their departments. The following sections present useful **alternative scheduling** techniques. These techniques may also meet the needs of many employees and, properly implemented, could increase staff morale and job satisfaction.

Exhibit 5.10 Sample Schedule Worksheet

	6:00 a	7:00 a	8:00 a	9:00 a	10:00 a	11:00 a	12:00	1:00 p	2:00 p	3:00 p	4:00 p	5:00 p	6:00 p	7:00 p	8:00 p	9:00 p	10:00 p	11:00 p	12:00 p	1:00 a	2:00 a	3:00 a	4:00 a	5:00 a	Planned Total Hours

Day: _____Monday_____   Estimated Guests: A.M. | P.M.   Department: ____Food Service____

Date: ____8/1/00____ | 250   Position: ____Assistant Cook____

Shift: ____P.M.____

Position/Employee

Joe	7.0
Sally	6.5
Phyllis	4.5
	18.0

Position: ____Assistant Cook____

Standard Labor Hours: ____18____

Planned Labor Hours: ____18____

Difference: ____0____

Source: Jack D. Ninemeier, *Planning and Control for Food and Beverage Operations,* 3d ed. (East Lansing, Mich.: Educational Institute of the American Hotel & Motel Association, 1991), p. 360.

Stagger Regular Work Shifts of Full-Time Employees. Since the volume of business varies from hour to hour, there is no need for all employees to begin and end their shifts at the same times. By staggering and overlapping work shifts, the supervisor can ensure that the greatest number of employees are working during peak business hours.

Compress the Work Week of Some Full-Time Employees. For departments such as housekeeping, it may be possible to offer some full-time employees the opportunity to work the equivalent of a standard work week in fewer than the usual five days. One popular arrangement compresses a 40-hour work week into four 10-hour days. This technique can be beneficial to lodging operations whose primary market is the business traveler. A compressed work schedule for some full-time room attendants would meet the demands of high occupancy during the middle of the week.

Implement Split Shifts. A split shift schedules an employee to work during two separate time periods on the same day. For example, a day-shift dining room server may be scheduled from 8 A.M. to 10 A.M. to handle breakfast business and, on the same day, be scheduled from 11:30 A.M. to 1:30 P.M. to handle lunch business. While this technique helps the supervisor ensure that the greatest number of employees are working during peak business hours, it may meet the personal needs of very few full-time employees. However, offering split shifts to part-time employees may enable them to conveniently increase their earnings.

Increase the Number of Part-Time Employees. Employing a substantial number of part-time workers provides the supervisor with greater scheduling flexibility. Part-time employees can easily be scheduled to match peak business hours.

Evaluating the Scheduling Process

Using the department's staffing guide and a reliable business forecast to develop an employee work schedule does not guarantee that the hours employees actually work will equal the number of hours for which they were scheduled to work. Supervisors must monitor and evaluate the scheduling process by comparing, on a weekly basis, the actual hours each employee works with the number of hours for which the employee was scheduled to work. Information about actual hours worked is usually obtained from the accounting department or from a staff member assigned to maintain payroll records.

Exhibit 5.11 presents a sample weekly labor hour report. Actual total hours worked during the week are recorded in column 9. These actual hours worked can be compared with the scheduled labor hours shown in column 10. Significant variances should be investigated and corrective action taken when necessary.

The sample report shows that during the week of July 14, 216.5 labor hours were scheduled for dining room employees, but the actual hours worked totaled 224.5. This indicates a variance of 8 hours. Is 8 hours a significant variance? Should the supervisor investigate it? To answer these questions, let's do some quick calculations. For illustrative purposes only, let's assume that if the average hourly wage for the staff is $5.00, the variance of 8 hours costs the operation a total of $40 for the week of July 14. If actual hours worked differed from scheduled labor hours at this rate for the entire year, it would cost the operation a total of $2,080.

As pointed out in the beginning section of this chapter, the $2,080 represents lost profits. Since few food service operations can afford to lose any amount of their potential profit, the answer to both questions is, "Yes!" The variance is significant and should be investigated. The supervisor's remarks recorded at the bottom of the report address the variances in relation to each employee. If similar variances and remarks occur over a period of several weeks, corrective action may be necessary. For example, the supervisor may need to do a better job at planning and scheduling necessary cleaning for the dining room and storeroom areas.

Supervisors can also use the weekly labor hour report to monitor overtime labor costs. Any number of situations may arise that force a supervisor to schedule overtime for some employees. However, most operations require management approval for any scheduled overtime. Unscheduled and excessive overtime costs are generally signs of poor forecasting and/or scheduling procedures. While supervisors have little control over the forecasting methods used by the operation, they are directly responsible for scheduling errors that may result in overtime.

The weekly labor hour report alerts the supervisor to all situations in which an employee's actual labor hours exceed the number of hours for which that employee was scheduled. If previous approval of a variance was not granted, the discrepancy

Exhibit 5.11 Weekly Labor Hour Report

Weekly Department Labor Hour Report

Week of: _7/14/00_   Department: _Food Service_   Supervisor: _Sandra_

Shift: _P.M._

Actual Labor Hours Worked

Position/ Employee	7/14 Mon	7/15 Tues	7/16 Wed	7/17 Thurs	7/18 Fri	7/19 Sat	7/20 Sun	Total Labor Hours Actual	Std.
DINING ROOM									
Jennifer	7	—	7	6.5	7	6	—	33.5	31.0
Brenda	—	7	6.5	7	6.5	6.5	5	38.5	38.5
Sally	—	5	8	7	8	10	—	38.0	36.0
Patty	8	6	6	4.5	—	—	6	30.5	31.0
Anna	4	4	6.5	—	4.5	—	5	24.0	22.0
Thelma	6	5	5	5	5	—	—	26.0	24.0
Elsie	6	—	—	6	6	8	8	34.0	34.0
								224.5	216.5
COOK									
Peggy	4	4	4	4	4	—	—	20.0	20.0
Kathy	4	4	4	—	—	4	4	20.0	20.0
Tilly	4	—	—	4	4	4	4	20.0	18.0
Gert	—	4	4	4	4	4	—	20.0	20.0
Sam	4	4	—	—	—	—	4	12.0	12.0
								92.0	90.0
DISHWASHING									
Terry	—	—	6	6	6	—	—	18.0	18.0
Andrew	6	6	—	—	8	5	5	30.0	30.0
Robert	8	8	8	8	—	—	6	38.0	38.0
Carl	5	—	5	5	5	6	—	26.0	26.0
								112.0	112.0
				Total (all personnel)				428.5	418.5
Remarks:				Difference				+10.00	

Remarks: 7/18 — Jennifer, Sally and Elsie given extra hours to learn tableside flaming
7/19 — Sally stayed 2 hours—special cleaning
7/20 — Tilly stayed 2 hours—cleaned storeroom shelves

Source: Jack D. Ninemeier, *Planning and Control for Food and Beverage Operations*, 3d ed. (East Lansing, Mich.: Educational Institute of the American Hotel & Motel Association, 1991), p. 363.

may signal an attempt by one or more dishonest employees to steal through payroll fraud.

Monitoring and Evaluating Productivity Levels

A supervisor is often evaluated on the basis of how well he/she manages the productivity of the department's employees. This chapter presented practical procedures with which supervisors can:

- Develop productivity standards based on established performance standards.

- Construct a staffing guide based on productivity standards.

- Create employee work schedules by using the staffing guide in conjunction with business forecasts.

However, even if a supervisor carefully follows these procedures, the actual productivity of employees on a given day will rarely, if ever, correspond to the established standards. This is because forecasts of business volume are themselves rarely, if ever, exact. Therefore, some variance in productivity is to be expected. For example, when the actual volume of business is greater than the forecasted volume, productivity generally increases—but only because the department is understaffed. Conversely, when the actual volume of business is less than the forecasted volume, productivity generally decreases—but only because the department is overstaffed.

The supervisor's responsibility is to minimize variances in productivity when, for whatever reason, the department is understaffed or overstaffed. Supervisors must plan for these occurrences so that appropriate action can be taken quickly the very day (or shift) that the situation arises. For example, on a day that the department appears to be understaffed, a supervisor could call in the appropriate number of full-time or part-time employees who were not scheduled to work. Part-time employees may be preferred to avoid possible overtime costs for full-time employees working an extra shift. On a day that the department appears to be overstaffed, a supervisor could check if any scheduled employees would volunteer to take the day off or work shorter shifts.

These are the sorts of adjustments that supervisors must make on a daily basis to ensure the productivity of employees in their departments. A challenge for all hospitality supervisors and managers is to continually seek ways to increase the productivity of employees. Understaffing the department is not an effective solution to increasing productivity.

Increasing Productivity

One of the most difficult and challenging tasks for supervisors is to create new ways of getting work done in the department. Too often supervisors get caught up in routine, day-to-day functions and fail to question the way things are done. The best way to increase productivity is to continually review and revise performance standards. The following sections present a five-step process for increasing productivity by revising performance standards.

Step 1—Collect and Analyze Information about Current Performance Standards. Often this can be done by simple observation. If you know what must be done in order to meet current performance standards, observe what is actually being done and note any differences. When analyzing tasks listed in performance standards for positions within the department, supervisors should ask the following questions:

- Can a particular task be eliminated? Before revising how a task is performed, the supervisor needs to ask whether the task needs to be carried out in the first place.

- Can a particular task be assigned to a different position? For example, instead of room attendants stocking their own carts at the beginning of their shifts, the task could be assigned to a night-shift houseperson. This could increase the productivity of day-shift room attendants by half a room.

- Are the performance standards of another department decreasing the productivity of employees in your department? For example, the on-premises laundry area may not be supplying the correct amount of clean linens your department needs. Productivity suffers when room attendants or dining room staff must make frequent trips to the laundry area to pick up clean linens as they become available.

Step 2—Generate Ideas for New Ways to Get the Job Done. Generally, when work problems arise, there is more than one way to resolve them. Performance standards for many hospitality positions are complex, and it is often difficult to pinpoint the exact reasons for current problems or new ideas about how to get the job done more efficiently.

Employees, other supervisors, and guests are important sources of information that can help a supervisor pinpoint tasks for revision. Employees who actually perform the job are often the best source for suggested improvements. Other supervisors may be able to pass on techniques which they used successfully to increase productivity in their areas. Also, networking with colleagues often results in creative ideas that you can apply to your own area of responsibility. Completed guest comment cards and/or personal interviews with selected guests may reveal aspects of the department that supervisors may consistently overlook.

Step 3—Evaluate Each Idea and Select the Best Approach. The actual idea you select may be a blend of the best elements of several different suggestions. When selecting the best way to revise current performance standards, you must be sure that the task can be done in the time allowed. It is one thing for a "superstar" employee to clean a room or register a guest within a specified time; it may not, however, be reasonable to expect that an average employee—even after training and with close supervision—can be as productive. Remember, performance standards must be attainable in order to be useful.

Step 4—Test the Revised Performance Standard. Have only a few employees use the revised performance standard for a specified time so you can closely monitor whether the new procedures do indeed increase productivity. Remember, old habits are hard to break. So, before conducting a formal evaluation of the revised performance standard, employees will need time to become familiar with the new tasks and build speed.

Step 5—Implement the Revised Performance Standard. After the trial study has demonstrated that the new performance standard increases productivity, employees must be trained in the new procedures. Continual supervision, reinforcement, and coaching during the transitional period will also be necessary. Most important, if the increased productivity is significant, you need to make the necessary changes to the department's staffing guide and base your scheduling practices on the new productivity standard. This will ensure that increased productivity translates to increased profits through lower labor costs.

Endnotes

1. For more information on this subject, please see Margaret Kappa, et al., *Managing Housekeeping Operations* (East Lansing, Mich.: Educational Institute of the American Hotel & Motel Association, 1990), Chapter 2.

2. Readers interested in more information are urged to consult Raymond S. Schmidgall, *Hospitality Industry Managerial Accounting*, 3d ed. (East Lansing, Mich.: Educational Institute of the American Hotel & Motel Association, 1995).

3. For information on more sophisticated forecasting methods, please see Schmidgall, Chapter 9.

Key Terms

alternative scheduling
fixed staff positions
performance standards
productivity standards
staffing guide
variable staff positions

Discussion Questions

1. Why is it impossible to identify productivity standards that would apply throughout the hospitality industry?

2. How are productivity standards determined?

3. What is the relationship between performance standards and productivity standards?

4. What is the difference between fixed staff and variable staff positions?

5. What purpose does a staffing guide serve?

6. Why is it important for the budgeted labor expense for a department to be based on the same productivity standards as the department's staffing guide?

7. How does short-term forecasting differ from long-term forecasting?

8. How does a base adjustment forecast differ from a moving average forecast?

9. How can supervisors use a weekly hour labor report to control and evaluate the scheduling process?

10. What steps can supervisors take to increase productivity by revising performance standards?

REVIEW QUIZ

When you feel you have covered all of the material in this chapter, answer these questions. Choose the *best* answer. Check your answers with the correct ones found on the Review Quiz Answer Key at the end of this book.

True (T) or False (F)

T   F   1. Productivity standards should apply equally throughout the hospitality industry.

T   F   2. A dining room supervisor can determine productivity standards by observing and tracking the time it takes for his/her head server to perform tasks.

T   F   3. Previously established productivity standards can be used to determine the total labor hours for positions that must be scheduled when the hotel is at specific occupancy levels.

T   F   4. Forecasts should not be revised every time there is a change in the circumstances on which the forecasts were based.

T   F   5. One of the most difficult forecasting methods involves using the most recently collected data as the basis for the forecast.

T   F   6. Properly implemented labor scheduling techniques could increase staff morale and job satisfaction.

T   F   7. Supervisors must monitor and evaluate the scheduling process by comparing the actual hours each employee works with the original schedule.

T   F   8. Supervisors can use a weekly labor hour report to monitor overtime labor costs.

T   F   9. When work problems arise, there is normally one "best" way to resolve them.

T   F   10. It is generally easy to pinpoint the exact reasons for problems and find solutions to them.

Alternate/Multiple Choice

11. Fixed labor needed to operate a lodging or food service facility regardless of business volume represents:

    a. minimum labor expense.
    b. maximum labor expense.

12. Historical activity may not be a strong indicator of future activity, but it is considered a reasonable:

    a. starting point.
    b. ending point.

13. When full-time employees work the equivalent of a standard work week in fewer than the usual five days, they are working:

    a. a compressed work week.
    b. a split shift.

14. Fixed staff positions would most likely be filled by:

    a. department managers.
    b. shift cooks.
    c. room attendants.
    d. none of the above.

15. The *best* source for suggested improvements in performance standards is:

    a. other supervisors.
    b. guest comment cards.
    c. employees who actually perform the job.
    d. personal interviews with selected guests.

Chapter Outline

Benefits of Performance Evaluations
Obstacles to Effective Performance
    Evaluation
        Supervisor's Insufficient Skills
        Ineffective Forms
        Incorrect Procedures
        Irregular or Infrequent Evaluation
        Fear of Offending Employees
        Failure to Use Performance Evaluation
            Information
        Failure to Follow Up
        Concern About Errors
        Fears of Being Unfair
Approaches to Performance Evaluations
    Comparative Methods
    Absolute Standards Method
    Management by Objectives Method
    Direct Index Method
The Supervisor's Role in Performance
    Evaluations
        Performance Standards and the
            Review Process
Steps in the Performance Evaluation Process
    Before the Session
    During the Session
    After the Session
Coaching
    Common Concerns
    Principles of Coaching
    Coaching Actions
Informal On-the-Job Coaching
    Use Positive Reinforcement
    Re-State Expectations
    Stay Involved
Formal Coaching
    Preparing for Formal Coaching
        Sessions
    Conducting Formal Coaching Sessions
    Following Up Formal Coaching
        Sessions

Learning Objectives

1. Describe the benefits of performance evaluations to the employee, the supervisor, the property, and the guest.

2. Identify several obstacles that might interfere with an effective performance evaluation program.

3. Identify several comparative methods of evaluating performance and describe how they differ.

4. Describe three approaches to the absolute standards method of evaluating performance.

5. Describe how evaluators and employees work together to determine goals in the management by objectives (MBO) method of performance evaluation.

6. Identify the important points of the direct index method of performance evaluation.

7. Identify the supervisor's role in conducting performance evaluations.

8. Describe the steps the supervisor should take when conducting performance evaluations.

9. Describe the common concerns and principles of any planned coaching session.

10. Identify several coaching actions a supervisor may take to help an employee improve behavior and attitudes.

11. Explain how formal coaching differs from informal on-the-job coaching.

12. Describe what steps a supervisor should take before, during, and after a formal coaching session.

6

Evaluating and Coaching

By DEFINITION, supervisors spend most of their time overseeing and evaluating employee performance. Even so, you may think you can't afford the time to sit down with employees to discuss job-related performance, its improvement, or its problems. However, all employees want to know how well they are performing their jobs. Therefore, despite the many demands on your day, you must take the time to talk with employees regularly, especially when problems arise.

This chapter discusses two of your most important responsibilities as a supervisor:

1. Conducting employee performance evaluations

2. Providing coaching when evaluation sessions indicate that this is necessary

This chapter begins by describing the benefits that performance evaluations have for the employee, the supervisor, the property, and the guest. It also explains why some properties do not conduct performance evaluations on a regular basis or, if they do, why they do not derive full benefit from the process.

The chapter next discusses the different methods and approaches that properties commonly use in conducting employee performance reviews. It goes on to define the important role that you, as supervisor, play in the process, whether you are assigned to evaluate or whether your manager is the evaluator, as is sometimes the case.

The chapter further presents a list of tasks that an effective evaluator should carry out before, during, and after conducting a performance evaluation. During these review sessions, the evaluator may determine that an employee will benefit from further coaching. Coaching actions are recommended that can help change a situation for your employee's benefit or change your employee's perception, skills, and objectives.

Finally, the chapter shows how you can extend an employee's training and development through informal coaching on a continual basis. It further describes a procedure you can use to conduct a performance improvement session to resolve specific problems. This session is also known as formal coaching.

In all interactions between you and your employees through evaluation and coaching, you will need to give your employees support and encouragement. The result should be improved employee-supervisor relationships as well as improved employee performance and increased productivity.

Benefits of Performance Evaluations

Performance evaluations benefit the employee, the supervisor, the property's management, and even its guests.

133

First of all, performance evaluations help identify employee strengths as well as areas which need improvement. During the performance review, the evaluator typically points out the employee's strengths and compliments the employee for his/her good performance. The compliments boost the employee's self-esteem and make him/her feel good. Conversely, if the evaluator needs to identify employee weaknesses, the evaluator can focus on improvements which the employee can make during the next evaluation period.

Second, through performance reviews, a supervisor can recognize individual employees who have contributed valuable ideas about work improvement or other professional development activities. Third, a properly conducted performance evaluation will, in part, address an employee's career plans. The evaluator can encourage the employee to consider long-range career programs and can offer helpful suggestions. In this case, evaluation sessions can also focus on specific career development strategies and the progress which the employee has made during the evaluation cycle.

Finally, performance evaluations can pinpoint coaching and counseling needs for employees who experience job-related problems. Together, the supervisor and employee can agree on action plans to solve these problems. If personal problems surface during performance reviews, the supervisor may offer assistance or refer a troubled employee to professionals who can help him/her.

The benefit that the supervisor receives is centered in an improved relationship with his/her employees. Since the supervisor and the employee must work closely together during the performance review sessions, they learn about each other in the process. The dialogue at the core of a properly conducted evaluation process can lead to understanding between a supervisor and his/her employee even if the evaluation is, at times, negative. Employees see that performance standards are "real" measures which, although set high, are reachable. They understand the supervisor's commitment to monitoring compliance with the standards, and recognize the supervisor's commitment to employees in the way he/she provides feedback with an action plan that will help employees improve. Further, employees recognize the supervisor's commitment to teamwork to improve performance, which leads to his/her employees' career growth and eventually to increased business for the property, from which everyone benefits.

The property's management benefits through its use of the information obtained during the evaluation process. This information forms the basis for property decisions that affect compensation, job actions, and training programs.

Wages, salaries, merit increases, and bonuses are linked to job performance. Although employee unions may have critical interests in compensation matters, wage and salary adjustments should focus on job performance.

Justification for job actions by management results from effectively conducted evaluation sessions. Employee abilities recognized during the evaluation cycle and documented in performance evaluations can lead to promotions, transfers, and other positive job actions. Likewise, the employee's inability to perform according to property standards can lead to demotions, terminations, or other negative job actions. Obviously, it is important that all evaluations of employee competence be done regularly and as objectively as possible.

Furthermore, from the information obtained during evaluation sessions, trainers and supervisors can determine the need for property-wide training programs or evaluate the effectiveness of programs already established. If the evaluation process indicates that several employees are weak in various skills, the property may want to schedule group training sessions. Similarly, the property may authorize supervisors to schedule individualized training programs or coaching sessions to resolve individual employee problems.

Every employee of the property has an important role to play in the organization's goals. Regularly held performance evaluations remind employees of their commitment to the property's high standards of performance and productivity. Performance evaluations produce motivated employees who can be counted on to perform at levels which consistently meet or exceed guest expectations.

Thus, performance evaluations spread benefits beyond the employee and the supervisor to the property in general and especially to satisfied guests, who will keep coming back and will tell others of their positive experiences.

Obstacles to Effective Performance Evaluation

Some properties don't conduct formal performance evaluations at all. This may be because there are several obstacles to conducting them successfully.

Supervisor's Insufficient Skills

Because of the busy nature of the hospitality industry, supervisors may not receive sufficient training in conducting performance evaluations. In some cases, the supervisors themselves have never been evaluated.

An organization that requires supervisors to conduct performance evaluations—but doesn't teach them how to go about it—may unintentionally send the message that such evaluations are unimportant. However, organizations may find that an effective performance evaluation process has a positive effect on employee productivity. Such organizations give priority to teaching supervisors about the importance of the evaluation process.

Ineffective Forms

When evaluation forms do not contain factors that relate to job performance or become too complicated and lengthy, the forms themselves may cause problems. Furthermore, some evaluators may not know how to complete the forms. Others may not know how to use the information gained in the evaluation process in planning actions to improve employee performance.

Incorrect Procedures

Some hospitality operations may have few, if any, organized procedures for conducting reviews. Supervisors or managers may conduct performance evaluations only when they wish to discipline employees—not as opportunities to gain the benefits of evaluation discussed at the beginning of this chapter. (For more information on discipline, please see Chapter 7 of this book.)

Irregular or Infrequent Evaluation

Some properties conduct performance evaluations infrequently and irregularly. Performance evaluations should be conducted regularly and frequently. Even if you formally review employee performance only once or twice a year, you should conduct informal reviews more frequently. Such a program will provide employees with the repeated feedback necessary to improve their performances.

Fear of Offending Employees

It is easy and enjoyable to congratulate an employee for an outstanding performance. However, it is hard to tell an employee that his/her performance does not meet standards. Supervisors may fear offending employees who are performing inadequately and may be less than completely honest when evaluating them. Such supervisors defeat the purpose of the performance evaluation process and, therefore, miss opportunities to improve productivity.

When evaluating an unsatisfactory performer, you must concentrate on criticizing the poor performance and not the employee. Remember to make it a business decision, not a personal one. In doing so, point out specific evidence, rather than general, to support your observations. Then, explain which specific steps the employee must take to improve performance.

When evaluations are tied to wage or salary increases, employees often challenge supervisors when they receive unsatisfactory evaluations. Many employees believe their performance is better than it really is when compared with the standards. This issue highlights the importance of setting measurable (observable) performance standards, keeping accurate records, and giving the employee frequent feedback throughout the evaluation period.

Failure to Use Performance Evaluation Information

Supervisors and managers in some hospitality operations may fill out and file performance evaluation forms, but do nothing else with them. In fact, some supervisors may fill out the forms but fail to tell employees or to even show them the forms. In order for performance evaluations to work, employees must be actively involved in the process. Furthermore, information gained in the evaluation process must be used to improve employee performance.

Failure to Follow Up

It is important that supervisors follow up on employee performance evaluations. The supervisor must follow up performance reviews with the necessary coaching, counseling, or re-training to help employees improve performance. It is useless to conduct and discuss evaluations with employees if the evaluations are going to be forgotten until the next review.

Concern About Errors

Evaluators may be so afraid to make errors in the evaluation process that they are unable to start an evaluation program. Alternatively, they may develop so many safeguards that the entire process becomes unmanageable. No supervisor can expect the performance evaluation process to be perfect, so it's useless to wait for that to happen. A supervisor or manager can work to make the performance evaluation process as objective and fair as possible. While the chance of error can never be entirely avoided, it can be decreased.

Fears of Being Unfair

Effective supervisors try to be fair in all interactions with employees. Therefore, some evaluators may be concerned that negative information surfacing in performance evaluations will become part of an employee's permanent **personnel file.** Such data could affect the employee even after performance problems are resolved.

As you are coaching an employee during the time covered by a review, you may notice areas of performance that do not meet the standards. You must give the employee feedback on these areas promptly and initiate actions to improve the employee's performance. These discussions and actions must be documented. To keep these records from becoming a permanent part of the employee's file, write the information on plain paper and keep it in your working files. You will need these notes to support any unsatisfactory ratings given on the evaluation if the employee's performance does not improve. However, if performance improves and is highly rated on the evaluation, you may decide to throw out the support notes you've kept in the working files.

Approaches to Performance Evaluations

Supervisors are not likely to have significant input in determining which type of performance review system the organization or department uses. Ideally, though, upper management will have considered input from supervisors. However, this chapter presents a brief overview of different types of performance reviews so that you may understand the wide range of possible performance evaluation systems and potential advantages and disadvantages of each. This section will consider some of the more common approaches used in the hospitality industry.

Comparative Methods

Comparative performance review methods involve comparing employees with each other. There are four approaches to comparative methods: the simple ranking approach, the alternative ranking approach, the paired comparison approach, and the forced distribution approach.

Simple Ranking Approach. The evaluator classifies employees in order, from the best to the worst (or those needing the most attention). This is done subjectively, that is, the evaluator makes a judgment of the overall performance of each employee. Ranking should consider how consistently employees meet performance standards. It should not consider how one employee compares with another.

Serious disadvantages of this approach include the supervisor's possible bias and the chance that comparisons will focus on personality or relationships instead of job performance.

Alternative Ranking Approach. This is a modification of the simple ranking approach. First, the evaluator places the best employee at the top of the list, and the worst employee at the bottom. The evaluator then places the second best employee in the place second from the top, and the second worst employee in the second place from the bottom. This process continues until the evaluator has included all employees in the ranking list.

Paired Comparison Approach. The evaluator must rank each employee from best to worst—in terms of a single factor only—such as overall performance, quality of work, or receptivity to new ideas. Employees are "matched" not only with each other, but also against a specific factor important to effective job performance.

Forced Distribution Approach. The evaluator is permitted to rank only a certain percentage of all employees "superior" and the same percentage "unacceptable." The evaluator is then forced to place a required percentage of the remaining employees in each of the other categories such as "above average," "average," and "below average."

Employers often decide that comparative evaluation methods are neither useful to management nor helpful to employees. Employees feel that a performance evaluation should focus on the employee's ability to perform required work—not on how the employee compares with others. Furthermore, since it is unlikely that all of a supervisor's employees perform identical tasks, it is difficult—if not impossible—to use any of the comparative approaches consistently, fairly, and objectively.

Absolute Standards Method

With the **absolute standards method,** the evaluator assesses each employee's work performance without regard to the performance of other employees. Generally, there are three popular approaches through which to incorporate absolute standards into performance reviews. These include the critical incidents approach, the weighted checklist approach, and the forced choice approach.

Critical Incidents Approach. The supervisor or other manager responsible for the evaluation keeps a "diary" (also called a tickler file or manager's log) of incidents that indicate acceptable and unacceptable job performance. When using this approach, remember that such a diary should be kept up to date during the entire time period between evaluations. The worst results of waiting until the last minute to write something down are entries that are inaccurate, incomplete, and unfair. Furthermore, avoid dwelling only on negative incidents. While these are important, it is equally important to consider the positive aspects of an employee's performance.

A sample of a critical incidents format is shown in Exhibit 6.1.

Weighted Checklist Approach. Supervisors and others familiar with departmental work flow and positions develop checklists of duties making up each job. Each listed duty is weighted to represent the relative value of "good" and "bad" performance aspects. A sample of a checklist format is shown in Exhibit 6.2.

Exhibit 6.1 Sample of Absolute Standards Evaluation: Critical Incidents Approach

Instructions: Provide examples of employee activity in regard to each of the following. Indicate positive and negative incidents.

Name of Employee: _____

Activity	Date	Observed Activity
Follows Directions		
Work Quality		
Makes Suggestions		

Signature of Supervisor: _____ Date: _____

Forced Choice Approach. This approach requires the evaluator to select one statement that describes how the employee performs certain factors considered important for successful job performance. A sample format is shown in Exhibit 6.3. Many hospitality operations use the forced choice approach. The number of work factors addressed in this method may vary. When using this method you should consider all the specific tasks that are important to a position.

Management by Objectives Method

In the **management by objectives (MBO) method,** the evaluator works with the employee to determine a set of goals. The evaluator and the employee consider how the employee will reach the goals. They then work together to establish evaluation procedures. Procedures in an MBO plan consist of four steps:

1. Goals are set for the employee to reach by the next performance evaluation.

2. The employee is given time on the job to master applicable tasks in order to reach goals. Strategies for training, coaching, and other developmental activities should be built into this plan.

Exhibit 6.2 Sample of Absolute Standards Evaluation: Weighted Checklist Method

Instructions: Check (✓) each of the statements that apply to the employee being evaluated.

Name of Employee: _____

(✓) if applicable	Activity	Scale Value
_____	1. Turns off equipment when finished	2.0
_____	2. Keeps work area clean	1.5
_____	3. Gathers all work supplies/utensils needed at one time	1.5

Signature of Supervisor: _____   Date: _____

Exhibit 6.3 Sample of Absolute Standards Evaluation: Forced Choice Method

Instructions: Check (✓) the box for each factor which exemplifies the quality of work performed by the employee.

Name of Employee: _____

FACTOR	PERFORMANCE				
	Excellent	Above Average	Average	Below Average	Unacceptable
KNOWLEDGE OF JOB	Understands all aspects of work	Understands almost all aspects of work	Understands basic aspects of job	Has fair job knowledge	Has poor job knowledge
WORK QUALITY	Very accurate and neat	Seldom makes mistakes	Work normally acceptable	Work often unacceptable	Work seldom meets quality requirements

Signature of Supervisor: _____   Date: _____

3. During the next evaluation, the goals actually reached are compared with the goals originally set. If the employee did not reach the goals, the evaluator and the employee try to understand why. The evaluator asks for the employee's

views on the level of goal-reaching and which actions to take. It is important that the evaluator meet periodically with the employee during the time frame allowed to accomplish the goals. The evaluator should measure progress and provide additional coaching when necessary. It is particularly helpful to set intermediate **benchmarks** to measure progress.

4. New goals and strategies for attaining them are developed for the next evaluation period.

Recall that job lists and job breakdowns developed for training programs are helpful for evaluating employees. The evaluator and employee agree on which specific tasks the employee performed well, and on those activities toward which the employee must use extra effort. Give copies of job lists and job breakdowns to the employee so that he/she can use them to perform tasks accordingly.

Direct Index Method

The direct index method quantifies tasks and measures the employee's performance. For example, a receiving clerk could be evaluated against the actual number of unacceptable products the clerk received. (This would be compared with records of the number of product returns initiated after supplies were in inventory.) Or the clerk could be evaluated against the number of times stockouts (shortages) occurred because the employee failed to inform the purchasing department according to established operating procedures.

Measurements against productivity, quality, or quantity of work standards are also possible. These measures may be best applied in the evaluation of non-managers. However, a manager or supervisor can be evaluated on the basis of how his/her employees perform.

The Supervisor's Role in Performance Evaluations ——————

Evaluating employee performance is one of the supervisor's chief duties. There is no hard and fast rule in the hospitality industry about what exactly the supervisor's role should be. If your property is large, your department manager or assistant manager may evaluate employee performance. He/she may rely on input from several supervisors, including you. In smaller properties, the shift supervisor may report directly to the department manager. In such a case, the ultimate responsibility for performance evaluations would still lie with the department head or manager.

An employee's immediate supervisor may not be the staff member who conducts performance evaluations. However, performance evaluations are most effective when the employee's immediate supervisor is responsible for preparing and conducting the evaluation. Higher-level supervisors may be involved in a follow-up session with the employee. In most systems, the evaluation forms require the signatures of at least two levels of supervisors. The department's size may be a factor. As the number of department employees increases, it becomes more difficult for the department head to make evaluation decisions. In larger departments there probably are more intermediate-level managers or supervisors who assume this responsibility. While the department head ultimately is responsible for employee evaluations, the authority to conduct them may be delegated to a supervisor, depending on the organization's structure.

Suppose the department head or another manager assumes performance evaluation duties. In this case, you, as an immediate supervisor, must be able to answer employees' questions about the evaluation process. Furthermore, you must provide appropriate information to the manager conducting the evaluation and also must be able to understand the results of the evaluation. For example, you will need to know whether the evaluator and the employee agreed on problem areas and suggested resolutions and whether they discussed plans for the employee's professional development. This will allow you to help the employee, through on-site supervision, training, and coaching, to resolve job-related problems cited in the evaluation session. If you think of ways to improve the performance evaluation system, share your ideas with the managers responsible for developing and running the system.

For example, encourage your managers to establish appeal procedures if the company hasn't already done so. Employees who believe that a performance evaluation was administered unfairly should be allowed to appeal to the next higher management level. If this is not allowed, the credibility of the entire evaluation process will be questionable. Normally, procedures for such an appeal are provided for in a clearly stated policy.

Performance Standards and the Review Process

Since the evaluation should focus on employee performance, the evaluator must fully understand the employee's responsibilities and levels of acceptable performance. Recall that you learned (in Chapter 4) to develop job lists, which identify all tasks making up a job, and job breakdowns, which review specific procedures for performing each task. You also learned to identify corresponding performance standards. The evaluator must be familiar with exactly *what* the employee is expected to do and the agreed-upon levels of expected performance for each task. This information forms the basis for the review. The supervisor compares the employee's actual performance with performance standards. If the employee's level of performance falls below the level of expected performance, the difference between the two levels represents the improvement the employee must make.

Give employees as much freedom as possible to participate in the performance review process. Allow employees to react to the evaluator's opinions, defend your position pleasantly but firmly, help plan goals for the next evaluation period, and offer any opinion or advice about their jobs.

Steps in the Performance Evaluation Process

The performance evaluation must be a two-way communication process that permits you to help the employee develop goals to reach by the next evaluation. At the end of the session, you and the employee should agree about areas in which the employee is performing well, areas which need improvement, and specific action plans for improving performance. The evaluation session should not end until the

Exhibit 6.4 Conducting Performance Evaluations: Guidelines

1. Interview in a setting that is informal, private, and free of distraction.
2. Provide a courteous, supportive atmosphere.
3. Encourage the employee to participate actively.
4. Clearly explain the purpose of the interview.
5. Explain problem areas thoroughly but tactfully.
6. Listen when the employee talks; don't interrupt.
7. Criticize job performance, not the employee.
8. Criticize while you're calm, not angry.
9. Avoid confrontation and argument.
10. Emphasize the employee's strengths, then discuss areas which need improvement.
11. To set goals for improvement, focus on future performance, not past.
12. Assume nothing; instead, ask for clarification.
13. Ask questions to gather information, not to "test" the employee.
14. Expect the employee to disagree.
15. Try to resolve differences; don't expect total agreement.
16. Avoid exaggerations (such as "always" or "never").
17. Help the employee maintain self-esteem; don't threaten or belittle.
18. Keep your own biases in check.
19. Allow the employee to help you set goals for improvement.
20. Assure the employee that you will help him/her reach the goals.
21. Maintain appropriate eye contact.
22. End on a positive note.

employee and supervisor have agreed on these points. When the review is over, you must complete any required paperwork. Managers frequently require performance review information for the employee's personnel file; it is often used in wage and salary decisions. See Exhibit 6.4 for a set of guidelines to help you conduct performance reviews.

Exhibit 6.5 lists tasks which the supervisor should complete before, during, and after a performance evaluation session.

Before the Session

Prepare for the discussion. Set the date and time in advance. Review the employee's job description. Gather information, such as material about job incidents you observed, that is directly related to outstanding, acceptable, or poor performance. Get input from others, too. List objectives you wish to accomplish. Find a

Exhibit 6.5 Supervisors' Performance Evaluation Tasks

A wide variety of tasks must be done before, during, and after the evaluation session.

Before the Session

- Review the previous evaluation form and any records about the employee's performance since the previous evaluation.

- Allow the employee to review information from the previous evaluation.

- Complete a first draft of the evaluation form for the current session. Have the employee complete one too.

- Schedule a time and place for the evaluation meeting which is acceptable to both you and the employee.

- Prepare for the session by thinking about the results you desire and specific procedures which will achieve those results.

- Make a list of questions you have and matters you wish to resolve.

- Think about your suggestions for the employee's performance improvement and professional development plans.

- Focus the evaluation on the employee's performance, how it has improved, and how it can improve even further.

During the Session

- Create a friendly, relaxed atmosphere.

- Review the evaluation forms thoroughly; highlight areas in which the two of you agree. Be sure to note areas of disagreement as well.

- Solicit feedback from the employee.

- Focus on the employee's performance, not on the employee; be specific about areas of acceptable performance and areas where improvement is possible.

- Take notes about the most important points covered during the session.

- Be sure that the employee knows exactly what you expect.

- Have the employee sign the evaluation.

- End the evaluation on a professional note, offering any possible assistance to help the employee further reach goals formed during the evaluation.

After the Session

- Review the notes you took during the session; make any additions while the interview is fresh in your mind.

- Complete any necessary forms; route copies as necessary to the human resources department.

- Give the employee a copy of the evaluation.

- Follow up; do appropriate coaching, counseling, and so forth.

- Discuss any important points with your own supervisor.

private, non-threatening place to hold the interview. Plan what you're going to say, and rehearse your opening remarks.

We must emphasize the importance of preparation by both the evaluator and the employee. (Refer to Exhibit 6.6 for a list of questions to give employees to help

Exhibit 6.6 Questions to Prepare Employees for Performance Review

Before conducting an employee performance evaluation, help employees prepare mentally for the session. Ask them to think over a set of questions like the ones listed below.

- What have I personally done to improve my skills since my last performance evaluation?
- In which areas of responsibility did I excel? In which did I fall short?
- What aspect of my position do I especially enjoy? What has been the most challenging aspect of my position?
- What were my three major accomplishments in the past year?
- What have I done personally to improve morale within my department?
- How could my supervisor help me do a better job?
- How does my present position make the most of my capabilities?

Courtesy of Opryland Hotel, Nashville, Tennessee

them mentally prepare for a performance review.) There are two kinds of preparation which the evaluator makes: preparing the *content* of the interview and preparing the *process*. When you prepare the content, you plan *what* topics the evaluation will cover. Process planning determines *how* the topics will be discussed.

Ask the employee to do some content planning also and provide him/her with a blank evaluation form ahead of time. Ask the employee to review it and conduct a self-evaluation. The employee can make notes on the form or even fill it out completely. During the evaluation session, ask the employee to explain his/her self-evaluation. Then, state how you rated the employee, and explain what factors contributed to your decisions.

Asking employees to rate themselves has certain advantages. For instance, employees are often quite accurate when rating themselves and can recognize how good their performances have been. In addition, such a system ensures that both evaluator and employees focus on the same topics, and that no important subject is overlooked. Bear in mind, also, that sometimes employees rate themselves more harshly than their supervisors do. This gives you an opportunity to provide additional positive feedback. Asking employees to rate themselves helps you spot those areas in which you agree on performance levels. You should quickly cover these areas so that you can spend more time discussing those areas in which you disagree. Giving employees an opportunity to rate their performance also gives them a chance to remind you of their accomplishments that you may have forgotten. Finally, this approach may help put employees at ease because they know in advance exactly what topics the evaluation session will cover.

Good content planning offers several advantages, one of which is that it lets the evaluator appraise employee performance more objectively. With adequate, thoughtful preparation, the evaluator will be less likely to rely on suspicions and rumors, someone else's opinions, or his/her own unclear memories. Moreover, thorough content planning, when focused on facts, helps keep both the evaluator and the employee from becoming too emotional. In addition, careful planning saves time in the interview itself; you won't have to go searching the files for facts or records if they're already assembled. Finally, in the course of your planning, you will have formulated a schedule of topics to keep your discussion within bounds.

In process planning, you decide how to introduce the content you've already planned. This involves guessing how you think the employee will rank himself/herself, whether and to what degree the employee will challenge your evaluation, and how you will handle the employee's resistance, among other matters.

During the Session

As you make your opening remarks, be friendly and sincere. Clearly explain why you are holding the interview. Encourage the employee to participate, and interact positively with him/her. Make sure that the employee knows this is a two-way conversation.

Ask the employee to discuss previously established performance objectives (if any) and the results reached in each area. Have the employee rate his/her own performance and explain the ratings. Make sure you understand what the employee is saying. Actively listen to the employee—don't interrupt.

Next, explain your appraisal, focusing on the employee's performance rather than his/her personality. Then, explain why you appraised the performance as you did. Discuss both the employee's strengths and the areas which need improvement. Finally, discuss points about which you and the employee agree and disagree.

Praise the employee's good work. Discuss and summarize areas in which the employee needs to improve. Discuss the evaluation objectives you agree on. Review and resolve performance points on which you haven't agreed.

The next phase involves the **performance improvement plan.** Determine specific actions the employee will need to take to improve job performance. Avoid trying to change everything all at once. Instead, choose one area of performance, making sure that you and the employee agree. Then, set practical, time-oriented, and specific action plans and approaches the employee will take. Ask for and obtain the employee's commitment. Ask the employee what he/she needs from you to improve performance. Due to the length of the performance evaluation discussion, it may be better to deal with the performance improvement plan in a separate session. This approach gives the employee and supervisor a chance to consider each other's input, identify improvement strategies, and focus completely on this important element of the process.

In many hospitality organizations, pay increases are directly related to the performance evaluation and become effective at the time the review is given. In these systems, it is a good idea to begin by stating your overall rating, what the salary increase will be, and when it takes effect. Usually, the money issue is foremost in the employee's mind. Once you address it, you can focus more easily on the specifics of job performance.

At the end of the session, summarize the performance evaluation and action plans. Schedule follow-up dates, and have the employee sign the evaluation form.

After the Session

Evaluate the interview and think about how you might have improved the session. Give the employee a copy of the final version of the written performance evaluation.

Then, meet the employee on the determined follow-up date. In the meantime, give the employee appropriate help, support, and rewards for improving performance. Provide coaching or further training if it's necessary. Lastly, if the employee desires, allow him/her to ask for additional evaluation sessions, which would be held before the next "official" session.

Coaching

Through training, employees learn how and why to perform in a certain way. Through coaching, employees learn how to apply what they learn in training sessions. When coaching, a supervisor persuades, corrects, and inspires employees to perform effectively. The supervisor uses positive reinforcement to achieve desired results.

Coaching may be informal or formal. **Informal coaching** is usually conducted at the employee's actual work station. It occurs in the course of normal day-to-day operations. It often is conducted to improve a skill, communicate a single piece of knowledge, or adjust an inappropriate behavior.

Formal coaching is usually conducted privately, away from the work station. It focuses on knowledge, skills, or attitudes that negatively affect a large part of the employee's job performance. A formal coaching session may also be referred to as a performance improvement session. The supervisor should plan an agenda and keep a formal record of the session.

Coaching differs from **counseling,** which uses a one-on-one process to help employees solve their own problems. Job-related counseling concentrates on the employee's attitudes toward the job and the work environment. Non-job-related counseling involves personal problems not directly connected with work. However, personal concerns often negatively affect job performance. Personal counseling issues are usually referred to professionals trained to handle them.

Common Concerns

In any planned coaching session, supervisors should address at least three concerns:

1. The specific problem which needs solving

2. The relationship between the supervisor and the employee

3. The employee's general growth and development

Planned coaching sessions should be similar to an interview in form and approach. In a coaching session, a supervisor should obtain facts, provide fair feedback, show understanding of the employee's feelings, and plan a course of corrective action. Planned coaching sessions help solve problems and build supervisor-employee relationships. They also help employees to perform more effectively and productively.

Generally, coaching sessions are problem-oriented. That is, they focus on problems which the employee encounters while on the job, or on problems resulting from ineffective performance.

Principles of Coaching

Job-related coaching is an important supervisory activity. Employee attitudes and performance are affected by how a supervisor directs or instructs, the supervisor's attitudes toward employees, and the supervisor's own performance. If you act as though you do not care about how employees perform, employees are also unlikely to care. If you expect work that meets established performance standards, that is exactly what employees are likely to produce. Coaching is most effective if supervisors develop a proper work environment that helps employees do their best.

Employee Involvement. If coaching is to succeed, employees must be actively involved in setting goals and responsible for meeting them. The more employees become involved in evaluating problems and seeking solutions, the more committed and successful they are likely to be.

Encourage employees to participate in the coaching process. Ask questions which the employee can answer to help solve problems.

Mutual Understanding. Both you and the employee must understand the topic you're discussing. To ensure this, ask the employee to define the problem in his/her own words. Then, re-state the employee's views to see whether the employee understands. If you do not do this, both of you might leave the session with entirely different ideas about the issues and solutions.

Listening. The supervisor must do more listening than talking. You and the employee may gain more from the coaching session if you allow the employee to talk while you actively listen. Allowing the employee to describe the problem will allow him/her to make suggestions and discuss job-related issues and problems.

Coaching Actions

Supervisors coach when they want to improve employee behavior and attitudes. A supervisor may help employees by changing a situation, an employee's perception, an employee's skills, or an employee's objectives.

Changing a Situation. The supervisor may (1) change his/her own behavior or leadership style, (2) alter the work group by encouraging employees to change their own behavior or by separating problem employees, or (3) change work resources or conditions. A supervisor making any of these changes may help an employee to modify his/her own behavior.

Changing Employee Perception. A supervisor can help change an employee's attitudes toward work by making sure the employee is accurately informed about company objectives, problems, and so forth. In addition, the supervisor can point out how the employee can effectively perform in order to meet personal goals. The supervisor can provide positive feedback when the employee meets—or doesn't meet—established performance standards.

Changing an Employee's Skills. A supervisor can help an employee learn more about the job and how to solve its particular problems. This will help improve the employee's attitude and **self-esteem** (confident, positive feelings about oneself; self-respect).

Changing an Employee's Objectives. A supervisor can help employees set objectives which they can reasonably meet. Supervisors should regularly review job performance standards. If standards are too high, or if employees expect too much of themselves, employees may become discouraged. Help them by setting up short-range goals that they can reach.

Informal On-the-Job Coaching

When coaching is conducted informally, it is a routine part of supervision. A supervisor coaches whenever he/she stops and talks to an employee about the employee's performance, and then goes on to interact with another employee in the same way. When coaching employees informally, you should reinforce good performance, re-state performance expectations, and stay involved with the employees.

Use Positive Reinforcement

The purpose of informal, everyday coaching is to point out which job behaviors meet performance standards and which do not. In cases of sub-standard performance, demonstrate correct procedures and explain why incorrect procedures are unacceptable.

When you want an employee to continue meeting established performance standards, you must notice the employee doing so and immediately compliment him/her. It's a good idea to try to "catch" an employee doing something right, and then immediately praise the employee. Positive reinforcement is most effective when it is specifically connected to correct behavior. Behavior that is positively reinforced is more likely to be repeated.

Re-State Expectations

As you coach, expect to state and re-state your expectations to get your points across. Employees may not even try to meet desired standards unless they understand and remember your expectations. Re-stating expectations will reinforce employee learning, and will also remind employees of established performance standards. Employees base their performance goals on performance standards.

Hospitality industry supervisors may use "over-the-shoulder" supervision, in which a supervisor watches from a distance as the employee works. The supervisor compliments the employee for tasks that the employee is doing well. Then, the supervisor tactfully corrects sub-standard performances while re-stating job expectations.

Employees welcome positive "over-the-shoulder" coaching. They feel that their supervisors are interested in them as people, not as machines. However, supervisors should make sure that they never hang over their employees as they work. Supervisors should not crowd employees or criticize every action.

Stay Involved

Involved, effective supervisors make coaching a regular part of every workday. Good supervisors make continuous efforts to reinforce, teach, and re-teach correct procedures. Effective supervisors must master all job skills themselves or know which employees they can rely on to demonstrate or teach skills.

Formal Coaching

Formal coaching is often conducted in sessions resembling interviews. A formal coaching session is essentially a performance improvement session. There are two primary types of interviews used in formal coaching: directive and non-directive interviews.

Directive interviews are those which the supervisor directs by asking certain questions. Directive interviews are held to give and receive information, but they are also conducted to discuss feelings and attitudes. The interviewer may gain more or less benefit from directive interviews, depending on how the interviewer communicates and asks questions.

In *non-directive interviews,* problems are discussed in a less structured format. The supervisor begins with general questions or statements about the problem and gives the employee freedom to discuss the issues from his/her own perspective. Non-directive interviews are generally conducted to explore the employee's feelings and attitudes.

Supervisors often discover that employees try to hide or misrepresent their true feelings and do not always say what they really mean. In non-directive sessions, supervisors analyze employee attitudes which affect job performance.

Provide an understanding, open-minded atmosphere. When you do, the employee is more likely to say exactly what he/she feels. Although you may need to start the session by announcing that there is a problem, quickly give the employee the lead. When the employee believes that you will listen in a non-threatening way, the employee might be more able to discuss the problem.

Listen to the employee. The session will succeed if you listen with understanding and acceptance (in this usage, "acceptance" indicates that you accept the employee's right to a viewpoint and that you accept the employee as a worthwhile human being). Withhold criticism of the employee. In addition, you do not need to agree with everything the employee says. In a non-directive session, your criticism or judgment of the employee's viewpoint, statements, or attitudes will make the employee stop talking. If the employee stops talking, you may never discover the cause of a problem.

Respond briefly and positively to show understanding of the employee. Nods or simple responses such as "Yes" or "I see" show understanding. You will probably receive similar signals from the employee.

In addition, you might try repeating key statements that the employee makes. For instance, the employee may say, "I want my job to have more responsibility." Your non-directive response might be, "You feel that you want more responsibility." Be sincere when you say this. Say something which will be matter-of-fact and which will prompt the employee to further clarify his/her point. You could follow this re-statement with a question, such as, "Could you tell me what type of extra responsibility you would like?" (For a more thorough discussion of listening and other communication skills, please see Chapter 2, "Effective Communication.")

Preparing for Formal Coaching Sessions

When preparing to conduct a formal coaching (or performance improvement) session, you must first decide what you hope to accomplish in the session. You should have a definite objective in mind before scheduling it. The session will be more productive if you write down exactly what information you want from the employee, what issues you will stress, and even some questions to ask.

Then, gather background information. Supervisors should know their employees. In large organizations, this is difficult. If this is true in your case, you should seek as much background information as possible about the employee, including strengths and areas which need improvement. You can do this by reviewing written records and speaking to other supervisors who work with the employee.

Before scheduling the coaching session, consult the employee and review the weekly schedule. The coaching session is an expanded training session, but it should not interfere with the employee's regular work. Notify the employee as far in advance of the session as possible. Don't spring any surprises on the employee.

It often takes extra time for an employee to feel free enough to talk openly with an interviewer, especially when the interviewer is the employee's supervisor. In addition, this may be the employee's first chance to associate personal experiences and goals with the organization's goals. Allow the employee time to make the connection.

Be aware of your attitudes toward coaching, the session, and the employee. You should also consider the employee's attitudes. The employee's biases and behaviors may influence job performance. The session may be more productive if you try to understand how the employee feels about the coaching process and the topics under discussion.

Conducting Formal Coaching Sessions

Conduct the session privately. When possible, do not allow any interruptions. Hold the interview in a private area, not in a busy public place. Use a private office or conference room suitable for thoughtful, productive discussion.

Establish a comfortable atmosphere. The employee must feel free to talk and express ideas. You must be willing to listen to the employee without getting angry, even if the employee questions your effectiveness. To establish a relaxed atmosphere, give the employee time to get used to the setting. Help the employee feel that he/she is relating to you as an equal. Put the employee at ease by reassuring him/her that you are meeting to clarify the issues and work toward improvement. Show your understanding by honestly answering every comment the employee makes.

Start slowly. When the session begins, the employee may respond to your questions or statements slowly or unclearly. In fact, the employee may feel confused and frightened. Therefore, you should allow the employee extra time to think before responding. If you seem calm and patient, the employee will not feel threatened. Adjust to the employee's thinking and conversational abilities.

Describe the problem in a caring, positive way. Make it clear that you want to discuss the problem and how to solve it rather than blame the employee. When the employee realizes this, he/she will be more willing to talk about the problem. Avoid accusing the employee or causing him/her to withdraw. Assure the employee that you realize he/she wants to do well. When you outline the problem, be as specific as you can. Discuss the department's performance standards and tell the employee exactly how his/her performance is falling short of expectations. Support your views with specific evidence. Remember to focus on the performance problem, not on the employee's personality or attitude.

Ask the employee to help you solve the problem or identify its cause. If you can obtain the employee's commitment, your chances of solving the problem will be greater. Ask for the employee's help in deciding what steps to take to work out the problem. When the employee understands that you really value employee ideas, he/she is more likely to cooperate. This will help raise the employee's self-esteem, too.

To obtain more information, ask the employee general questions (beginning with "What," "How," "Who," "When," etc.). As the employee becomes more relaxed, ask more specific questions to clarify the problem. Be sure to listen and show understanding, especially when the employee seems worried or upset. Your empathy will help the employee maintain self-esteem. If you take notes, keep them brief so you can focus more fully on what the employee says and also maintain frequent eye contact. However, it is better to take your notes when the discussion is over. Be sure to put the notes on plain paper and store them in your working file.

In addition, you'll have ideas of your own to discuss. As you do so, remain friendly and safeguard the employee's self-esteem. Before beginning to talk about solutions, summarize the causes the two of you have identified to help ensure that you both understand all the information discussed.

As employees start to think the session is about to end, their remarks often become more pointed and significant. The last several minutes of the session may be the most productive if you pay close attention to the employee's final comments. These may be more significant than the employee's beginning remarks, which he/she may have made thinking you wanted to hear them.

Ask the employee for ideas about solving the performance problem. Taking brief notes at this time will make the employee feel good and will also produce a record of possible solutions. Such a record may prove helpful if the first remedy you try doesn't work out. Record as many ideas as the two of you can produce. When possible, use the employee's suggestions to solve the problem.

After deciding on a course of action, work together to determine exactly who must do what by a certain date. Add this information to your written record. Stress that, while you will do what you can to help the employee succeed, the employee is responsible for improving. Express confidence in the employee's ability to improve performance. This will strengthen the employee's commitment to solving the problem.

Before ending the discussion, schedule a follow-up session. This emphasizes that you expect the employee to solve the performance problem and that you want to track progress. A follow-up discussion ensures that you and the employee will meet to explore progress or any problems the employee continues to have. If necessary, you'll be able to plan a different course of action.

End the discussion in a positive, caring manner. Again, express your confidence in the employee's ability to solve the problem, and indicate your support.

Following Up Formal Coaching Sessions

Give the employee help and encouragement as he/she takes steps to improve performance. Provide further coaching or training, if necessary. Let the employee ask for additional coaching sessions, which would be held before the next "official" session. Keep written records of all sessions, especially of the improvements the employee makes.

Key Terms

absolute standards performance
   review method
benchmark
comparative performance review
   method
counseling
formal coaching

informal coaching
management by objectives (MBO)
   performance review method
performance evaluation
performance improvement plan
personnel file
self-esteem

Discussion Questions

1. What are the benefits of conducting performance evaluations?

2. What obstacles interfere with effective performance evaluation programs?

3. What are some comparative methods of evaluating employee performance? How do they differ?

4. What are various methods through which to evaluate employee performance?

5. What are three approaches through which to incorporate absolute standards in performance evaluations?

6. How do evaluators and employees work together to determine goals in the management by objectives (MBO) method of performance evaluation?

7. What is the supervisor's role in conducting performance evaluations?

8. What steps should the supervisor take when conducting performance evaluations?

9. What common concerns should a supervisor address in planned coaching sessions?

10. How does formal coaching differ from informal on-the-job coaching?

REVIEW QUIZ

When you feel you have covered all of the material in this chapter, answer these questions. Choose the *best* answer. Check your answers with the correct ones found on the Review Quiz Answer Key at the end of this book.

True (T) or False (F)

T   F   1. Effectively conducted employee evaluation programs should address the employee's career plans.

T   F   2. Performance evaluations usually help identify employee strengths or areas that need improvement.

T   F   3. A negative performance evaluation can result in an improved employee-supervisor relationship.

T   F   4. A cause of poorly executed evaluations may be due to the evaluator/supervisor's insufficient training.

T   F   5. Ineffective evaluation forms may be a cause of inefficient performance evaluations.

T   F   6. Performance evaluations needn't be conducted regularly in order to be considered effective.

T   F   7. Employers often decide that comparative evaluation methods are among the most useful.

T   F   8. Performance evaluations are most effective when the employee's immediate supervisor is responsible for preparing and conducting the evaluation.

T   F   9. It is often best to deal with the performance improvement plan in a separate session, not in the performance evaluation session itself.

T   F   10. Coaching activities are generally not influenced by work environment.

Alternate/Multiple Choice

11. The critical incidents approach to comparative evaluations involves:

    a. developing checklists.
    b. keeping a diary.

12. The person ultimately responsible for employee evaluations is the:

    a. supervisor.
    b. department head.

13. The evaluator is responsible for two kinds of preparation before conducting a performance evaluation:

    a. discussion and planning.
    b. content and process.

14.   The purpose of everyday, informal coaching is to:

   a.   schedule a performance improvement plan.
   b.   point out which job behaviors meet performance standards and which do not.
   c.   change employee objectives.
   d.   conduct directive interviews.

15.   The two primary types of interviews used in formal coaching are:

   a.   weighted checklist and forced choice.
   b.   absolute standards and critical incidents.
   c.   directive and non-directive.
   d.   questions and answers.

Chapter Outline

The Myths of Discipline
A Close Look at Rules and Regulations
    Positive Reinforcement
    Enforcement of Rules
Causes of Disciplinary Problems
Administering Discipline
    Minor Corrections
    As the Seriousness Increases
Progressive Discipline Programs

Learning Objectives

1. Describe four myths of discipline that many supervisors continue to believe, and why they should change their beliefs.

2. Explain why it is important to review rules and regulations, enforce them, and justify them to employees.

3. Define positive reinforcement and why you should use it.

4. Identify possible causes of disciplinary problems.

5. Describe how to administer discipline effectively.

6. Describe how a supervisor should handle minor corrections.

7. Identify what to do when the seriousness of a discipline problem increases.

8. Identify the steps making up a disciplinary discussion.

9. Describe the steps which might be included in a property's progressive discipline program.

7

Discipline

SUPERVISORS AND MANAGERS try to change employee behavior with the use of **discipline.** In a positive sense, discipline involves activities that correct, strengthen, and improve employee performance.

However, many supervisors dread disciplining more than any other aspect of their jobs. They dread it because they do not understand how to do it properly. This lack of understanding leads supervisors to employ disciplinary actions that either work poorly or don't work at all.

The Myths of Discipline

Most of the problems surrounding the use of discipline arise when a supervisor doesn't understand its purpose or the proper way to handle it. If a supervisor bases disciplinary actions on any of the following myths, discipline will be ineffective. It may, in fact, be counterproductive. Therefore, we begin this chapter by discussing four myths of discipline.

Myth 1: Discipline Is a Form of Punishment. This is probably the most commonly believed of the four myths. Sometimes, supervisors use punishment when they're angry, tense, or don't know what else to do. Some supervisors may punish in order to get revenge or to show the employee who's boss. However, punishment is not an effective long-term strategy in the workplace. Any positive effects resulting from the use of punishment usually will not last long.

The long-term negative effects, however, may overwhelm your department. Punished employees may react by hiding mistakes or by becoming resentful and hostile. They may try to get even by decreasing their output whenever their boss isn't looking. Too often, employees simply stop trying. Feelings of low self-esteem replace creativity and the desire to do a good job—both factors you want to encourage in your employees. Most important, perhaps, is the fact that punishment fails to deal with what's actually causing the problem.

Myth 2: Being the Boss Means People Have to Do What You Say. Many supervisors think that their employees will do everything their supervisors tell them to do just because they must. In fact, some supervisors try to threaten and force employees to behave in the ways they want them to behave. This usually results in a power struggle which no one can win. Employees make their own power plays, the supervisor responds with a greater display of power, and the struggle continues until both sides run out of ideas. A supervisor's final threat may be **termination,** but you can't fire your entire staff. If employees challenge the threat of termination and don't get fired, they've won the battle: the supervisor loses all credibility and authority.

The problems resulting from such "control by power" are like those which result from the use of punishment. The causes of problems aren't looked into, and employees become defensive, uncommunicative, rebellious, unhappy, hostile, and stubborn.

Being the supervisor doesn't make you "better" than your employees. Effective supervisors must function within a value system which prizes high ethical principles, a belief in the dignity of employees, and respect for employee rights. There are fewer and fewer employees who are helpless or part of a captive work force. Employees who are unhappy working for an unusually strict supervisor will go somewhere else to find a job. If a supervisor continues to use power over those employees who have no other choices, the employees' hostility can develop into hatred and even violence.

Myth 3: If You're Nice to Your Employees, You Won't Need to Discipline Them. Because they fear disciplining employees, supervisors often become too lenient. They want to believe that they're ensuring employee loyalty, friendship, and productivity when they ignore mistakes and broken rules and give in to employee demands. Instead, employees tend to expect more of such treatment, and lose respect for the supervisor or loyalty to the department. Employee morale and productivity might actually suffer. Employees might begin to believe that the rules don't apply to them. Employees in other departments with harsher supervisors might experience drops in morale, too.

The overly lenient supervisor can grow to resent employees who take advantage. If the resentment reaches a breaking point, the supervisor could unleash hostilities on the next employee who appears or, moreover, might punish the entire department. Further problems arise as employees become confused about what to expect from their supervisor. Employees could believe they're unfairly treated, since their own behaviors aren't any different from the ways they've behaved all along. The fact is, it's the supervisor's inconsistent behavior that has worsened.

Myth 4: Every Disciplinary Situation Must Be Handled in Exactly the Same Way. Union contracts, labor laws, and government regulations are made to ensure that all employees are treated fairly. However, many managers and supervisors think this means they must treat all employees in exactly the same way under all circumstances. It's true that you must be able to justify handling similar infractions differently. However, while two problem behaviors might be similar, the causes may be different—and that means your solutions may differ as well. Your choice of a disciplinary approach depends on the factors involved in a given situation.

For example, it would be unfair to use the same disciplinary approach for a dependable 15-year employee who is late twice because of the serious illness of a spouse, and a second employee—new and still on probation—who's late twice because an alarm didn't go off.

In other words, enforce the spirit, rather than the letter, of the policy. Keep your overall purpose in mind, which is to get employees to improve their behavior. Be consistent, but flexible, within the guidelines established by your property.

It's important to handle each situation properly and effectively from the start, maintain thorough records, and document every instance of disciplinary action. Be sure to include reasons for any exception you make. As long as you apply the same set of goals and values to all, you may treat each employee and each case individually.

It's easier and more effective to improve your approach to discipline than it is to change employees' behaviors. No book can tell you how to handle *every* disciplinary challenge. However, changing your belief in these four myths will help you decide for yourself how to handle a disciplinary situation—and keep employees productive in the process.

A Close Look at Rules and Regulations

One objective of employee disciplinary efforts is to ensure employee compliance with reasonable rules and regulations. Many hospitality operations have numerous rules and regulations, sometimes referred to as red tape. Other operations do not. The number and types of rules vary according to the philosophy and leadership styles of the top management staff. The rules that cause trouble and that employees often break are probably those that do not make sense to employees.

Therefore, it is important to review rules, especially those frequently broken, to make sure that they are reasonable. Once management confirms that the rules are reasonable, you should explain and justify these rules to employees. If you can improve employee attitudes toward the rules, disciplinary problems likely will decrease. Employees working in organizations with too many rules often feel that management is saying, "Employees are not intelligent and mature enough to discipline themselves. We must issue rules to manage their behavior." This kind of management attitude can create problems. For example, employees may feel that they are misunderstood or not to be trusted. As a result, they may respond to management by becoming distrustful and even rebellious.

Positive Reinforcement

Positive reinforcement tends to increase the likelihood of acceptable behavior and decrease the likelihood of unacceptable behavior. It can be a powerful tool in your strategy if you are starting a positive discipline program. Typically, supervisors are more effective in maintaining acceptable behavior through positive reinforcement than they are in eliminating undesirable behavior after it begins. In part, this is because employees who comply with rules and work according to procedures do not need to change behavior. You need only motivate them to continue the acceptable behavior. By contrast, employees whose behavior is unacceptable must change their behavior. It is then up to you to encourage consistent repetition of the desired work practices. Reinforce employees positively by rewarding them with praise, compensation, or other incentives when their work behavior corresponds to expectations. This practice encourages employees to even exceed the expectations management places on them.

In order for positive reinforcement to work, the reward being offered must be meaningful to the affected employee. In addition, the reward must be timely and frequent. There must be a relationship between the desired activity and the positive reinforcement action. Positive reinforcement must also recognize group or team efforts, since one employee's work is frequently dependent upon another's.

Praise is one of the best positive reinforcement techniques. Sincere praise is a strong reward, and people tend to repeat behavior that's been rewarded. Praise employees for trying to improve behavior. Be sincere, though, and don't overdo it. The following sentences of praise, though simple, can be very powerful:

"You learn fast."

"You're really doing a good job here."

"Keep up the good work."

"These tables look great."

"You handled that last guest really well."

"I'm proud of you."

You can't build a relationship with your employees if you talk to them only when they're doing something wrong. Positive reinforcement will help you store up goodwill and mutual respect. Another advantage of bestowing praise is that it only costs a few minutes of your time.

Enforcement of Rules

Once rules or policies are in place, supervisors must consistently enforce them. Consistent enforcement of rules tells employees that the rules are valuable to the successful operation of the property. Reasonable rules and regulations set the guidelines within which employees must work. They also tell employees where they do and do not have the authority to make "on-the-spot" decisions, and, therefore, are important elements in the operation's basic management program.

Causes of Disciplinary Problems ──────────────────────

Specifying the types and numbers of negative discipline problems that arise in hospitality operations is a difficult undertaking. While some companies may collect this information, no industry-wide statistics are available. Exhibit 7.1 lists examples of problems that, unfortunately, occur regularly in many hospitality operations.

Why do disciplinary problems occur? It is largely because policies and procedures are not written, understood, or enforced. Larger operations and those that are unionized are more likely to have written rules than are their small, non-unionized counterparts.

Some research indicates that possible causes of disciplinary problems can be attributed to (a) inadequate aptitudes and abilities, (b) inadequate knowledge and skills, (c) personality and motivational problems, and (d) troublesome environmental factors.[1]

To minimize disciplinary problems among your employees, you must be a good communicator. Talk with and listen to your employees. Sometimes you will need to probe below the surface to identify the real problems.

You're likely to find that there are two major types of unacceptable behavior:

Exhibit 7.1 Examples of Discipline Problems

Minor Problems

1. Failure to report accidents/injuries
2. Leaving assigned work areas without permission
3. Unauthorized breaks/rest periods
4. Gambling
5. Unauthorized selling
6. Smoking-related problems
7. Absenteeism
8. Negligence-related problems
9. Troubles with other employees
10. Insubordination
11. Miscellaneous rule violations

Serious Problems

1. Purposeful destruction of property
2. Immoral, indecent, dishonest actions
3. Carrying weapons
4. Falsifying records
5. Illegal strike; restriction of production
6. Substance abuse on the job
7. Time clock violations

- That which results from a purposeful decision made by the employee (such as stealing, willful damage to equipment, or lying)

- That which is beyond the employee's control (due to lack of training, improper tools, poor supervision, or other conditions)

Unacceptable behavior that is *within* the control of the employee must be managed through effective disciplinary action procedures. Unacceptable behavior *beyond* the control of the employee is really your problem. You must do a better job of helping employees meet job requirements. In every discipline case, you should look at yourself and your organization to assess whether causes of discipline problems are, or are not, within the employees' ability to control.

Administering Discipline

Disciplinary programs must be designed to yield positive benefits for the hospitality operation. If they are not, they can create serious problems in the form of poor human relations, lowered job performance, potential legal or union controversies, and personal problems for both the supervisors and the employees involved. Normally, your own manager will be directly involved in the disciplinary process. For example, you may need to ask your manager to clarify whether a policy violation warrants disciplinary action. Many employees feel that management input regarding the appropriate disciplinary action assures them of some degree of consistency and fairness. Sometimes a supervisor may request that his/her own boss be directly involved in any disciplinary interview. However, this is not typically advisable, because the supervisor loses power and authority in the eyes of the employee.

If infractions continue or increase, causing you to take further disciplinary measures, other levels of management will become involved. For example, you may have the authority to reprimand an employee and place a written report in his/her personnel file. However, you may not be authorized to discharge an employee without the full knowledge and approval of managers in higher levels of the organization.

In unionized operations, union officials are likely to be involved in aspects of the discipline program. For example, the result of some disciplinary actions may be mediation or arbitration by an outside, disinterested party.

Policies, rules, and procedures should pertain to all employees of the operation, not just to some. Furthermore, they should be enforced on a consistent basis and should be reasonable and fair from both management and employee perspectives. They should also be written and included in employee handbooks, and explained during orientation sessions. You should inform employees of major changes in policies, rules, and procedures before these changes are implemented. There should be no surprises.

Discipline is a management or supervisory skill that you can learn only through practice and by following guidelines. It is not a skill that you should just "know." Exhibit 7.2 presents general guidelines for taking disciplinary action.

If you have been experiencing problems disciplining your employees, you'll first have to work toward changing the way *you* behave. Indeed, you can't change your employees' behavior; they must change their own. True, brute force on your part can sometimes bring about short-term changes. However, if you want to make long-term changes, you have to modify the way you interact with your employees. When you are able to do that, then you are ready to help employees change themselves.

Many supervisors and managers mistakenly think that discipline equals punishment. If you think of discipline as a form of punishment, you'll spend all your time waiting for employees to do something wrong. Instead, think of discipline as a way to give employees the opportunity to improve themselves and their behavior to meet the expectations of your department. If you do, you and they will be better able to discuss the "gap" that exists between your expectations and their behavior. The goal of the discipline process is to close that gap.

Rather than acting as judge, jury, and executioner of your employees when you discipline them, your role is that of a *coach* who's trying to motivate employees to perform to the best of their abilities. Adopting this attitude will put discipline in a much more positive light, and will help you to act immediately when a discipline issue arises. Moreover, if you take this more positive attitude toward discipline, you

Exhibit 7.2 Some General Guidelines for Disciplinary Action

1. Be consistent and predictable. The certainty of discipline is a stronger deterrent than the severity.

2. Don't overreact. Use only enough discipline to get the job done. There must be some equity between the violation and the amount of discipline taken. If you threaten to fire someone for a first offense or mistake, you have no back-up position as a further step in your progressive discipline approach. In addition, if the offense later recurs and you don't fire the person, but rather have to back down from your threat, you'll lose much of your effectiveness as a manager.

3. Discipline should take place immediately. Don't delay with statements such as, "We'll talk later," or "Next week, we're going to make some adjustments." If you aren't going to deal with it right away, don't even bring it up at this time. The exceptions to taking immediate action include providing a very short cooling-off period, allowing time to arrange for a private location, or giving the employee an opportunity to practice self-discipline. Remember, however, that some employees are much harder on themselves than you would be or than the situation dictates when they make a mistake, and you may have to *un*-discipline them by saying, "Yes, it was a mistake, but it wasn't that bad. Don't get discouraged."

4. Don't compare one person to someone else in the department. It won't help the employee come to grips with the problem, and can open the door for responses such as, "Yes, but there are others in the department who do it worse." These types of comparisons can also cause a more difficult working relationship between the two employees by creating unwelcome competition or resentment.

5. Don't pre-judge. Making premature judgments is one of the biggest mistakes inexperienced managers make; then, after hearing what the employees have to say, they're often forced to back down. Listen to all sides of the story, collect all the facts, and then decide.

6. By all means, never back down when you're right, even if the employee disagrees with your actions or the outcome. If necessary, repeat the same message after each objection: "I understand how you feel; however, the results of your action are still the same, and that's what we're talking about. It can't happen again or further action will have to be taken." You don't have to specify the action, since doubt is sometimes a stronger deterrent and you can't always predict what the circumstances of the next offense will be.

7. When the discipline is over, put it behind you. Don't harbour a grudge. Don't use the incident against the employee again later unless it figures in discipline for a subsequent offense.

Source: David Wheelhouse, *Managing Human Resources in the Hospitality Industry* (East Lansing, Mich.: Educational Institute of the American Hotel & Motel Association, 1989), p. 357.

need not fear confrontations—because, when discipline sessions are effectively conducted, confrontations rarely occur.

Minor Corrections

Training, performance discussions, and discipline often overlap in the supervision process. Suppose you notice that one of your employees, a cook, isn't wearing a hat. You step in, tell the employee what is wrong, and explain why. In this case, the process of correction really is part of training. Finally, you praise the employee for the work he/she is doing well, and affirm that you're glad the employee is part of the team. Even though this interaction is casual, it will tell the employee that your standards are high, that you're checking his/her work, and that the employee is

Making minor corrections in a casual, friendly manner allows the employee to maintain self-esteem. With many employees, this level of correction is all that's necessary.

Exhibit 7.3 Making Minor Corrections

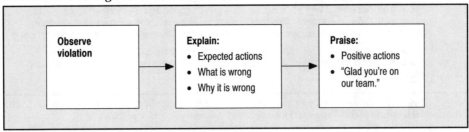

meeting your expectations. Exhibit 7.3 summarizes the steps to follow when making minor corrections.

Progressive discipline usually starts with this kind of casual, friendly correction. In fact, making this kind of correction is a normal part of the supervisor's everyday job. If you correct employees when you first spot them making mistakes, you can keep small errors from turning into major problems. With many employees, this level of correction is all that's necessary. After all, most employees come to work hoping to perform well, not poorly.

If you notice the employee still making the mistake, say something like, "I don't know if I said this or not, but this is how I'd like you to do this." Such a

Exhibit 7.4 Sample Employee Incident File

INCIDENT FILE	
Name _____	Telephone _____
Date of Employment _____	
Personal:	
Spouse's name _____	Spouse employed?_____
Names & Ages of Children _____	
Hobbies, special skills, etc. _____	

Date	Incident and Action Taken

(Continue on Back)

Source: David Wheelhouse, *Managing Human Resources in the Hospitality Industry* (East Lansing, Mich.: Educational Institute of the American Hotel & Motel Association, 1989), p. 360.

statement allows the employee to maintain self-esteem. Express confidence that the employee can correct the problem and learn the right way to perform. Such feedback is similar to the kind of feedback and correction you use when training employees.

Don't criticize too much in areas in which the employee can make only small improvements. Naturally, we'd all like to have error-free employees who always meet department standards, but that is unrealistic. The truth is that no employee will ever be perfect. Constant criticism wears away employee morale and self-esteem, causing even bigger problems in the process. With service industry employees, a little discipline tends to go a long way. Because service employees want to please others, unkind criticism can be very harmful.

It's important to follow up every act of discipline, however minor. First, make a brief note about the incident and place it in the employee incident file (see Exhibit 7.4 for a sample form). All you'd need to do is list the date, the time, the incident itself, and any action you and the employee agreed upon. The note reminds you that you've given the employee the chance to correct his/her behavior. If the employee successfully changes the behavior, you'll be able to show that you've recognized the change. In addition, creating a well-documented paper trail for your files is an important way to protect yourself, the operation, and your right to supervise. Without such records, it could be hard to prove that you ever tried to correct the problem. Also, such a habit allows you to help employees change their behavior. Careful documentation helps you to keep track of important dates, facts, and patterns of behavior.

Many supervisors hesitate to document negative incidences if it means creating a permanent written record for inclusion in the employee's personnel file. This concern may be addressed, however, if the operation's policies permit removal of the information after a certain period of time or after corrective action has proven effective.

Supervisors and managers should also remember that the incident file is the best place to record positive achievements, as well as personal information about employees.

As the Seriousness Increases

More serious problems require more of the supervisor's time and attention. When it's apparent that you need to make more than minor corrections, disciplinary discussions may be in order. Such discussions should take place as soon as possible after you observe the employee's incorrect behavior. Hold the discussion in a place with as much privacy as possible. Before meeting with the employee, you'll have to do some investigating. Asking yourself the following questions may help you decide how to conduct the meeting:

- Did the employee knowingly break the rule?

- What were the consequences of the behavior?

- What is the employee's disciplinary record?

- Is a temporary personal problem contributing to the discipline problem?

- Is the incorrect behavior or rule violation entirely the employee's fault?

- Have you overlooked the behavior in the past, both in this employee and in others?

In fairness to your employees and in the best interest of your organization, try to follow the principle that an individual is presumed innocent until proven guilty. With this principle as a guide, it is your responsibility as a supervisor to prove that an infraction has occurred. It is important to consider all applicable circumstances. Determine whether the problem resulted from the employee's purposeful actions or whether the problem was beyond the employee's control.

When the meeting begins, explain your view of the discipline problem. If you have held previous discussions with the employee, discuss what actions the employee has and hasn't taken. Acknowledge the progress the employee has made so far, if any. Exhibit 7.5 summarizes steps to follow during a disciplinary session with an employee. These steps are discussed in detail in the following sections.

Be Specific. When you're discussing the problem, be as specific as possible. Refer to data that you've kept in the employee incident file. Focus on how the problem

Exhibit 7.5 Conducting a Disciplinary Session

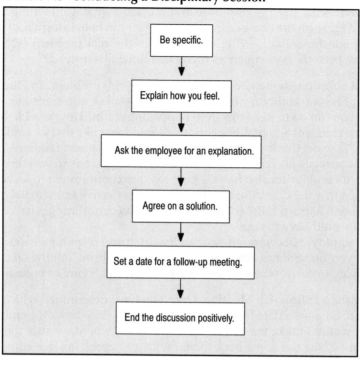

behavior falls short of your expectations; do not focus on the employee's attitude. Don't attack the employee's personality. For example, instead of saying, "You're rude," tell an employee, "It's rude to turn your back on a guest who's obviously coming to ask you a question." If you concentrate on the act instead of on the employee, you'll help the employee maintain self-esteem. This may enable the employee to talk about the problem objectively instead of reacting defensively. Throughout the interview, it is important not to threaten, argue, or display anger. These actions will only serve to move the focus of the discussion away from your objectives.

Explain How You Feel. It is always helpful to explain to the employee how you feel about the problem behavior. Statements like, "When I saw you turn away from the guest, I was disappointed, because guest relations are very important to me and to this company," are better and more effective than, "Because *you* turned your back on that guest, *you* ruined the company's good reputation for guest service." Telling how you feel encourages the employee to talk freely, too. It also may help the employee see that it is his/her problem, and that the employee is responsible for solving it.

Ask the Employee for an Explanation. Ask the employee to explain why the behavior occurred. Give the employee the chance to explain his/her side of the story while you listen attentively and objectively. Encourage the employee to talk by using active listening responses, such as "Uh huh," "Go on," "I see," or by just nodding your head. Ask the employee to summarize what went wrong. The two of you should agree on the cause of the problem. You can help bring about agreement by asking questions like, "What do you think the real problem is?" or "What would have been the consequences if you had done this instead?"

Agree on a Solution. Remember, this is the employee's problem, and the employee must accept responsibility for his/her own actions. Ask questions like, "What do you think you can do to keep this from happening again? How can I help?" If possible, offer a choice of acceptable solutions: "Would you like to try working another shift?" or "Do you think you need further training in guest relations?" Offering choices discourages power struggles which each of you has to win. Involving the employee in the solution also helps secure his/her commitment to solve the problem. Explain that the disciplinary action becomes effective immediately. Then, explain what will happen if the problem is not resolved, outlining what disciplinary action you would have to take.

If the employee becomes upset or angry, listen and respond with empathy. Explain that you understand how he/she feels, but be firm. Tell the employee that you are trying to correct the performance problem, not trying to punish him/her.

Set a Date for a Follow-Up Meeting. Once you have determined which disciplinary action to take, set a date for a follow-up meeting. This shows the employee that you really want to make the solution work. In addition, make sure the employee knows that he/she can come back to you with any problems that come up in the meantime.

End the Discussion Positively. Your focus in the meeting should be future-oriented, unless, in extreme circumstances, you terminate a person's employment. That is, you want the employee to correct the problem behavior because he/she is important to your company. Offer the employee support and encouragement, and express confidence that he/she can improve. Shake hands with the employee when the meeting ends.

Finally, it's important to communicate with the employee again before the day ends, even if you just talk about something else. This tells the employee that you're not holding a grudge and that you still value him/her.

Appeal procedures should be designed and incorporated into the discipline process. When you have made a disciplinary decision affecting an employee, the employee's route of appeal normally would begin with your boss. In unionized operations, these and other aspects of the disciplinary process will likely be covered in the bargaining agreement.

Progressive Discipline Programs

Many hospitality operations adopt **progressive discipline programs.** Such programs might include the following steps:

1. An oral warning may be appropriate at the time of the first offense.

2. A second warning may also be oral, but should be followed up by a written statement signed by the employee and supervisor. A copy should be retained for the personnel files.

3. An official reprimand—in writing—is often the third step and is also placed in the employee's file.

4. A suspension of, perhaps, a few hours or several days without pay may be the next step. A decision to suspend an employee will depend upon the seriousness of the offense and the surrounding circumstances.

5. A disciplinary transfer or demotion may be the next logical step. This can be necessary when, respectively, there is a personality conflict between the supervisor and the employee, or there is a problem resulting from the employee's incompetence.

6. Immediately before termination, some organizations may grant an offending employee "one last chance" to correct a problem. Typically, supervisors specify exactly what must be done and when. For example, you might ask an employee with a substance abuse problem to participate in an appropriate employee assistance program. If the employee agrees, you might give the employee extra time to solve the problem in an effort to avoid terminating his/her employment. After all, disciplining a current employee, with whom you already have a relationship, is always preferable to starting all over again with a new employee.

7. Employment termination is typically the last step in the discipline process. However, in some operations termination may be the immediate and only response to the more serious problems of violence, theft, or falsification of employment records.

Endnotes

1. J. Clifton Williams, *Human Behavior in Organizations,* 3d ed. (Cincinnati, Ohio: Southwestern, 1986), p. 483.

Key Terms

discipline
positive reinforcement
progressive discipline programs
termination

Discussion Questions

1. What myths of discipline do many supervisors believe?

2. Why do supervisors dread disciplining employees?

3. Why is it more effective to improve your approach to discipline than it is to change employee behavior?

4. What are the objectives of an employee discipline program?

5. Why should you use positive reinforcement when dealing with employees?

6. What are some causes of disciplinary problems?

7. How should you administer discipline effectively?

8. How should supervisors handle minor corrections?

9. What steps should you take when the seriousness of a discipline problem increases?

10. What steps do many hospitality operations include in their progressive discipline programs?

REVIEW QUIZ

When you feel you have covered all of the material in this chapter, answer these questions. Choose the *best* answer. Check your answers with the correct ones found on the Review Quiz Answer Key at the end of this book.

True (T) or False (F)

T   F   1. Punishment is an effective long-term strategy in the workplace.

T   F   2. Supervisors often become too lenient because they fear disciplining employees.

T   F   3. According to the chapter, discipline can be thought of as a way to force people to improve themselves and their behavior.

T   F   4. Discipline leads to confrontation when the supervisor takes a positive attitude.

T   F   5. A supervisor seldom makes minor corrections in the course of an average workday.

T   F   6. Constant criticism helps employees develop high levels of self-esteem and confidence.

T   F   7. Because service industry employees tend to want to please just themselves, constant criticism of employees is necessary.

T   F   8. Some supervisors hesitate to document incidences if it creates a permanent written record for the employee's personnel file.

T   F   9. In the best interest of your organization, it is your responsibility to assume an infraction has occurred.

T   F   10. Employees must see the problem behavior as their own problem, which they are responsible for solving.

Alternate/Multiple Choice

11.   As a supervisor, your choice of a disciplinary approach should depend on:

   a. the factors involved in a given situation.
   b. the problem behavior itself.

12.   The overall purpose of discipline is to get employees to:

   a. learn who's boss.
   b. improve their behavior.

13.   When you are discussing a disciplinary problem with an employee, be as:

   a. general as possible.
   b. specific as possible.

14. Consistent enforcement of the rules tells employees that the rules are:

    a. valuable to the successful operation of the property.
    b. not important.
    c. made to be broken.
    d. more important than the employee.

15. The major purpose of a discipline conference is to:

    a. terminate the employee.
    b. correct a problem behavior.
    c. explain why the company views the behavior as a problem.
    d. all of the above.

Chapter Outline

The Labor Shortage
The Supervisor's Legal Role
    Equal Employment Opportunity Laws
    Sexual Harassment
Safety and Security
    Risk Management
Supervising a Multi-Cultural Work Force
Ethics
Substance Abuse
    Employees
    Guests
Unions
    Structure of Unions
    Impact of Unions on Management
    Collective Bargaining
    Union Organizing Campaigns
    Working with the Union

Learning Objectives

1. Describe the labor shortage.

2. Explain how equal opportunity laws affect hospitality operations.

3. Describe the supervisor's safety and security role.

4. Describe the special challenges of supervising a multi-cultural work force.

5. Discuss ethics.

6. Explain the supervisor's role in combating drug abuse by employees and guests.

7. Describe typical reasons that employees join unions.

8. List actions that supervisors can take to influence a union organizing campaign.

9. List actions that supervisors cannot take to influence a union organizing campaign.

10. Describe special considerations of working with a union.

11. Contrast mediation with arbitration.

12. List examples of management rights that should be protected when negotiating with a union.

8

Special Supervisory Concerns

THE JOB OF THE SUPERVISOR in today's hospitality industry is very complex. Not only do supervisors have to know their jobs and most or all of the jobs of their employees, they have to be knowledgeable in areas as diverse as guest relations, safety, security, civil rights, risk management, business ethics, substance abuse, union relations, multi-cultural work force issues, and other areas.

Large hospitality operations may have specialists to help you in these areas when necessary. Small organizations will probably hire consultants to provide help and advice. However, all managers and supervisors must have at least a general knowledge of these special areas so that they can effectively manage potentially serious problems.

The Labor Shortage

In the past few years one of the most serious and talked about problems in the hospitality industry has been the shortage of workers. The numbers tell the story. The industry will need 25% to 40% more workers by the year 2000. However, the population group from which the industry draws most of its new employees—people 16 to 24 years old—is expected to decline 26% in the 1990s. The total job force—the pool of workers from which all businesses must draw—will grow by only 1%.

To combat the labor shortage, your property will need to revise its recruiting and hiring procedures to accommodate non-traditional workers. When interviewing job applicants, you must have an open mind and consider applicants that you might not have considered ten years ago. You and other supervisors and managers in your organization need to ask yourselves some hard questions, including:

- How can we alert non-traditional employees to job opportunities within our organization?

- Can we modify our orienting, training, and work procedures to accommodate non-traditional employees without lowering our standards?

- How exactly will we need to revise training and work procedures?

- What can we do for non-traditional employees to ease the transition from new-hire to productive employee, and shorten that transition time?

- Will I need to modify my leadership style to accommodate non-traditional employees? If so, how?

- What can I do to help non-traditional employees become productive and remain with the organization? What supervisory skills will I need to improve?

- What reward systems and benefits are important to non-traditional employees?

Your answers to these and other questions will help determine whether your organization thrives or merely survives during the labor crisis of the 1990s.

The Supervisor's Legal Role

There are many laws that affect what a supervisor can and cannot do. You may think that your organization's attorneys and top-level managers are the only ones who need to keep up with these laws. Not true! In fact, if you break a law out of ignorance, you and/or your employer may still be held responsible.

This brief section will give you an idea of some of the laws you must be knowledgeable about. Of course, supervisors should check with their boss or their company's legal counsel if they are unsure of the legal ramifications of a given situation.[1]

Equal Employment Opportunity Laws

Discrimination is the practice of treating someone differently—usually wrongly—based on a factor such as the individual's race or nationality. When you discriminate, you don't bother to get to know people as individuals and relate to them according to their merits as persons. Rather, you put people in categories based on their color, religion, sex, etc., and treat everyone in that category the same. Since this treatment is based on ignorance of the individuality of the members of these various categories, these people usually are subject to whatever stereotypes and prejudices you hold about the category you happen to place them in.

Employment discrimination at all organizational levels is prohibited by law in the United States. The amended Civil Rights Act of 1964 contains a section, **Title VII**, that deals with employee selection and guarantees the right of an individual to work in an environment free from discrimination based on race, sex, religion, or national origin.[2] All employees must be treated equally by both managers and co-workers. In fact, a hospitality organization may be held liable for the discriminatory acts of its employees even if company officials were unaware of those acts. Discrimination includes practices where discrimination may not have been intended, such as supervisors allowing employees to tell ethnic or racial jokes.

Dress codes and standards for personal appearance also have discrimination implications. Men and women, of course, are allowed to dress differently, but the same general standards must apply to each sex and the standards must be reasonable, appropriate, and consistent. For example, if a hotel or restaurant requires food service employees to be clean shaven, this requirement should be imposed on other service employees at the bell-stand, front desk, and garage. There must be property-wide consistency in the interpretation of what is appropriate for employees; individual departments or managers must not be allowed to make contrary decisions or rules.

Religious discrimination must be avoided. You must allow employees time off for religious purposes and will need to make whatever schedule and other adjustments are necessary to meet these special requests. An employee's personal

Many older employees are more responsible and motivated than their younger counterparts, making it unwise as well as unlawful to discriminate against them when hiring.

appearance may reflect his/her religious heritage (length of hair, for example) and personnel policies must accommodate these special circumstances.

Supervisors must not discriminate on the basis of sex. For example, personnel specifications such as weight or height that discriminate against women are unlawful unless they reflect essential attributes required for performing the job. These essential attributes are called **bona fide occupational qualifications (BFOQ).** Discriminating against pregnant women and refusing to hire women because of uniform, locker space, or other problems are examples of unlawful practices.

Laws prohibit direct or indirect discrimination against individuals because of their national origin. Employees must be allowed to use their native language unless they must interact with the public in a situation where English is the only language understood.

Age discrimination is also illegal and applies to persons over the age of 40. Offering different fringe benefit packages to older workers, refusing to train or promote them, and mandating their retirement are all examples of illegal acts.

Handicapped persons' right to work is also protected by law. Most recently, the Americans with Disabilities Act of 1990 stipulated that a disabled individual can't be discriminated against in hiring if he/she can perform the job and does not pose a threat to the safety and health of others. The law further stipulates that an employer must provide work areas and equipment that are wheelchair-accessible unless this is not "readily achievable" and it would be an "undue hardship" to provide such areas and equipment.[3]

Some laws require companies doing business with the government to protect the rights of veterans. Generally, organizations must re-hire employees who complete military service if they re-apply. Further, time off (without pay) must be provided to those employees with Military Reserve obligations.

Federal and state laws also protect employees against invasion of their privacy. The Federal Right of Privacy Act covers employee records, locker and personal inspections, background investigations, and other matters. Normally, employees are entitled to a reasonable expectation of privacy and, if this is denied, legal liability can result.

Sexual Harassment

Today, **sexual harassment** in the workplace receives significant attention and is one of the most frequent reasons for employee litigation. Title VII of the Civil Rights Act of 1964 and similar state laws focus on this issue. The Equal Employment Opportunity Commission (EEOC) has confirmed that sexual harassment is a violation of Title VII and has presented information about conduct that constitutes unlawful sexual harassment. Simply stated, in order for conduct to be considered sexual harassment, the conduct must be (1) sexual in nature, and (2) unwelcome. Sexual harassment may be physical, verbal (including suggestive comments), or visual (for example, displaying pornographic photographs).[4]

While the laws and their interpretations may change, some principles appear established. You and/or your employer will probably be held liable for sexual harassment if an employee is deprived of a tangible job benefit—for example, if an employee is fired for refusing a supervisor's sexual advances. If an employee's work environment is negatively affected (in the employee's opinion) by the sexual harassment of a supervisor or co-worker, and if the employer knows or should have known of this conduct and does not take immediate action, the employer will probably be held liable. You and your organization could also be found liable for the harassment of employees by guests and vendors if unwanted activities occurred, you were aware of them, and did not take immediate corrective actions.

Your organization must exercise reasonable care to prevent sexual harassment. General strategies include:

- A written and distributed policy statement prohibiting sexual harassment.

- A reasonable and well-publicized grievance procedure for reporting and processing sexual harassment allegations.

- Ongoing training for supervisors and managers to make sure they are aware of their responsibilities to guard against sexual harassment.[5]

In the event you are informed that an employee is being sexually harassed, you should take the following steps:

1. Notify your boss.

2. Investigate the situation according to company policy.

3. Confront the accused party, and get the accused party's side of the story.

4. Take any necessary disciplinary actions.

Exhibit 8.1 Sample Safety Rules for Employees

SAFETY RULES AND REGULATIONS

1. All fires and accidents must be reported immediately.
2. Any unsafe act or condition must be brought to the attention of your supervisor.
3. Smoking is permitted only in designated areas.
4. No running, horseplay, or fighting is permitted.
5. If you are unfamiliar with an assigned task, check with your supervisor before beginning.
6. Do not operate hazardous equipment if you are unauthorized to do so or if you do not know how to operate it.
7. Use of liquor or drugs is prohibited. Those reporting for work in an intoxicated condition are subject to immediate discharge.

Safety and Security

As a supervisor, you have a significant role to play in your property's safety and security programs. A primary concern of every hospitality operation is to protect the health and well-being of employees and guests. This is best done through efforts to prevent accidents and promptly investigating problems that do occur.

Hospitality operations must comply with regulations established by the **Occupational Safety and Health Administration (OSHA).** This federal agency is responsible for developing and managing regulations and standards for employee safety and health in the workplace. OSHA personnel inspect businesses and have the authority to issue citations to those that are not in compliance with safety and health requirements.

There are a number of ways you can assist in a property's safety program. Observe employees as they work and correct any unsafe practices immediately. Make sure first aid kits are well stocked and conveniently located. Check work areas for safety hazards on a regular basis. Inspections must be continual, not put off until "we have more time." Promptly correct any problems identified during an inspection, such as leaky pipes or employees incorrectly working with hazardous equipment. Keep records of all inspections and actions taken to fix problems.

Take an assertive role in alerting your boss to potential safety problems in the workplace. Maintain safety records and promptly complete all required reports. If your firm has a safety committee, serve on it.

You should also motivate employees to make safety a priority at work (see Exhibit 8.1). Train employees to perform their job tasks in a safe manner. Encourage them to report all accidents and injuries and take prompt follow-up action when necessary.

Ideally, you and your employees should be trained in first aid techniques. Food service supervisors and employees should be trained in the **Heimlich Maneuver**—a first aid technique that forces air through a choking person's lungs to dislodge an obstruction in the windpipe. Several people at the property should be trained in cardiopulmonary resuscitation (CPR)—a technique to provide artificial

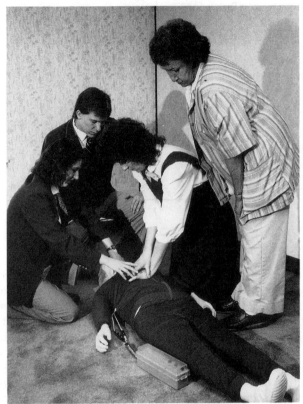

Supervisors and employees should be trained in such first aid techniques as cardiopulmonary resuscitation (CPR).

circulation and breathing to someone whose heart or lungs have stopped because of a heart attack or some other health threat.

Safety is as much an attitude as it is a set of rules and procedures. Many of the cuts, slips, burns, and falls that happen to employees and guests can be prevented and the severity of many others can be reduced if you constantly look for potential problems and take immediate action to prevent them.

You also have a role to play in keeping your property secure. You must know exactly what to do when there is a threat or an occurrence of a fire, severe storm, bomb threat, or other emergency. During an emergency, every moment is critical. You must know what actions to take and how to guide your employees and guests through the crisis.

Your role in property security programs includes helping to guard against the unlawful acts of others. To protect employees and guests, you should be trained in guestroom security, including key control; control of the building's perimeter (grounds and entrances); and the protection of assets—money, employees' and guests' personal effects, equipment, inventories, and so forth.

Your employees are an important part of your organization's security team. Alert employees can help prevent events that may threaten lives or property.

You should train your employees to:

- Report suspicious activities or persons anywhere on the property.

- Avoid confronting a suspicious individual, go to a secure area, and call you or another supervisor for help.

- Report drug paraphernalia or other suspicious items they see while working.

- Make sure posters, tent cards, and other security information for guests are available and properly located.[6]

Risk Management

The objective of a **risk management** program is to avoid losses. As such, it's closely aligned with many of the safety and security concerns we've just discussed. Risk management is much more than just buying insurance. It involves the study of risky situations at your property such as unsecured stair rails, poorly located swimming pool safety equipment, or flammable materials in guestrooms, and then remedying the situations before an accident occurs.

While risk management programs are generally planned at upper-management levels, many aspects of program implementation are clearly within your responsibility. You are directly involved with day-to-day operations and therefore are a vital element in your property's loss prevention efforts.[7]

Supervising a Multi-Cultural Work Force

People of many different cultural backgrounds work in the hospitality industry. Today, food and lodging properties employ many Asians, Hispanics, and others from cultures and ethnic groups with unique values and attitudes. The resulting diversity creates significant challenges and opportunities for supervisors.

Many supervisors do not know how to manage people whose backgrounds are significantly different from theirs. They may believe in inappropriate stereotypes—for example, that all people in a particular ethnic group are overly aggressive. They may be insensitive to cultural differences and lack the ability to effectively communicate. Communication problems not only involve language difficulties but also actions. For example, being honored as "employee of the month" may be embarrassing for employees from some ethnic groups.

Several principles can help you get maximum effort from employees no matter what their cultural background. Keep in mind that ideas about the value of work differ between cultures. Definitions of what is socially acceptable differ from culture to culture also. Words and phrases have different meanings; one phrase may be complimentary to one group and insulting to another. Recognize that members of ethnic groups are often victims of racism and stereotyping. Finally, keep in mind that trying to force members of different cultural or ethnic groups to conform to your "norm" is often unproductive.

Training can help you become a better multi-cultural supervisor. You should make an honest attempt to understand the basic values and beliefs of various ethnic groups and try to modify your management strategies accordingly. Otherwise, tensions and misunderstandings may plague your work group and you may be continually fighting such problems as low productivity, high absenteeism, and turnover.

Ethics

Ethics involve standards about what is "right" and "wrong." Some organizations create a code of ethics for their personnel. This code helps employees decide between right and wrong when called on to make a tough decision at work. Professional associations may develop ethical guidelines for their members. Unfortunately, ethical codes and guidelines tend to be general in nature and may not be very helpful when it comes to the day-to-day decisions and actions of supervisors. There are few, if any, absolutes when it comes to making an ethical decision. While federal and state laws and a firm's policies establish guidelines for a supervisor, there are still many "gray areas" not covered by laws or regulations in which you have latitude.

Let's look at a common situation in the hospitality industry. An employee arrives a half hour late for work with a reasonable excuse and asks you to (1) rewrite her schedule so that it appears she wasn't late, and (2) extend it a half hour so she can receive full pay. If there is no company policy or rule that dictates what to do in this situation, the decision is yours to make. What should you do? On the one hand, the employee has a good reason for being late, will still work a full shift, and needs the full pay. On the other, the company expects employees to arrive on time and you needed her for the half hour she missed, not for the half hour she's now asking for. What should you do? There may be no "right" or "wrong" answer to this question. And, in that sense, this situation is like many others where ethical questions come up (see Exhibit 8.2).

Opportunities to cheat your guests provide other examples of ethical dilemmas that arise in the hospitality industry. You know it's against truth-in-menu laws but you also know you won't get caught—so is it acceptable to use frozen chicken rather than fresh chicken in a recipe when the menu specifies fresh chicken? Is it okay to advertise a special sales package with "limited availability" when only a few guests can be accommodated and the main objective of the ad is to sell guests on other, more expensive, packages?

Regardless of the extent to which policies, rules, and regulations exist, there will always be gray areas in which you will need to make a decision. Your boss and other upper managers expect you to put the long-term interests of the organization ahead of any other considerations.

Substance Abuse

Drug-abuse problems are all around us. Many of us see it daily in our communities and in the properties where we work. The drug problem is significant among all age groups, particularly young adults.[8]

Exhibit 8.2 Ethics Quiz for Supervisors

1. You drop some loaves of bread on the floor in the kitchen; you do not have time to prepare new ones. No one will know if you pick them up, re-plate them, and serve them. What would you do?

2. You want to buy some products used by your property for personal use. You talk with the salesperson, who says, "I can get you those items at no cost if you'll look favorably on additional purchases by the property." What would you do?

3. One employee is an excellent worker; another is your friend who is not as good. There is an opportunity for you to promote one of your employees in the near future. What would you do?

4. As a sales supervisor, you have booked a function room for a small party and now have an opportunity to sell the room to a larger group that will generate significantly higher revenues. There is no other place to put the small group. What would you do?

5. You supervise a friend who is unable to perform to required standards. According to company policy, you should meet with your friend to discuss the situation and write a report about his shortcomings for his personnel file. What would you do?

6. You are in charge of receiving products for the hotel. Through a delivery error, a larger quantity of products is received than is entered on the delivery invoice; the property will only need to pay the smaller amount unless the supplier is notified of the error. What would you do?

7. You are in the middle of writing a report for the general manager to advise her about which company the hotel should select to put in an expensive water-heating system. One supplier's representative offers you a free weekend of hunting if you "put in a good word for our product." What would you do?

Employees

Employees who abuse drugs—including alcohol—cost their firm in many ways. Drug-abusing employees are not as productive as those who are drug-free. Drug abusers use more sick time and have a much higher accident rate than drug-free employees. Income is lost when guests do not return to a property because of a bad experience with one or more intoxicated employees. A substantial percentage of industrial deaths or injuries can be traced to employee **substance abuse.**

It's important to recall that drug abuse is not limited to entry-level employees. Staff at all organizational levels may abuse drugs and pose a hazard to themselves and others.

Unfortunately, hospitality industry supervisors frequently neglect the problem of drug abuse among their employees. Reasons include:

- Difficulty in estimating the scope and cost of the problem

- Difficulty in identifying employees with substance abuse problems

- Difficulty in estimating the effects of substance abuse on job performance

- Uncertainty about whether to refer employees to treatment centers

- Potential for lawsuits by employees accused of substance abuse

What can you do to combat drug use among employees? First, you must become aware of how many—if any—of your employees are abusing drugs.

Exhibit 8.3 Behaviors and Characteristics Associated with Possible Substance Abuse

PERSONAL

Appearance

- Sloppy
- Inappropriate clothing

Mood

- Withdrawn
- Sad or depressed
- Mood swings, high and low
- Suspiciousness
- Extreme sensitivity
- Nervousness
- Frequent irritability with others
- Pre-occupation with illness or death

Actions

- Physically or verbally assaultive
- Unduly talkative
- Exaggerated self-importance
- Rigidity—inability to change plans with reasonable ease
- Making incoherent or irrelevant statements on the job
- Over-compliance with any routine: making it a ritual
- Frequent argumentativeness
- Frequent outbursts of crying
- Excessive use of the telephone

JOB PERFORMANCE

Absenteeism

- Multiple instances of improper reporting of time off
- Excessive sick leave
- Repeated absences which follow a pattern (Fridays and Mondays; absence on days following days off)
- Leaving work early
- Excessive lateness in the morning, or on returning from lunch
- Peculiar and increasingly improbable excuses for absences
- High absenteeism rate for colds, flu, gastritis, general malaise, etc.
- Frequent unscheduled short-term absences, with or without medical explanation
- Frequent use of unscheduled vacation time

On-the-Job Absenteeism

- Unusually large amounts of time spent away from job location
- Frequent trips to water fountain or restroom
- Long coffee breaks

Accidents

- More than the usual number of accidents on the job
- More than the usual number of accidents off the job

Source: Daniel T. Davis and Jack Ninemeier, *Controlling Drug Abuse: A Handbook for Managers* (East Lansing, Mich.: Educational Institute of the American Hotel & Motel Association, 1987), p. 23.

Unexplainable changes in attendance, discipline or performance problems, and unusual outbreaks of temper are all signs that an employee may be using drugs. Exhibit 8.3 lists other appearance, mood, behavior, and job performance characteristics frequently associated with substance abuse.

Confronting an employee about a drug problem is never easy. To avoid complaints of slander or discrimination, make sure that your talk with the employee concentrates on lowered job performance and other measurable job-related factors. Avoid accusations or general comments about substance use or abuse. Exhibit 8.4 summarizes some of the principles important in identifying and dealing with substance-abusing employees.

Exhibit 8.4 Summary of Guidelines for Supervisory Action in Suspected Drug-Abuse Cases

- Know whom to notify when you suspect an employee of drug abuse.
- Watch for strangers who visit the employee frequently or at odd times.
- Try to determine whether the change in the employee's behavior is caused by a reason other than drug abuse.
- Before meeting with the employee, make sure you know your property's substance abuse policy.
- Become familiar with drug-abuse programs offered by your company and/or the community. In most cases, offer this information only if the employee asks for it.
- Meet with the employee at a formal review session. In most situations it's best to have your boss or some other person present at the meeting.
- Assure the employee that the meeting and what is said during the meeting will be kept confidential.
- At the meeting, focus on the employee's decline in job performance. Have written documentation of job performance problems available to back up your statements.
- Don't get involved with the employee's personal life or try to analyze the employee. Unless you are a trained counselor, do not try to counsel the employee at all.
- Don't moralize. Be factual and specific—not judgmental—about the problems you see.
- Be firm and formal yet have a considerate attitude.
- Explain in very specific terms what you want the employee to do to remedy the situation.
- Troubled employees manipulate others by emotional pleas and defensiveness; don't get caught in this trap.
- With the employee's input, decide on the amount of time appropriate to correct the situation.
- Set a time limit for demonstrating improvement.
- Only talk about possible disciplinary measures if you're willing and able to do what you say.
- If your boss was not present at the review session, discuss the employee's case with him/her. Explain your intended plan of action and ask for advice.
- Try to involve your boss at each step of the process. At the very least, keep him/her fully informed.

Several elements are necessary in an effective program to manage substance abuse. First, an appropriate company policy for dealing with the threat is required. While this will be developed by top-level managers with advice from legal counsel, you will be required to communicate it to your employees. Exhibit 8.5 illustrates a typical policy. Companies can also create employee assistance programs that try to restore employees to their former productivity levels by providing measures to help employees free themselves of chemical dependency.

Guests

You have a duty to report any illegal activity that occurs in a hotel's guestrooms or public areas. If your employees, in the course of their required work activities, see guests who may be abusing or selling drugs, they should notify you immediately.

Exhibit 8.5 Sample Company Substance-Abuse Policy

Sample Company Policy Statement: Abuse of Alcohol and Drugs

"(Name of Company) recognizes that the future of the company depends upon the physical and psychological health of all its employees.

"The abuse of alcohol and drugs threatens both the company and its employees. Commonly abused or improperly used drugs or substances include the following: alcohol, painkillers, sedatives, stimulants, and tranquilizers, in addition to such illegal substances as marijuana, cocaine, heroin, etc.

"It is the responsibility of both employees and the Company to maintain a safe, healthful, and efficient working environment. Therefore, the Company has adopted the following policy:

1. The possession, use, or sale of alcohol, unauthorized, or illegal drugs or the misuse of any legal drugs on Company premises or while on Company business continues to be prohibited and will constitute grounds for termination of employment.

2. Any employee under the influence of alcohol or drugs that impair judgment, performance, or behavior while on company premises or while on Company business will be subject to disciplinary action, including termination of employment.

3. The Company has a number of jobs that pose special safety considerations to employees, such as use of moving machinery, transportation of goods and persons, and the handling of chemicals. The Company will require all employees whose jobs involve special safety considerations to be tested periodically for use of drugs. Positive test results may result in the withdrawal of qualification to work on those jobs.

4. All prospective employees will be tested for use of drugs before being hired. Positive test results will be considered in employment decisions and may result in the withholding of medical qualification for employment.

5. It is the responsibility of each employee to report promptly to his/her supervisor the use of any prescribed medication that may affect judgment, performance, or behavior.

"The Company will institute such procedures as are required to effectively enforce this policy. This may include the requirement that employees cooperate in personal or facility searches when the presence of drugs or alcohol is indicated and performance is impaired or behavior is erratic. Refusal to cooperate with these procedures may subject employees to discipline and/or termination of employment.

"The Company has developed an Employee Assistance Program (EAP) and strongly encourages employees to use the program for help with alcohol or drug-related problems. It is each employee's responsibility to seek assistance from the EAP prior to reaching a point where his or her judgment, performance, or behavior is negatively affected.

"Any provision of this policy in conflict with applicable law in any jurisdiction will be modified to comply with such law."

Source: Daniel T. Davis and Jack Ninemeier, *Controlling Drug Abuse: A Handbook for Managers* (East Lansing, Mich.: Educational Institute of the American Hotel & Motel Association, 1987), p. 40.

You must then alert your boss. If there truly is a drug problem, the next step is to alert the appropriate law enforcement agency.

How much cooperation to offer police in conducting searches is largely dependent on whether a search warrant has been issued. In the absence of a search warrant, you should only provide the police with information about the guest's automobile registration. A search warrant should be produced before you release folio information (telephone call information, room charges, etc.) or allow access to

Exhibit 8.6 Indicators of Criminal Activity

1. Guests checking in without prior reservations, paying cash and extending the length of their stay on a day-to-day basis. Guests who check out prematurely or at an unusual time of the day or night.
2. Guests visiting from cities considered to be "source" cities—Los Angeles, Miami, San Diego, and Orlando, and others—who exhibit one or more of the other indicators listed below.
3. Guests from foreign countries whose luggage and/or personal effects are not consistent with their length of travel or stay.
4. Guests displaying large amounts of U.S. currency. These individuals will generally pay cash for their lodging, meals, and expenses on a day-to-day basis.
5. Guests whose general appearance does not fit with their clothing or general attire—i.e., seedy in appearance and yet wearing expensive clothing or jewelry.
6. Several guests checking into different rooms, requesting different floors, and later meeting in one room with excessive communication between the rooms.
7. Unusual foot traffic to and from a guest's room. The guests have late-night visitors and a high volume of telephone communication.
8. Drug-related paraphernalia found in a guest's room. Examples include plastic baggies, scales, rubber bands, money wrappers, empty luggage, large amounts of currency, etc.
9. Guests who exhibit unusual behavior such as never leaving the room, constant use of the "Do Not Disturb" sign, refusal of cleaning services, etc.
10. Unusual alteration of room furnishings or tampering with room fixtures.
11. Guests who use pay telephones instead of the telephones in their rooms.
12. Guests whose registration information does not fit the driver's license and other identification they carry or whose registration information is scant or vague.
13. Packages containing white or brown powder substances. Any unusual chemical odors.
14. Evidence that a guest may have a firearm—loose ammunition cartridges, empty handgun holsters, empty ammunition containers, etc.

Source: U.S. Justice Department.

guestrooms. However, if police are in "hot pursuit," there is no need for them to present a warrant for room entry.

How do you know if guests are dealing in drugs? The U.S. Department of Justice suggests 14 potential indicators of criminal activity (see Exhibit 8.6). If you or any of your employees observe any of the indicators listed in the exhibit, you should report them to your superiors immediately.

Unions

Employee unions have recently been successful in organizing large hospitality properties located in large metropolitan areas. While the lodging and food service industry is labor-intensive, its employees are spread among thousands of operations throughout the country. Traditionally, **labor unions** have not organized small, scattered properties because it's not economically feasible.

While it may appear that this section is applicable only to supervisors now working in unionized properties, this is not necessarily true. First, your career may take you to a unionized property. Second, many of the principles discussed in this section can be useful in dealing with all employees, not just those who are members of a union.

Employees who join unions usually have several reasons, including:

- *Inattentive management.* Employees usually turn to unions because their managers are not responding consistently to employee issues and concerns.

- *Increased bargaining power.* Individual employees believe they have little power in an organization. Often, they think their only bargaining tool is threatening to quit. Unions present an opportunity for employees to make demands as a group.

- *Desire for self-expression through a third party.* Unions allow employees to communicate their concerns, feelings, and complaints to management through an organized structure. Many employees think a third party will represent them more fairly than the employee can.

- *Minimizing favoritism.* With union bargaining agreements, fewer management decisions are based on personal relationships. Treatment based on seniority as a top priority is a common practice of employee unions.

- *Social reasons.* Employees are influenced by the attitudes and behaviors of their peers. They associate with persons they like and the desire to "go along with the crowd" becomes important.

- *Problems with advancement opportunities.* If employees believe they cannot receive reasonable pay increases, better jobs, and greater professional status, they often turn to employee unions for assistance.

Most hospitality employees do not belong to unions. There may be other reasons for this besides the fact that existing unions do not try to organize small properties with relatively few employees. Employees may distrust unions because of past experiences, because they want to control their own destinies, or because of perceptions that unions encourage lower productivity. Some employees want to represent their own interests to management—they would rather work things out by themselves. Other employees, especially those aspiring to management positions, identify with management. Even though employees are protected by various laws, some employees may be anti-union out of fear that they will be punished if they join a union.

Structure of Unions

There are approximately 280 national and international unions and 46,000 locals in the United States.[9] A local is a union's basic unit of organization. For example, a union local may represent all of the carpenters or electricians in a city, or it may represent only union members within a specific property—this is the case prevalent in the hospitality industry.

Most unions have a president. Normally, the union president has a regular job at the property, is paid by the employer, and uses some time from the job—in addition to personal time—for completing union duties. Typically, union stewards are elected in each department to represent the employees of that department. Unions carry out contract negotiations, build memberships, charge dues, administer grievances, manage the union bargaining agreement, and conduct strikes or other work actions when necessary.

Impact of Unions on Management

Once a union represents hospitality employees, management's options in dealing with individual employees are altered. Managers no longer can make one-sided decisions or deal individually with employees. They must closely follow all requirements imposed by the union bargaining agreement. Regardless of an employee's skill or ability, managers must give equal treatment to employees in the same job classification. Seniority becomes the most important determinant of management actions regarding promotions, schedule preferences, and other personnel decisions.

Collective Bargaining

Collective bargaining involves (1) negotiations between employers and unions when union contracts are up for renewal, and (2) day-to-day negotiations between employees and unions over routine situations or problems. Most union contracts in the hospitality industry involve a single property dealing with a single union. A single hospitality operation also may have separate bargaining agreements with a number of different unions. For example, a large urban hotel may have agreements with ten or more separate employee unions.

Union agreements or contracts are typically negotiated for three or more years. Preparing for contract bargaining is difficult and time-consuming. Managers must gather information about wage rates, fringe benefit practices, and the firm's current financial position. Analysis of the current contract's provisions and speculation about new union demands also must be addressed. Management and union representatives meet during negotiations, bargain in good faith, reach decisions, and write down what they agree to. While there are many topics that might be negotiated, Exhibit 8.7 lists those typically covered in union bargaining agreements.

Union Organizing Campaigns

As a supervisor, you can have an impact on whether your employees want to join a union. This section reviews actions you can and cannot take during a union organizing campaign. Your property will need competent legal advice when it faces possible unionization; the following section presents general guidelines only.

Management Do's and Don'ts. There are many actions you can take to affect the outcome of a union organizing campaign. All employees should be encouraged to vote, for example. In many cases union advocates could be out-voted if the "apathetic majority" that opposes unions took the time to vote. Under the direction of higher-level managers, you can also:

- Inform your employees of employee benefits that equal or exceed industry averages.
- Relate management's past successes in dealing with employee grievances.

Exhibit 8.7 Topics Typically Covered in Union Bargaining Agreements

1. Union recognition
2. Union security
3. Management security
4. Wages and benefits
5. Strikes and lockouts
6. Duration of agreement
7. Union dues procedures
8. Union representation
9. Duties and responsibilities of stewards
10. Grievance procedures
11. Seniority rights
12. Probationary periods
13. Promotions and job openings
14. Leaves of absence, vacations, and sick leave
15. Discipline and discharge procedures
16. Hours of work, scheduling, and overtime
17. Prohibition of discrimination
18. Safety concerns
19. Meals, uniforms, and dressing rooms
20. General provisions—breaks, layoffs, posting of jobs, etc.

- Indicate how management has developed and improved benefits and working conditions.

- Inform employees about management policies that favor them.

- Publicize details about the union that your employees may not be aware of.

- Describe disadvantages of union membership.

- Explain that, even if the union wins the election, it still must bargain with management. In other words, union organizers may not be able to deliver on all they promise.

- Remind employees that all sides lose when there is a strike.

- Tell employees that they do not need to vote for the union even if they have signed a union authorization card to hold the election.

- Point out statements made by the union that management feels are untrue.

There are actions that by law you cannot take during a unionizing campaign:

- You cannot promise benefits to employees who vote against the union and cannot make any type of threat (a layoff, for example) to employees who vote for the union.

- You cannot withhold benefits from union organizers.

- You cannot discriminate against employees because of their pro-union activities, including subjecting pro-union employees to unfair working conditions to which other employees are not subjected.

- You cannot attend union organizing meetings or attempt to secretly determine which employees are participating.

- You cannot grant unscheduled wage increases, special benefits, or concessions to employees during the pre-election period.

- You cannot keep employees from wearing union buttons unless the buttons are extremely large or are considered in poor taste.

- You cannot stop union organizers from soliciting employee membership during their *non-working* hours as long as they do not interfere with the work of other employees.

- You cannot hold private meetings with employees to discuss unions or the upcoming election. You also cannot question employees about their union activities.

- You cannot ask employees about how they intend to vote.

- You cannot meet with employees within 24 hours of the election.

- You cannot refuse to recognize the union if it's chosen to represent the employees.

Working with the Union

As mentioned earlier, once hospitality employees have unionized, the relationship between you and your employees will change. You must continue treating all employees fairly and consistently, but you will likely find that some of your authority has been eroded. You must comply with all contract provisions, even those you don't agree with or particularly like. Most important, you cannot discriminate against employees who join the union (see Exhibit 8.8).

Perhaps the most frustrating change will be that you no longer will deal directly with your employees on matters covered by the union contract. Instead, your employees' union steward acts as an intermediary. Therefore, the relationship between you and the steward is very important.

Stewards and Supervisors. You and the steward are in unique positions within a hospitality operation. Both of you rank between employees and higher management. As a supervisor, you have to represent management to your employees and represent your employees to management. In the same way, the steward represents higher union officials to employees and vice versa. In these positions, you and the steward share similar types of pressures and experience similar conflicts of loyalty at times. Therefore, you should try to look on the union steward as someone who is

Exhibit 8.8 After Unionization

There are many laws that prevent discrimination against unions and their members. Some restrictions that apply to supervisors include:

1. You cannot interfere with, restrain, or coerce employees from exercising their right to participate in union activities.

2. You cannot fire, demote, or discipline employees solely because of union activities.

3. You cannot refuse to hire employees because of pro-union sentiments.

4. Special benefits cannot be given to employees who do, or do not, participate in the union.

5. You cannot interfere with the management of the union.

6. There are limits on the degree to which you can participate in employees' union activities. Generally, the lower the organizational level, the greater the amount of union activity which is permitted.

7. You cannot transfer or lay off employees for anti-union reasons nor can you refuse to reinstate employees after strikes if they otherwise are eligible to be rehired.

8. You cannot fire or discriminate against employees who file grievances or testify in any union proceedings.

9. You cannot refuse to bargain with union representatives if you are part of management's bargaining team.

10. You cannot refuse to provide the union with information it needs to bargain intelligently.

11. In cases where there is more than one union at your property, you cannot show favoritism, link benefits to membership in a union that is sanctioned by the employer, or give financial aid to any union.

12. You should consider any anti-union activity by you or any of your employees to be a violation of the law.

in a tough position, just as you are, and try to work together rather than making him/her the enemy. You both have the responsibility to understand, interpret, and enforce the union contract while protecting management and employee rights. This can be accomplished much easier with less possibility of frustration, misunderstandings, and anger if you can establish and maintain a good working relationship with the steward.

Grievances. If the steward agrees, an employee may file a formal grievance when he/she is not satisfied with the way you have resolved a complaint. While a different grievance process is outlined in every union contract, certain components of the process are typical.

In most grievance procedures, you first meet with the steward and employee in an attempt to resolve the problem. If you can't resolve it, your boss or another manager may meet with the union's grievance committee to reach an agreement. If unsuccessful, top managers meet with the grievance committee to search for a solution. If necessary, top management can discuss the problem with high-level representatives at the union's national or international offices. If resolution is impossible at this level, the matter then goes to **mediation** or **arbitration**. With mediation, the two sides sit down with an unbiased third party—a mediator—who reviews the dispute and gives advice on how to resolve it. The parties involved in the dispute do not have to take this advice. Arbitration involves sitting down with an unbiased third party—an arbitrator—who reviews the dispute and makes whatever decisions he/she believes are necessary to resolve it. The parties in dispute must then abide by those decisions.

As you can see, an employee complaint can develop into a serious grievance that can take great amounts of time and money to resolve. It's in the best interests of you and your company to resolve employee complaints before they become grievances that must be handled according to provisions of the union contract.

Management Rights. Management rights may be limited to those that are expressly included in the union contract.[10] A list of basic rights that management must protect includes the rights to schedule and allocate overtime; to establish, change, and enforce work rules, policies, and procedures; to discipline and fire employees; to develop or change work schedules as needed; to adjust or change job tasks; to increase workloads of staff members when necessary; and to have jobs performed by employees that management believes are qualified.

Other management rights that should be protected include the rights to assess employee eligibility for merit increases and job promotions, to require tests for employment, to set work standards, and to close down departments or the entire property if a strike occurs.

Management rights should belong to and be retained by supervisors. Unfortunately, these basic rights can be jeopardized during contract negotiations or day-to-day bargaining. Practices that can diminish these rights include careless wording of contracts and failure to understand the implications of contract wording.

Endnotes

1. Readers desiring more information about hospitality law are referred to Jack P. Jefferies, *Understanding Hospitality Law,* 3d ed. (East Lansing, Mich.: Educational Institute of the American Hotel & Motel Association, 1995).

2. Details about employee selection, including legal aspects, are included in David Wheelhouse, *Managing Human Resources in the Hospitality Industry* (East Lansing, Mich.: Educational Institute of the American Hotel & Motel Association, 1989).

3. "Will the Disability Law Impact YOU?" *Lodging,* September 1990, page 11.

4. EEOC Guidelines on Discrimination Because of Sex. 29 C.F.R. Section 1604.11. Sexual harassment.

5. Readers desiring further information about legal aspects of personnel management are referred to Wheelhouse, *Managing Human Resources.*

6. Additional information about hospitality security is found in Raymond C. Ellis, Jr. and the Security Committee of AH&MA, *Security and Loss Prevention Management* (East Lansing, Mich.: Educational Institute of the American Hotel & Motel Association, 1986), and Jefferies, *Understanding Hospitality Law.*

7. Additional information about risk management is found in John Tarras, *Reducing Liability Costs in the Lodging Industry: A Planned Approach to Risk Management* (East Lansing, Mich.: Educational Institute of the American Hotel & Motel Association, 1986).

8. Some of the information in the following section is taken from Daniel T. Davis and Jack Ninemeier, *Controlling Drug Abuse: A Handbook for Managers* (East Lansing, Mich.: Educational Institute of the American Hotel & Motel Association, 1987).

9. U.S. Department of Labor, Office of Labor Management Standards. Washington, D.C., 1989.

10. This discussion is based on Herbert K. Witzky, *The Labor-Management Relations Handbook for Hotels, Motels, Restaurants and Institutions* (Boston: CBI, 1975), pp. 236–238.

Key Terms

arbitration

bona fide occupational qualifications (BFOQ)

discrimination

ethics

Heimlich maneuver

labor union

mediation

Occupational Safety and Health Administration (OSHA)

risk management

sexual harassment

substance abuse

Title VII

Discussion Questions

1. What are some strategies that supervisors can use to combat the labor shortage of the 1990s?

2. How do equal opportunity laws affect a hospitality organization?

3. What is sexual harassment?

4. What is the supervisor's role in safety and security programs?

5. A multi-cultural work force presents what kinds of challenges to supervisors?

6. What are some signs that an employee is abusing drugs?

7. What is the best way to confront an employee you suspect is abusing drugs?

8. Why do employees join unions?

9. What are some management do's and don'ts in a union organizing campaign?

10. What is the difference between mediation and arbitration?

REVIEW QUIZ

When you feel you have covered all of the material in this chapter, answer these questions. Choose the *best* answer. Check your answers with the correct ones found on the Review Quiz Answer Key at the end of this book.

True (T) or False (F)

T F 1. To combat the labor shortage, your property will need to consider applicants that you might not have considered ten years ago.

T F 2. Discrimination includes practices where discrimination may not have been intended, such as supervisors allowing employees to tell ethnic or racial jokes.

T F 3. Widely varying differences in general standards of dress are allowed men and women in the work place without the possibility of discriminatory implications.

T F 4. Displaying pornographic photographs would not be interpreted as sexual harassment under the law.

T F 5. CPR and the Heimlich maneuver are first aid techniques that you and your employees should be trained in.

T F 6. Safety is simply a set of rules and procedures that everyone must learn and follow.

T F 7. It's important to remember that drug abuse is usually limited to low-paid, entry-level employees.

T F 8. If police are in "hot pursuit," there is no need for them to present a search warrant for room entry.

T F 9. Generally, individual employees believe they have little power in an organization.

T F 10. Once hospitality employees have unionized, the relationship between supervisor and the employees will go back to normal.

Alternative/Multiple Choice

11. The federal agency responsible for developing and managing regulations and standards for employee safety and health in the workplace is called:

    a. the EEOC.
    b. OSHA.

12. If employees see guests who may be abusing or selling drugs, they should immediately:

    a. call the police.
    b. notify their supervisor.

13. When two sides sit down with an unbiased third party who reviews the dispute and gives advice, it is called:

    a. mediation.
    b. arbitration.

14. Treatment based on _____ is not discriminatory by nature.

    a. race
    b. sex
    c. individuality
    d. religion

15. Your employees are an important part of your organization's security team. The text suggests that you train your employees to:

    a. report suspicious activities.
    b. confront suspicious individuals.
    c. appropriate what appears to be drug paraphernalia.
    d. keep security information out of the hands of guests so they won't be frightened.

Part III

Supervisory Tools

Chapter Outline

Formal Work Groups
    Types of Formal Work Groups
    Communication Between Formal
        Work Groups
Informal Groups
    Types of Informal Groups
    Communication Between Informal
        Groups
Stages of Team Development
The Supervisor as Team Leader
    Roles Individuals Play in Groups
Managing Effective Meetings

Learning Objectives

1. Describe how formal work groups are organized in a hospitality organization.

2. Explain how the flow of information between formal work groups differs from the flow of information between informal groups.

3. Describe what a supervisor can do in response to rumors circulating in the organization.

4. Identify the stages through which members of a group become an effective team.

5. Describe important roles that supervisors play as team leaders.

6. Identify positive and negative roles that individuals play as members of a group.

7. Explain how a supervisor can use an agenda to plan and conduct an effective meeting.

8. Identify techniques supervisors can use at meetings to draw out silent members of the group.

9. Identify techniques supervisors can use at meetings to stop disruptive side conversations.

10. Describe situations that may arise during a meeting which indicate that the supervisor should stop the group's discussion.

9

Building an Effective Team

In order to prepare the products and provide the services desired by guests, employees in hospitality operations must work together as a team. The role of the supervisor is to build the employees within a specific work section into productive members of a team. Therefore, knowing about the various types of groups and how they function within a hospitality organization will enable you to fulfill your important role as a team leader.

This chapter identifies some of the formal and informal groups within hospitality operations. The supervisor's role of ensuring effective communications within these different types of groups is described in detail.

However, building a group of employees into a productive team involves more than establishing effective communications. An important section of this chapter looks at how groups develop into productive teams. Specific stages of a team's development are examined in the context of a hospitality operation. Knowing how a group evolves into a team allows you, the team leader, to establish the right atmosphere and develop appropriate strategies which will encourage the growth of individuals as productive team members.

In addition to leading a group of employees in a specific work section, a supervisor often functions as a member of a larger team—a group of supervisors in a specific department or division within the hospitality organization. Therefore, it becomes doubly important that you, as supervisor, learn the positive and negative roles that individuals play when in a group—whether it is your employee work group or the management group. This knowledge will help you to better lead the employees under your supervision, and at the same time enable you to function more productively as a member of the management team. A final section describes in detail how you can plan and conduct successful meetings.

Formal Work Groups

A hospitality organization is itself made up of a group of employees. At the highest level, all employees of the organization have the same boss: the general manager. However, as work is organized, smaller, formal work groups must be established. Therefore, the organization may be divided into divisions such as rooms, food and beverage, engineering, sales, etc.

In many organizations, divisions are too large and unwieldy for one person to manage effectively. A further subdivision into departments is necessary. For example, a food and beverage division might be divided into food, beverage, and banquet departments. The rooms division might be divided into such departments as front office, housekeeping, and laundry.

Exhibit 9.1 The Supervisor and Command Groups

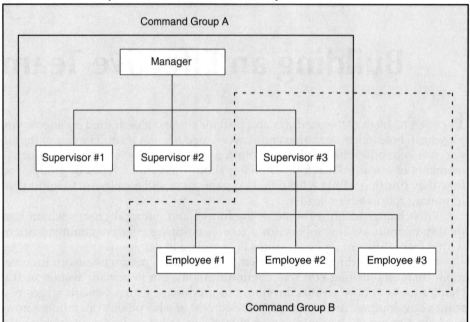

Departments can be further divided into work sections. For example, specific floors of a hotel may be divided into work sections of the housekeeping department. Or specific areas of a kitchen (such as the pantry, bake shop, etc.) may be designated as work sections of the food department.

Divisions, departments, and work sections are examples of formal work groups. Each has a formal manager or supervisor who coordinates, directs, and controls the work of the group.

Types of Formal Work Groups

The most common type of formal work group is a **command group,** which may include a manager, supervisors, and employees. Depending upon the level in the organization, a supervisor directs the work of some employees and, at the same time, reports to a manager. Managers and supervisors are generally members of at least two command groups.

Exhibit 9.1 diagrams how a supervisor (Supervisor #3) serves as a "linking pin" between Command Group A and Command Group B. The supervisor is the primary channel through which communication flows between the two command groups.

A second type of formal organizational group is called a **task group.** This type of group works on essentially non-routine tasks. A special committee, formed to address a specific situation or problem, is an example of a task group. Activities of a task group might involve creating a new menu or developing performance standards for positions in a department. Once their work is done, task groups normally disband. Command groups, on the other hand, are permanent formal work groups in the organization.

Communication Between Formal Work Groups

Every hospitality organization establishes a formal means of communication between work groups. The routing of information is often mapped by the "chain of command" diagrammed by the organization chart. For example, policies, rules, and regulations are developed at the higher levels of the organization (ideally, with input from affected managers, supervisors, and employees). This type of information is then sent down the organization to middle and lower levels. Information generated at lower levels of the organization includes records, attitudes toward policies and procedures, and ideas to improve the organization. This type of information moves up to supervisors and managers, who, in turn, communicate it to the higher levels of the organization. Much of the formal communication between work groups takes the form of memos, letters, reports, presentations, meetings, and personal conversations.

Hospitality organizations also establish a formal means of communication across divisions and departments. The managers of divisions may meet regularly as an executive committee to discuss issues of importance to all areas of the operation. Similarly, a department manager or supervisor may meet with counterparts in other departments to resolve common problems.

Informal Groups

Informal groups develop for many different reasons. When individuals have common interests, backgrounds, and experiences and work in close proximity with one another, an informal group is bound to develop. Exhibit 9.2 diagrams how employees can be members of formal and informal groups at the same time. The informal group marked with the dotted line is made up of members from four different formal work sections. The informal group marked with the solid line has members from three separate formal groups. It is also common for several members in a large formal work group to form an informal group within the same work section.

Informal groups are not, by definition, "good" or "bad." They might help or hinder the efforts of a department, division, or organization to achieve its goals. Depending on the situation, informal groups might support or oppose management actions. As a supervisor, your job is to create a climate in which members of informal groups work with you, not against you.

There are some common sense techniques you can use to identify informal employee groups. You can gather information from casual conversations with employees in your own department. You may be able to learn which employees spend time together off the job. Observe interactions in the employee dining area, and note those employees who consistently take breaks with each other. By interacting with employees and supervisors from other departments, you may be able to identify the employees in your area who are members of informal groups

Exhibit 9.2 Overlap of Formal and Informal Groups

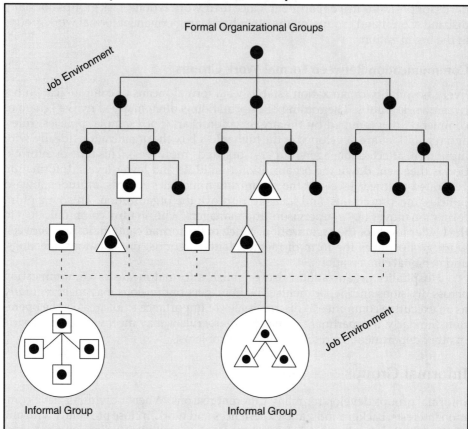

that extend to other areas in the organization. When gathering information about informal groups, make sure you don't give others the impression that you are "snooping" or "spying." Such an impression creates an atmosphere of distrust, and may severely reduce your effectiveness as supervisor in achieving goals set by the formal work group in the organization.

Every group has a leader who influences the behavior of members of the group. As a supervisor, you are the leader of a formal work group. Informal groups also have leaders. Find out who they are, and, if possible, establish a relationship of mutual trust and respect. You may be able to enlist their support on issues and activities that directly relate to the goals of the formal work group. Informal leaders are the ones who often set the work pace and also influence the work atmosphere. They're the employees whom co-workers go to with their personal and professional problems. Informal leaders communicate easily with employees at all levels of the organization. They're not necessarily the employees with the most experience, but they have earned the respect of others.

A supervisor can identify informal employee groups by observing interactions in the employee dining area and noting those employees who consistently eat with each other.

Types of Informal Groups

Informal groups are not as easily identified as are formal groups. Formal work groups exist to achieve the goals set by owners and top executives of the hospitality organization. Each group can be categorized in relation to the particular function it carries out in the attainment of the organization's goals. Informal groups, on the other hand, exist to achieve goals set by their own members. Each informal group may have its own unique set of goals. These goals may have little in common with the goals of other informal groups, or with the goals of the organization. For example, the goals of informal groups may be simply to socialize or to pursue common interests.

A potentially harmful type of informal group is a **clique.** A clique consists of two or more members of a formal group who have established their own set of goals which they view as more important than the goals of the formal group. While many informal groups are loosely structured, a clique is closely knit and often isolates itself from members of the formal group and from members of other informal groups as well. Cliques can be found in supervisory ranks as well as in employee groups.

As a supervisor, you cannot ignore a clique. Also, you may not be able to break up a clique. You can, however, provide opportunities for members of a clique to work more closely with other individuals in the work group. In addition, you can assign members of a clique to work together solving specific problems in the department. This strategy offers the clique a learning experience and may show its members that achieving the goals of the department can be a source of satisfaction.

Communication Between Informal Groups

As pointed out earlier, formal work groups often communicate with one another through a very structured process. Information passes up and down the organization through the chain of command. The flow of information is patterned and predictable because the organization is structured around a well-defined set of goals.

Since the goals of informal groups vary tremendously, there is no easily observed flow of information that is consistent among informal groups in the work environment. Information does not pass from group to group in a straight line; it twists and turns like a grapevine. Although seemingly without a pattern or design, the **grapevine** can spread information as fast as wildfire spreads through a forest. While it may take several days to communicate a directive from the general manager to employees, it may take only a few hours for everyone in the organization to learn who was fired that morning or where the party is that night.

To perform effectively as a supervisor, you need to recognize that a grapevine exists, and, when appropriate, use it to attain the goals of your department. You need to be connected with the grapevine because some of the information that passes along it may be incomplete or inaccurate. In some of these cases, you may be able to avoid later trouble by immediately clarifying issues and addressing concerns employees may have. Some of the information passed along the grapevine may be false or even deliberately misleading. In these cases, the grapevine has turned into a **rumor mill.**

A rumor is information that is not based on fact. It passes through informal communication channels. Rumors are often "gossip"—statements or stories which are not confirmed. When you hear a rumor, ask yourself the following questions:

*   Why is this person giving me this information?
*   Could the person have something to gain by telling me something that may not be true?
*   Does the person passing this information have direct access to the subject of the rumor?
*   How can I confirm this information?

You may or may not wish to take steps to confirm the rumor, but you should confront the person passing information to you. Ask the person directly how he/she obtained the information and why he/she is passing it on to you. Above all, do not participate in the rumor mill by passing this type of information on to others. If appropriate, alert your boss to the rumor, and discuss ways to address the issues which the rumor raises. If appropriate, you may wish to inform the person who is the subject of the rumor.

Stages of Team Development

As a supervisor, your job is to build the members of your formal work group into a productive team. Knowing how groups develop into teams will enable you to select the appropriate techniques to lead employees toward greater productivity and job satisfaction.

Members of a group typically pass through a number of stages as they develop into a team. These stages are:

1. Membership
2. Individual influence
3. Shared feelings
4. Respect for individual differences
5. Productive teamwork

These developmental stages can be identified by the kinds of questions that members often ask themselves about their relationship to the group. The following sections examine each stage in detail.

Membership. Individuals who are new to a work group generally pass through a membership stage during orientation and the first few days on the job. Although new members of the staff may want to become part of the work group, they rarely function as productive members until some of their initial concerns are addressed. These individuals are likely to have these concerns:

- How will I benefit from membership in the group? What can I contribute in order to be accepted?

- What will my supervisor and co-workers expect from me? What are my expectations of them?

- How will I find out what is really important to the group? What are the group's goals? Are they in line with mine?

- Will I find that being a member of the group is boring or exciting? threatening or rewarding?

- Is this a career or just another job?

On the other hand, existing members may have questions about a new member of the group. These questions or concerns often need to be resolved before the new member becomes accepted by the group. Existing group members are likely to have these concerns:

- Can I trust this person?

- Can I work effectively with this person?

- Will this person become a cooperative team player?

If there is high turnover in the department, new members will always represent a significant percentage of the work group. This can seriously slow the development of the work group into a productive team. Every effort should be made to address the concerns of new staff members. Supervisors who are caught up in the pressures of day-to-day operations may unintentionally overlook the very basic concerns of new employees. You can address many of these concerns by clearly communicating what you expect from the new employee in terms of compliance with company policies and progress in training sessions.

Individual Influence. After new employees understand what it means to be members of the work group, they begin to think about how they and others influence the way things get done in the department. For example, they may ask themselves such questions as:

- Who has the most power to influence people in this department? Who are the strong formal and informal leaders?

- How are others in the work group influencing me? Who am I learning from?

- How are others in the work group influencing each other? Is there really a team effort?

- What opportunities are there for me to influence others in the work group? Can I become an informal leader?

These are typical concerns that individuals have during the first few weeks on the job. Supervisors can address these concerns by interacting with the employee in ongoing training and coaching sessions. You can also create situations in which the employee interacts with the informal leaders who foster cooperation and teamwork within the department.

Shared Feelings. When individuals become comfortable with one another as members of the work group, the feelings of the members become more and more important. Concerns that individuals may have include:

- Can I freely express my feelings in this work group? Will the other members accept constructive criticism? Is the work atmosphere open and honest?

- When I'm under stress, frustrated, or angry, can I work things out with the group?

- When members criticize ideas or express negative feelings, do others see it as honest feedback that can help produce better results, or do they see it as a clash of personalities?

- When members agree with others or express positive feelings, do others see it as honest feedback that can help produce better results, or do they see it as insincere patronizing?

This is a critical stage in the development of the work group as a team. When feelings are properly addressed, members will value what they have in common. This bond of shared feelings is the basis for members to develop respect for individual differences.

Respect for Individual Differences. If enough trust develops within the work group during the stage of shared feelings, the group will become even more successful as members feel free to contribute their unique abilities and talents. During this stage, members come to value their differences more than their similarities. The focus of each member switches from individual to group concerns. Members are more likely to phrase their concerns in terms of the full group. The word "we" begins to replace "I." A new set of questions becomes important:

- Do we take the time and effort to learn about the knowledge, experience, feelings, and attitudes of one another?

- In sharing ideas, do we look forward to the reactions of others and value their feedback?

- Do we let others know that we appreciate their opinions and comments, even when we don't necessarily agree with them? Do we provide positive reinforcement even if we don't completely agree?

A good way of looking at this stage of development is to see the group as eager for a conflict of ideas—not for a conflict of personalities. Personality conflicts can be avoided if members are able to speak freely and see criticism as honest feedback.

Productive Teamwork. As the work group begins to value the individual differences among its members, the group becomes a productive and creative team. Members know they can learn from one another and they take advantage of opportunities to grow personally and professionally. At this stage, members are likely to express the following concerns:

- Are we spending our time looking for the causes of problems, or are we just complaining about problems and talking them to death? Are we using our time wisely as a team?

- When we identify problems, do we follow a process that analyzes them thoroughly, or do we jump at the first solution that comes along? Do we plan together?

- Do we take the time and effort to seek the ideas, opinions, and reactions of those affected by the problem we are trying to solve? Do we have a genuine concern for the welfare of others?

The Supervisor as Team Leader

Supervisors must be able to recognize the stages of their own work group's development into a team, and create the conditions for further growth by making sure to address the concerns of individuals. As the team leader, the supervisor must direct the efforts of the group without dominating meetings, smothering the individual initiative, or stunting the growth and development of the team. Several important roles that supervisors play as team leaders include the:

- Morale builder
- Conciliator
- Compromiser
- Standard setter

The supervisor acts as a morale builder by encouraging individuals to contribute toward the department's goals, creating a receptive atmosphere for new points

Exhibit 9.3 Team Leader Self-Evaluation Form

Think about your leadership experiences and rate yourself on each of the following skills or qualities. Evaluate your strengths and weaknesses as honestly as you can and chart your progress as a team leader. Use the following rating scale:

1 = Strong; 2 = Good; 3 = Unsure; 4 = Weak; 5 = Poor.

1. I can give a concise, clear description of the goals of my department.
2. When speaking before a group, I can project my voice and display enthusiasm.
3. While listening to a speaker, I am able to observe other people's behavior.
4. I am able to understand both spoken messages and non-verbal gestures.
5. I am able to ask open-ended questions which encourage others to share their ideas, feelings, or interests.
6. I can use effective openers to generate a lively group discussion.
7. I can focus a group's discussion by discriminating between significant and irrelevant information and comments.
8. I can re-state or clarify another person's ideas.
9. I can take an unexpected incident or event and use it to teach a concept.
10. I am able to give constructive pointers to individuals in a non-judgmental manner.
11. When working with a group, I can share my own feelings about the topic under discussion.
12. I am able to elicit participation from most people in a group.
13. I have a sense of timing for pacing discussions and planning activities.
14. I can accept anger or criticism from a person or a group without becoming defensive.
15. I am able to help others comfortably display their emotions or relate their feelings.
16. I have a sense of humor and can laugh at myself.

Source: Stephen J. Shriver, *Managing Quality Services* (East Lansing, Mich.: Educational Institute of the American Hotel & Motel Association, 1988), p. 218.

of view, and providing positive reinforcement for team members. As a conciliator, the supervisor recognizes differences of opinion, and tries to anticipate conflicts and relieve tensions by stressing common goals and the togetherness of the team. When acting as the compromiser, the supervisor reconciles conflicting views (even if it means modifying his/her own opinions), and seeks middle ground in the interests of team harmony. As a standard setter, the supervisor sets the example for others by treating employees fairly and maintaining reasonable, yet high, expectations for the team.

Exhibit 9.3 presents a team leader self-evaluation form. By honestly responding to each item on the form, you can assess your potential effectiveness as a team leader and identify areas for improvement. A score between 16 and 22 indicates strong leadership potential.

The stages of team development apply to all kinds of groups (both formal and informal) in hospitality operations. This section has focused on the employee work group under your supervision. As a supervisor, however, you may belong to a number of other groups. For example, a group of supervisors may meet regularly to discuss common problems and concerns. Before that group can function as a productive team, members will have to share feelings and develop a respect for individual differences. In order to lead a productive work team or to participate as a productive member of a supervisory team, you need to recognize the positive and negative roles that individuals may play in groups.

Roles Individuals Play in Groups

Supervisors need to recognize and encourage the positive roles individuals play in groups. When individuals play positive roles, their behavior advances the development of a group and increases its productivity. Exhibit 9.4 defines three dominant characteristics of six roles individuals may play. Also given are typical comments these individuals make when performing positively within a group. The identified roles are not necessarily personality types. One individual could play several different roles during a single group meeting. Supervisors should, of course, be alert to these positive roles and recognize when to adopt them to keep their work groups productive and on the right track.

Exhibit 9.5 presents five negative roles that individuals may play in group situations. When individuals play negative roles, their behavior hinders the development of the group and decreases the group's productivity. Supervisors must work to minimize the effect of these negative roles on the progress of the work group.

In some cases, the supervisor may wish to counsel some members individually and encourage them to adopt more positive roles. This can be done by explaining to individuals how their negative roles disrupt the group's productivity. You may also find it helpful to offer suggestions about how individuals could become more positive contributors to the group.

In other cases, you may wish to directly respond to the negative role played by an individual. For example, an individual may attempt to dominate the group with a comment such as, "Now, I've had a lot more experience at this sort of thing, so let me tell you what to do." You might respond by saying, "I appreciate your experience, but I want to hear some of the good ideas others in the group may have as well."

Managing Effective Meetings

As a supervisor you will participate in a number of different types of meetings. You may also be responsible for planning and conducting meetings in order to:

- Pass information on to employees in your department
- Explain a new department or company policy
- Obtain input from others about a problem or situation

The basic principles of successful meetings are similar regardless of whether your purpose is to be a productive participant or to be an effective organizer and leader.

Determine the Meeting's Objectives. For any meeting, proper planning is an absolute necessity. The first step in planning a meeting is to determine if a meeting is

Exhibit 9.4 Positive Roles Individuals Play in Groups

The Inquirer

1. Is concerned with the basics of reasoning.
2. Focuses the group's attention on the facts of a situation.
3. Encourages the group to interpret the facts in different ways.

Typical Comments:

- "Just how many times does this happen?"
- "Does this happen with just certain people or does it apply to everyone in that department?"
- "Does the problem arise because of the worker or because of the work method?"
- "Whose responsibility is this?"

The Contributor

1. Submits factual information.
2. Attempts to build a basis for sound decision-making.
3. Offers considered opinions about facts.

Typical Comments:

- "I think our decision should be based on the figures Denise got from the accounting department."
- "Let's see if we can combine that idea with the feedback we received from the dining room manager."
- "I think that we should listen to the facts and discuss what we should do about this later."
- "Let me give you the feedback I got from maintenance and housekeeping."

The Elaborator

1. Translates generalizations into concrete examples.
2. Builds on the ideas of others.
3. Projects a picture of what might happen if a solution is implemented.

Typical Comments:

- "Let's imagine what it would be like if we tried that idea in my department."
- "What do you think other employees would say about that?"
- "How do you think that would work at the front desk?"
- "How would this affect our guests?"

The Reviewer

1. Summarizes the progress of the group.
2. Clarifies relationships among the ideas that are being discussed.
3. Identifies points that the group agrees upon.

Typical Comments:

- "Let's recap what we've done so far."
- "Let me list the points that we seem to agree on."
- "Matt, let me try to rephrase what you just said and combine it with points that Andrew brought up at the last meeting."
- "So far we have identified five reasons why we need to do this. Let me list them and see if we all agree."

The Evaluator

1. Judges the group's thinking by its own standards.
2. Raises questions about facts and figures.
3. Explores the practical applications of proposed solutions.

Typical Comments:

- "Let's check these figures against the invoices in accounting."
- "Maybe we need a second and third opinion about this problem."
- "There could be another side to this story that we don't know about. We always try to get all of the information."
- "I think that we've tried things like this before and found out that we were on the wrong track."

The Energizer

1. Keeps the group's discussion moving along.
2. Stimulates new ideas that are pertinent to the topic.
3. Prods members to decide on a specific course of action.

Typical Comments:

- "Okay, we get the point, but what about this other idea?"
- "We're just spinning our wheels here. Let's move on to the next idea and come back to this later."
- "Let's wait on this point until we get the feedback we need from housekeeping. What's next?"
- "We've discussed this enough. Let's vote."

Source: Stephen J. Shriver, *Managing Quality Services* (East Lansing, Mich.: Educational Institute of the American Hotel & Motel Association, 1988), pp. 209–210.

really necessary. Meetings cost money. In order to justify holding a meeting, you need to decide exactly what you want the meeting to accomplish. There will likely be only one or two major objectives and, perhaps, a few secondary ones as well. If these objectives cannot be accomplished without a meeting, the next step is to develop an agenda.

Prepare an Agenda. An **agenda** is your plan for a successful meeting. It should list the meeting's objectives and a time limit for completing each objective. Stating time limits for discussion keeps participants on track and prevents them from pondering unrelated issues.

When preparing an agenda, you should carefully consider the sequence of activities that the group will perform to achieve the meeting's objectives. Generally, the first 20 minutes of a meeting are livelier and more creative than the last 20 minutes. So, if items on the agenda require energy, bright ideas, and clear heads, it may be wise to list them at the top of the agenda. Sometimes, it is effective to save an important item until near the end of the meeting. This may keep participants alert during the first half of the meeting as they gear up for the later activity. Exhibit 9.6 presents a sample format for preparing an agenda.

Exhibit 9.5 Negative Roles Individuals Play in Groups

The Dominator

1. Demands attention and tries to run the show.
2. Constantly interrupts other people.
3. Imposes personal opinions on the group.

Typical Comments:

- "Now, I've had a lot more experience at this sort of thing, so let me tell you what to do."
- "The only way we're going to make progress here is by following up on my idea."
- "Hold everything, I know exactly what to do."
- "You're wasting everyone's time discussing these things; let's just do what I suggested earlier."

The Blocker

1. Is a frustrated dominator.
2. Repeats arguments and refuses to listen to anyone else's reasoning.
3. When ignored by the group, the person becomes stubborn and resists everything the group wants to do.

Typical Comments:

- "None of you really understands what I'm trying to say."
- "We went over that idea at the last meeting and I didn't like it then either."
- "Well, that's my opinion and I think it's better than yours, so listen more carefully to me this time."
- "Why are we voting on this issue? There's a lot more I have to say."

The Cynic

1. Scoffs at the group's progress.
2. Tries to start conflicts and arguments among members of the group.
3. Is always negative.

Typical Comments:

- "I don't care what you do."
- "Do what you want; management won't approve it anyway."
- "You're just wasting your time if you're going to do that."
- "This whole thing is stupid; nobody cares what you guys think anyway."

The Security Seeker

1. Wants sympathy or personal recognition.
2. Always had it worse than anyone else.
3. His or her personal experiences are always more important than anyone else's.

Typical Comments:

- "I wish somebody would have told me what to do when that happened to me."
- "I never know what to do when that happens in my department."
- "The situation is so bad in my department that even this solution won't work."
- "I always have so many things going on, I'll never have time to do that."

The Lobbyist

1. Always plugs pet theories.
2. Is only concerned with problems that involve his or her own department.
3. Will keep talking about his or her own ideas even though the group has decided to do something entirely different.

Typical Comments:

- "I've been pretty open-minded about this, but don't you think we're being unfair to the people in my department?"
- "That's okay if that's what you guys want to do, but I don't think you really understand my idea."
- "That's a good idea you have, but I think you forgot to consider the things that I said last week."
- "I agree with everything you say, but I just can't buy your conclusion."

Source: Stephen J. Shriver, *Managing Quality Services* (East Lansing, Mich.: Educational Institute of the American Hotel & Motel Association, 1988), pp. 211–212.

Exhibit 9.6 Sample Meeting Agenda Format

Meeting Agenda

Meeting Room _____   Date _____

Starting Time _____   Ending Time _____

_____ Meeting Objectives _____   _____ Time _____

Review:

1.

2.

3.

4.

5.

6.

7.

Summary:

Source: Stephen J. Shriver, *Managing Quality Services* (East Lansing, Mich.: Educational Institute of the American Hotel & Motel Association, 1988), p. 224.

Depending on the type of meeting you are planning, you should review the agenda with your boss. During this review, your boss can offer tips and suggestions on how to conduct portions of the meeting, and advise changes in the meeting plan. You are responsible for distributing copies of the final version of the agenda to those who will be attending the meeting. This should be done early enough so that attendees are able to schedule the meeting in relation to their other responsibilities. Adequate notice is also necessary to ensure that attendees can properly prepare for the meeting and/or assign alternates if they cannot make the meeting themselves.

Again, depending on the meeting's objectives and the issues to be discussed, you may want to test the reactions of probable participants to items on the agenda. This allows you to find out what to expect at the meeting. Note any significant reactions on your copy of the agenda. Before conducting the meeting, review the agenda and make any additional notes on it that will facilitate discussion at the meeting.

Determine Who Should Attend the Meeting. In order to obtain the greatest value from a meeting, you need to carefully analyze the meeting's objectives and identify the best individuals to have present. Meetings can be costly business activities. The cost of a meeting includes not only the wages and salaries of attendees, but also the lost productivity of attendees as they devote the necessary time to preparing and eventually attending the meeting.

Assign a Participant to Record the Meeting Minutes. For some meetings, a record of the events and actions (referred to as **"minutes"**) will need to be taken. Most of the time, you will be too busy conducting the meeting to record the minutes. Assign this responsibility to a participant. Exhibit 9.7 presents a sample format that can be used to record the minutes of a meeting.

The first items listed on the meeting's minutes should be the meeting's objectives. Items listed as events are the discussions held and decisions made at the meeting. Names of individuals generally are not recorded in the events section. Actions are the steps that participants decided to take. Names of individuals may be listed in this section to indicate assignments and responsibilities. Within a few days after the meeting, the minutes should be distributed to all those who attended.

Keep the Meeting on Track. You should conduct a meeting by following the prepared agenda. The only way to start a meeting on time is to *start the meeting on time.* If you wait beyond the scheduled start time for everyone to arrive, all of your meetings will start late. By noting in the meeting's minutes those who arrive late or leave early, you can encourage members to be on time and to participate in the entire meeting. You may need to counsel repeat offenders. During the meeting, your primary responsibility is to accomplish your stated objectives. This is done by ensuring that all participants understand the issues and participate in the discussions.

In order to conduct a productive meeting, you must be able to control those members who wish to do all the talking and monopolize the discussion. You must also be able to draw out the silent members at the meeting. Silence may indicate a participant's hostility, shyness, lack of understanding, or indifference. You need to

Exhibit 9.7 Sample Meeting Minutes Format

Meeting Minutes

Meeting Room _____   Date _____

Starting Time _____   Ending Time _____

Members Present:

Late Arrivals:

Members Absent:

Non-Members Absent:

Objectives:

  1.

  2.

  3.

Events:

  1.

  2.

  3.

Actions:

  1.

  2.

  3.

Source: Stephen J. Shriver, *Managing Quality Services* (East Lansing, Mich.: Educational Institute of the American Hotel & Motel Association, 1988), p. 225.

identify and overcome the motive for a participant's silence. The following effective techniques may help you draw out silent members:

- Re-state the purpose of the group.
- Ask silent members for explanations or elaborations.
- Sit next to a quiet member and act like you are talking to him/her, one-on-one.
- Compliment normally quiet members each time they contribute to a discussion.
- Seek support from other participants.
- Go around the table and ask what each member is thinking about the issue under discussion.

Exhibit 9.8 Managing Special Group Members

What to do when a group member ...	Best Strategy
Wants to argue	Try not to get involved; put ideas "on the table" and allow the group to decide their value
Wants to help	Encourage ideas and ask for out-of-meeting assistance
Wants to discuss details	Recognize points being made but focus on the objective of the meeting and the time which is available
Wants to keep talking	Tactfully interrupt; ask a pointed question to help recall the focus of the discussion
Doesn't want to speak	Ask easy questions; make the group member feel important and give credit when possible
Defends self-interests	Recognize that there may be self-interests, ask for recognition of others' views and ask for a rational discussion of the situation
Is not concerned	Determine if there is any way the discussion is relevant; if not, perhaps the attendee can leave the meeting
Acts superior to others	Ask this individual the most challenging questions and recognize his/her ability
Wants to show "genius" and creativity	Be careful about "trick" questions; ask all group members for input to the discussion

You need to be sensitive to the body language of participants. For example, when two members look at each other and roll their eyes, ask for their opinions.

Some participants may not feel confident enough to fully participate in discussions. For example, young or new employees may hesitate to express their opinions in the presence of older or more experienced employees. Ask new members for their opinions before asking for the opinions of the more experienced employees.

Side conversations at meetings can disrupt the progress of the group. To decrease such disruptions:

- Ask the talkers if they wish to share their conversation with the other participants.

- Discuss their behavior with them after the meeting.

- Casually stand behind them when they are talking with each other.

- Call on them by name and ask them an easy question, or ask them to re-state the last comment and give their opinion.

During discussions, you should encourage members to express widely different ideas. This is the healthiest way to bring about a group decision. Examining the different sides of an issue generally produces the best solution. However, you must moderate the discussion to ensure that the "clash of ideas" does not become a clash of personalities. Exhibit 9.8 presents tips on how to handle problems that may arise

Exhibit 9.9 Checklist for Managing Meetings

Before the Meeting

1. Schedule the meeting.
2. Write an agenda for the meeting.
3. Discuss the agenda with the department manager.
4. Revise the agenda if necessary.
5. Distribute the agenda to attendees before the meeting.
6. Write the agenda on a flip chart sheet to be used at the meeting.
7. Set up the meeting room and secure necessary supplies, such as flip charts, marking pens, visual aids, and handouts.

During the Meeting

1. Assign a member to record the minutes of the meeting.
2. Review the agenda listed on the flip chart.
3. Write the objective of the meeting on the flip chart.
4. Direct discussion and keep participants on track.
5. Ensure full participation of all members.
6. Summarize the meeting's accomplishments.
7. Ensure that members understand their assignments.

After the Meeting

1. Review the meeting's accomplishments with the department manager.
2. Prepare for the next meeting.

during group discussions. Exhibit 9.9 presents a useful checklist for managing effective meetings.

End the Meeting on Time. Sometimes, supervisors fail to stop a discussion soon enough. It is important to stop a group's discussion when:

- The group needs more facts before it can make a decision.

- It is evident that the group must obtain expert opinions or technical advice.

- Participants need time to discuss an issue with co-workers.

- Events occurring outside the meeting will change or clarify the situation under discussion.

- There is not enough time to discuss the topic properly.

- It becomes clear that two or three participants can settle the issue outside the meeting and not waste other members' time.

At the end of the meeting, summarize what the group has accomplished, announce the time and place of the next meeting (if applicable), and remind participants of any tasks you assigned them during the meeting.

Key Terms

agenda
clique
command group
grapevine

meeting minutes
rumor mill
task group

Discussion Questions

1. How does a command group differ from a task group?

2. What are some of the ways that formal work groups communicate with one another?

3. How can a supervisor identify informal groups in a hospitality organization?

4. Why should supervisors try to be part of the informal communication system in the organization?

5. Why is it important for a supervisor to know how members of a group develop into a productive team?

6. What are some of the roles supervisors can play as team leaders?

7. What are some of the positive and negative roles that individuals may play in group situations?

8. How can a supervisor use an agenda to plan and conduct an effective meeting?

9. What are some techniques supervisors can use at meetings to draw out silent members of the group?

10. During the course of a meeting, what should a supervisor look for as signals to stop a group's discussion?

REVIEW QUIZ

When you feel you have covered all of the material in this chapter, answer these questions. Choose the *best* answer. Check your answers with the correct ones found on the Review Quiz Answer Key at the end of this book.

True (T) or False (F)

T   F   1. Divisions, departments, and work sections are examples of formal work groups.

T   F   2. Every hospitality organization establishes an unstructured and informal means of communication between work groups.

T   F   3. A rumor is information that passes through informal communication channels and is based on fact.

T   F   4. Supervisors should always take steps to confirm or deny rumors.

T   F   5. New employees should never consider their own individual influence in the department until at least six months on the job.

T   F   6. Groups become more successful as a unit as members feel free to undermine management's abilities and talents.

T   F   7. As respect for individual differences grows, each member of a group switches from individual to group concerns.

T   F   8. In some cases, the supervisor may wish to counsel negative members individually after a meeting and encourage them to adopt more positive roles.

T   F   9. It is not wise to test the reactions of probable participants to items on the agenda in advance, because it becomes too obvious that it is contrived.

T   F   10. During a meeting, if two members look at one another and roll their eyes, it's best to ignore them because they are troublemakers.

Alternate/Multiple Choice

11. Communication between work groups, which takes the form of memos, letters, reports, presentations, etc., is called:

  a. formal communication.
  b. informal communication.

12. The individual in the group who translates generalizations into concrete examples is called the:

  a. elaborator.
  b. cynic.

13. During the course of a meeting when it becomes evident that expert opinions or technical advice must be obtained, it is time to:

  a. call in some help.
  b. end the meeting.

14. A hospitality organization may be divided into all of the following divisions, *except*:

    a. rooms.
    b. food and beverage.
    c. general management.
    d. engineering.

15. Which of the following would be one of the initial concerns of new work group members?

    a. What can I do to influence this group?
    b. Can I freely express my feelings in this work group?
    c. Is this group really important?
    d. Will being a member of this group be boring or exciting?

Chapter Outline

Get to Know Your Employees
Motivational Strategies
Identifying Motivational Problems
Leadership Styles and Motivation
    Autocratic Leadership
    Bureaucratic Leadership
    Democratic Leadership
    Laissez-Faire Leadership
    Factors Affecting Leadership Styles
Increasing Employee Participation

Learning Objectives

1. Explain why supervisors can't motivate employees.

2. List ways by which supervisors can learn about the needs, interests, and goals of employees.

3. Explain how supervisors can turn basic human resource functions into motivational strategies.

4. Determine when the lack of motivation may be the cause of an employee's poor job performance.

5. Explain how the leadership of a supervisor relates to the motivational level of employees.

6. Describe four leadership styles.

7. Identify factors that affect the leadership style adopted by a supervisor.

8. Explain how supervisors can increase employee participation in department activities.

10

Motivation Through Leadership

Cᴏɴᴛʀᴀʀʏ ᴛᴏ ᴘᴏᴘᴜʟᴀʀ ʙᴇʟɪᴇF, a supervisor cannot motivate employees; employees must motivate themselves. A motive is a condition that is generated within an individual. This condition drives the individual's efforts to achieve a goal. The supervisor's primary strategy should be to provide a work environment in which employees can fulfill their personal needs, interests, and goals while achieving objectives of the department and of the organization.

Leadership is the ability to attain objectives by working with and through people. A leader creates conditions that motivate employees by establishing goals and influencing employees to attain those goals. Your role as a supervisor is to create the conditions that encourage employees to become motivated.

In the not-too-distant past, a supervisor might simply have told an employee what to do. If the work was done, employees and higher-level managers generally considered the supervisor a good leader. Today, however, changes in the workplace and changes in managers' and employees' perceptions of the supervisor's role have made this tactic less useful.

In today's workplace, leadership and supervision imply the need to guide and influence—rather than to order—employees to undertake specific actions. The role of the supervisor is fast becoming that of a facilitator (one who assembles resources and provides guidance) as opposed to the "dictatorial taskmaster" of yesterday. The supervisor who is flexible—able to select a style that is comfortable to work with and appropriate for the employee and situation—will likely be better able to provide an environment within which motivation can take place.

Get to Know Your Employees

Supervisors develop a motivated staff by creating a climate in which employees want to work *with*—rather than *against*—the goals of the department and those of the organization. In order to help employees become motivated, you must understand their needs, interests, and goals. What motivates one employee may have little effect on another because needs, interests, and goals vary from employee to employee. These motivational factors are a function of each individual's background, personality, intellect, attitudes, and other characteristics. Your challenge is to get to know employees under your supervision.

To be a successful motivator, you need to know what it takes for your employees to become motivated. This is not an easy task because some employees may

Exhibit 10.1 What Do Employees Want from Their Jobs?

Factors	Rank Given By	
	Employees	**Supervisors**
Full appreciation of work done	1	8
Feeling of being in on things	2	10
Help with personal problems	3	9
Job security	4	2
Higher wages	5	1
Interesting work	6	5
Promotion in the company	7	3
Personal loyalty of supervisor	8	6
Good working conditions	9	4
Tactful discipline	10	7

Source: Adapted with permission from John W. Newstrom and Edward E. Scannell, *Games Trainers Play: Experiential Learning Exercises* (New York: McGraw-Hill, 1980), p. 121.

not know, or at least cannot verbalize, their needs or goals. Much motivation is sub-conscious. For example, some "high energy" employees may be top performers be-cause they fear rejection from co-workers if they do not produce above-average results. These employees may not even be aware that they are seeking approval from their peers.

Exhibit 10.1 summarizes survey results and shows that significant differences exist between what supervisors *believe* employees want and what employees *actu-ally* want from their jobs. Workers across the country were asked to rate the factors that most affected their morale and motivation level. Likewise, supervisors were asked to indicate what they believed were most important to their employees. Note that the top three items ranked by employees (full appreciation of work done, feeling of being in on things, and help with personal problems) are the last three items ranked by supervisors.

The first two items judged most important by employees are fully within the control of a supervisor. In fact, there are a number of things you can do to improve the motivational climate at little or no cost to the organization. By acknowledging the good performance of employees and by providing appropriate recognition, you convey to employees that you appreciate their efforts. Also, a supervisor helps employees feel that they are "in on things" by effectively communicating the objec-tives of the department and significant events affecting the organization.

The third item judged most important by employees may not be fully within the control of a supervisor. Personal problems are generally better addressed by trained professionals. However, a supervisor can communicate understanding and concern for employees experiencing personal problems beyond the workplace. This kind of attention may be all that many employees expect and may be greatly appreciated.

Motivational Strategies

Your understanding of the needs, interests, and goals of employees forms the basis for developing motivational strategies. Exhibit 10.2 summarizes basic principles of

Exhibit 10.2 Principles of Motivation

1. **Compatibility with objectives.** People being motivated must (a) have clearly defined objectives, and (b) these objectives must be in concert with those of the organization.
2. **Motivational flexibility.** The type and degree of motivational efforts must be varied.
3. **Multi-directional force.** The manager must be the driving force behind the motivational efforts.
4. **Management maturity.** The type and direction of motivational efforts must change as the organization matures.
5. **Self-motivation.** Motivational efforts by the supervisor must be designed to yield self-motivation.
6. **Effective communications.** There must be an open and trustful atmosphere based upon respect in order for motivational efforts to be effective.
7. **Employee participation.** Employees must be able, to the extent possible, to be involved in matters which affect them.
8. **Credit and blame.** The supervisor must give credit to employees when due and accept responsibility to share blame when problems occur.
9. **Authority, responsibility, and accountability.** To motivate employees, a supervisor must give them the authority and responsibility necessary to perform their work and must, at the same time, hold them accountable for effective performance.
10. **Conscious self-motivation.** The most effective type of motivation comes from a serious and deliberate effort by the individual employee.
11. **Genuine respect.** A supervisor cannot be an effective motivator until he/she genuinely respects employees, recognizes their rights, and accepts their capacity for self-direction.

motivation. Incorporating these principles into the motivational strategies that you develop increases the likelihood that your efforts will succeed.

Many of the topics covered in earlier chapters are themselves motivational strategies. The following sections suggest how motivational strategies can be developed in relation to the basic human resources functions carried out by supervisors.

Recruitment and Selection. Your interviews with job applicants offer an excellent opportunity to learn about the individual needs, interests, and goals of prospective employees. With practice and experience, you can sharpen your interviewing skills and identify those candidates who seem motivated from the start to contribute to your department.

Orientation. New employees are usually highly motivated to succeed. It's your job to keep that motivational level high and lay the foundation for future success.

Training. Effective training programs create the conditions in which employees can become motivated. Training sends a strong message to employees. It tells them that the supervisor, the department, and the organization care enough to provide them the necessary instruction and direction to ensure their success. Tools such as organization charts, job descriptions, job lists, and job breakdowns all tend to make work requirements rigid and uniform. This need for consistency is good from the organization's perspective, but, at the same time, you should try to find ways within established restrictions to allow employees to address personal goals while on the job.

Cross-training can be a valuable motivational tool and can remove many of the obstacles that may block an employee's growth and advancement. From the employees' perspective, cross-training prevents the feeling of being locked into a particular job, and allows them to acquire additional work skills.

Coaching and Evaluating Performance. A critical motivational strategy is to formally and informally let employees know how well they are performing their jobs. Coaching and evaluating performance are among the best tools a supervisor has to increase employee motivation and improve department morale. This strategy is effective because it:

- Provides the employee with formal written feedback on job performance
- Identifies strengths in performance and offers a plan for improving weaknesses
- Gives the supervisor and the employee the opportunity to mutually develop specific goals and due dates to accomplish the desired results

Effective Communications. Communication is a key to any motivational program. Keeping employees informed about events and activities in the department and organization will yield positive results. Employees who are aware of what's going on feel a greater sense of belonging and value.

Developing a departmental or organizational newsletter is an excellent way to keep lines of communication open. Newsletter write-ups might be job-related or personal in nature and include such topics as:

- Promotions
- Transfers
- New hires
- Resignations
- Quality tips
- Special recognition
- Employee-of-the-month
- Birthdays
- Engagements, marriages, births

A bulletin board provides a place to post schedules, memos, and other important information. Bulletin boards are most effective when they are in an area accessible to all employees and when employees are asked to view the boards daily.

Identifying Motivational Problems

How can you determine when an employee has a motivational problem or when morale sinks in your work area? Common-sense observations can help; sophisticated studies are not always necessary. You can begin by investigating a number of factors that indirectly relate to low motivational or morale levels. These factors include:

- High absenteeism rates

- High turnover rates

- Increases in the number of accidents

- Excessive breakage or waste

- Unusually high number of complaints or grievances received from employees

Further observation may uncover a general lack of cooperation among employees or increasing conflicts in the work environment.

You also need to know how to determine when the lack of motivation may be the cause of an employee's poor job performance. Poor performance results when an employee's behavior falls short of established standards. A motivation problem exists when the difference between expected and actual performance on the job is due to a lack of effort on the employee's part.

The sample performance problem analysis worksheet shown in Exhibit 10.3 can help you to identify the possible causes of an employee's poor performance. Once you've identified the causes, you can generate the appropriate strategies by which to address the situation. The supervisor uses the worksheet by rating employees along two dimensions: how well the employee is performing on the job, and the level of knowledge or skill that the employee has in relation to the job. The job performance scale (low to high) is at the bottom of the worksheet; the job knowledge/skill scale (also low to high) is along the left side of the worksheet. The two ratings for an employee will intersect and, generally, fall into one of four areas:

- Box A—An employee rated high in the job knowledge/skill area but low in relation to job performance may indicate that a motivational problem exists.

- Box B—An employee rated high in the job knowledge/skill area and high in relation to job performance is probably a valued member of your staff.

- Box C—An employee rated low in the job knowledge/skill area and low in job performance may indicate a serious problem, especially if the employee has persistently rejected your training and coaching efforts. Transfer or termination of the employee may be the only alternatives open to you.

- Box D—An employee rated low in job knowledge/skill but high in job performance may indicate that the employee is somehow getting the job done in spite of a lack of training. Providing the necessary training and coaching could turn this employee into a valued member of your team.

Exhibit 10.3 Performance Analysis Worksheet

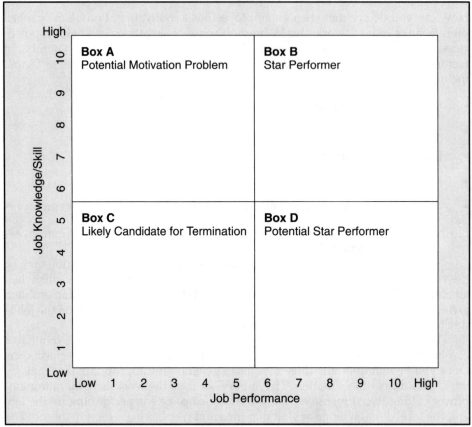

Source: Adapted with permission from John W. Newstrom and Edward E. Scannell, *Games Trainers Play: Experiential Learning Exercises* (New York: McGraw-Hill, 1980), p. 33.

Leadership Styles and Motivation

The following sections examine four leadership styles: autocratic, bureaucratic, democratic, and laissez-faire. Each leadership style creates conditions that can affect employees' motivational levels. Rather than adopting any one of these styles of leadership, you need to develop the flexibility with which to turn styles into strategies. For example, if you must give detailed instructions (such as when training a new room attendant) you will reflect that in the leadership style you use. Conversely, the food and beverage director who is supervising a creative chef will likely use a different approach.

Seen as strategies, leadership styles become the tools with which you can create the conditions in which employees become motivated to achieve department goals. Exhibit 10.4 summarizes some of the major points discussed in the sections that follow.

Exhibit 10.4 Overview of Leadership Styles

Name	Also Called	Basic Description of Leadership Style	Type of Employee with Whom It Might Be Used
Autocratic	Authoritarian or Dictatorial	Supervisor retains as much power and decision-making authority as possible. He/she is like a dictator, making decisions without consulting employees. Orders are given and must be obeyed without discussion.	New employees who must quickly learn work tasks, difficult-to-supervise employees who do not respond to other styles, and temporary employees.
Bureaucratic		Supervisor "manages by the book." Emphasis is on doing things as specified by rules, policies, regulations, and standard operating procedures. Supervisor must rely on higher levels of management to resolve problems not addressed by the ground rules.	Employees who must follow set procedures (such as accountants concerned with tax matters or purchasing staff who must comply with bidding/ordering requirements) and employees working with dangerous equipment or under special conditions.
Democratic	Participative	Supervisor involves employees as much as possible in aspects of the job which affect them. Their input is solicited; they participate in the decision-making process and are delegated much authority.	Employees with high levels of skill and/or extensive experience, employees who will need to make significant changes in work assignments (if time permits), employees who want to voice complaints, and employee groups with common problems.
Laissez-Faire	Free-Rein	Supervisor maintains a "hands off" policy. He/she "delegates by default" much discretion and decision-making authority to the employees. The supervisor gives little direction and allows employees extensive levels of freedom.	Highly motivated employees such as staff technical specialists and in some instances, consultants.

Autocratic Leadership

The **autocratic leadership style** is a classical approach to management. Supervisors adopting this style make decisions without input from their employees. They generally give orders without explanations, and expect those orders to be obeyed. Often, a structured set of rewards and punishments is used to ensure compliance by employees. While all supervisors must be results-oriented, the autocratic supervisor places results above concerns about the motivational level of employees. Employees are assumed to be already motivated, or at least motivated enough to simply follow orders.

Autocratic supervisors accept authority and responsibility delegated by their bosses, but are generally unwilling to delegate to employees under their own supervision. As a result, employees often become extremely dependent upon autocratic supervisors. Since they are given little, if any, discretion about how to perform their jobs, they learn to suppress their initiative and simply follow orders.

When practiced in the wrong situations or with the wrong type of employees, this leadership style can be disastrous. Low employee morale, high absenteeism and turnover, even work stoppage could result. However, there are times when this leadership style is both necessary and effective. Consider, for example, the situation when lunch business unexpectedly doubles the forecasted volume. The kitchen and dining room staff would need fast, specific instructions on how to vary accepted procedures in order to properly serve all of the guests. In this type of situation, employees might expect the supervisor to adopt an autocratic leadership style and tell them: "This is what must be done. Here is how to do it. Now let's get to work." Autocratic leadership techniques can also be successful when:

- The supervisor knows how to do the work of employees.

- There are a number of new, untrained employees who do not know which tasks to perform and/or which procedures to follow.

- Supervision is conducted through orders and detailed instructions.

- An employee does not respond positively to any other style of supervision.

- The supervisor's authority (power) is challenged.

Bureaucratic Leadership

The **bureaucratic leadership style** is one in which a supervisor focuses on rules, regulations, policies, and procedures. These supervisors manage by the rules and rely on higher levels of management to make decisions about issues not covered "by the book."

A bureaucratic supervisor is more a police officer than a leader. Normally, this enforcement style is adopted only when all other leadership styles are inappropriate, or when employees can be permitted no discretion in the decisions to be made. For example, it is important that rules and procedures are followed to the letter when an employee is assigned to operate potentially dangerous equipment. A bureaucratic leadership style may be appropriate in many situations in which procedures are established for employees performing routine or repetitive tasks. For example, clerical staff must follow the exact procedures established for filing documents and information.

Democratic Leadership

The **democratic** (also called participative) **leadership** style is almost the reverse of the autocratic style discussed earlier. The democratic supervisor keeps employees informed on all matters that directly affect their work, and shares decision-making and problem-solving responsibilities. This type of supervisor emphasizes the employees' roles in the organization, and provides opportunities for employees to develop a high sense of job satisfaction. The democratic supervisor seeks the opinions of employees and seriously considers their recommendations. Typically, the democratic supervisor:

- Develops plans to help employees evaluate their own performance

- Allows employees to help establish goals

- Encourages employees to grow on the job and be promoted

- Recognizes and encourages achievement

In effect, the democratic supervisor might be compared to a coach who is leading a team.

While this leadership style may seem vastly more appealing than autocratic or bureaucratic approaches, there are limitations and potential disadvantages to consider. For example, it may take longer to reach a decision or solution when a number of employees are involved in the decision-making or problem-solving process. Some situations call for more prompt action. Also, it may not be cost effective to involve employees in matters that are straightforward and easily resolved by the supervisor.

The democratic leadership style may be most appropriate to use with highly-skilled or experienced employees. This style can be effective when implementing operational changes or resolving individual or group problems.

Laissez-Faire Leadership

The **laissez-faire** (also called free-rein) **leadership** style refers to a hands-off approach in which the supervisor actually does very little leading. The supervisor provides little or no direction and allows employees as much freedom as possible. In effect, the supervisor gives all authority (power) to the employees, and relies on them to establish goals, make decisions, and resolve problems. The basic motto of this type of supervisor is "don't rock the boat."

While there are relatively few times when this approach can be effectively used, it may be appropriate to use with highly-skilled or experienced employees who have been trained in decision-making and problem-solving techniques.

Factors Affecting Leadership Styles

Ideally, an effective supervisor adopts the leadership style most appropriate to the situation. For example, the supervisor would know the needs, interests, and goals of each employee and then use the most appropriate leadership style to provide an optimal atmosphere for motivation. In practice, however, this is seldom possible. You have developed attitudes, feelings, and a personality based on your unique background. These factors generally limit your ability to move easily among radically different leadership styles.

The following sections examine major factors that influence a supervisor's leadership style. These factors include:

- The supervisor's personal background
- Characteristics of employees
- Organizational climate

The Supervisor's Personal Background. Your personality, knowledge, values, and experiences shape your feelings about and reactions toward employees. Some supervisors feel comfortable in freely delegating work and like to involve several employees in a team approach to defining and resolving problems. Other supervisors like to do everything themselves. Simply put, your feelings about appropriate leadership are important in determining the specific leadership style you will use. Also, the success you may have achieved with a particular style may affect your willingness to adopt a different style. If you experienced success with an autocratic style, chances are that you will use (and perhaps prefer) this leadership model in other situations. Conversely, if the democratic approach has proven successful for you, there is a strong likelihood that you will continue to use it.

Characteristics of Employees. Employees are individuals with differing personalities and backgrounds. Like their supervisors, they, too, are influenced by specific factors. Employees who want independence or decision-making responsibility, who identify with the property's goals, and who are knowledgeable and experienced may work well under a democratic leader. Conversely, employees with different expectations and experiences might require a more autocratic leader. The ability of employees to work effectively in groups also affects the usefulness of specific leadership styles.

Organizational Climate. The organizational climate, the composition of the work group, the type of work to be done, and related factors also influence leadership style. The traditions and values of the organization may influence your behavior. For example, some organizations stress human relations. Other organizations focus on the bottom line—at the sacrifice, if necessary, of extensive employee participation in the management process. To be effective in any organization, you must at least consider, and probably adopt, the prevailing organizational philosophy.

Increasing Employee Participation

The democratic leadership style attempts to raise the motivational level of employees by increasing their participation in decision-making and problem-solving activities. The following sections examine two formal techniques to use to increase employee participation: employee suggestion programs and departmental task groups. The final section suggests informal, democratic leadership actions that supervisors can take to increase the motivational level of employees.

Employee Suggestion Programs. Employee suggestion programs are examples of formal employee participation programs. The suggestion box and letters to the editor in the company newsletter are often used in the hospitality industry to increase communication between managers, supervisors, and employees.

While a formal employee suggestion program provides many useful ideas, some effort is required to implement and maintain the program. Employee suggestion programs must make it easy for employees to participate. For example, if employees are required to write their suggestions, some may believe that their suggestion is not worth the effort involved. The response of managers or supervisors to employee suggestions is critical to the success (or failure) of any formal employee suggestion program. For example, if you react to employee suggestions as if they were criticisms directed at your ability to supervise, you may discourage employees from providing additional comments.

Another critical element in the success of suggestion programs is feedback. Supervisors and managers must respond to employees offering suggestions. The response should inform employees about decisions made in response to the suggestions offered. This feedback not only may increase employees' knowledge of important business issues, it may also motivate more employees to participate in the suggestion program.

It takes a significant effort on the part of management to ensure the success of an employee suggestion program. These programs often fail because supervisors do not provide the necessary feedback and follow-through for them to succeed.

Employee Task Groups. A common employee participation activity involves the formation of task groups or work committees. This technique is used frequently at upper management levels but can be used at other organizational levels as well. Some properties have committees with representatives from all organizational levels who provide input on matters of property-wide interest. You can apply this same concept to generate participation in work decisions within a specific department or work section. For example, you could appoint a formal task group to develop job lists or job breakdowns, ideas for energy management techniques, new recipes, and so on. If you use this method, be sure that its benefits are not offset by high costs or time commitments.

Informal Participatory Techniques. In most operations it is relatively simple for a concerned and interested supervisor to use informal methods to gain employee participation. Consider, for example, the situation that arises when a decision must be made, perhaps about a recurring problem that must be resolved. You might begin by writing down all the ways to resolve the problem you can think of, then follow this up with a request for other ideas from affected employees. In doing this, you could talk to:

- Every employee affected by the problem
- Informal group leaders
- Experienced employees only
- Selected employees whom you think would have specific ideas or would have a special interest in solving the problem

Talking with any or all of the above employees will likely generate helpful alternatives. As you continue with the problem-solving task, participating employees could be involved in determining:

- Advantages and disadvantages of each alternative
- Procedures for implementing the selected solution
- Methods for evaluating the effectiveness of the solution
- Ways in which the solution may affect other aspects of the department

As you consider whether to involve employees in decision-making, be aware that disagreements can result—and that the disagreements must be managed. You will need to address conflicting interests and may need additional time for decision-making. Also, it's sometimes difficult for even the best-intentioned employees to remain objective; their own personal biases and concerns can influence their participation.

When you decide to involve employees in problem-solving and decision-making activities, it's important that the task at hand really involves employee participation and not just persuasion on your part. Effective supervisors must use persuasion to "sell" decisions and solutions to employees, but this should not be done under the label of employee participation. When you have a definite solution in mind, it's generally better to defend, justify, and sell it to employees rather than pretend that your employees have an active role in the process.

Key Terms

autocratic leadership style
bureaucratic leadership style
democratic leadership style
laissez-faire leadership style
leadership

Discussion Questions

1. Why can't supervisors motivate employees?

2. How can supervisors learn about the needs, interests, and goals of employees?

3. How can supervisory functions such as training, coaching, and evaluating become strategies by which to motivate employees?

4. What factors should a supervisor investigate to determine if there is a motivational or morale problem in the department?

5. How can a supervisor determine when a lack of motivation may be the cause of an employee's poor job performance?

6. How is the leadership of a supervisor related to the motivational level of employees?

7. What distinguishes an autocratic leadership style from a democratic leadership style?

8. How does a bureaucratic leadership style differ from a laissez-faire leadership style?

9. What factors affect the leadership style adopted by a supervisor?

10. How can supervisors increase employee participation in department activities?

REVIEW QUIZ

When you feel you have covered all of the material in this chapter, answer these questions. Choose the *best* answer. Check your answers with the correct ones found on the Review Quiz Answer Key at the end of this book.

True (T) or False (F)

T   F   1. An effective supervisor can motivate his/her employees.

T   F   2. Leadership is the ability to attain objectives by working through and with people.

T   F   3. A recent survey of employees and employers indicated that most supervisors know what motivates employees.

T   F   4. Employees should be allowed to address personal goals while on the job.

T   F   5. Cross-training is often an obstacle to an employee's advancement.

T   F   6. The number of accidents in a workplace is one indicator of motivational level.

T   F   7. An autocratic management style typically results in a high level of employee initiative.

T   F   8. A bureaucratic leadership style is best suited to highly experienced employees.

T   F   9. A supervisor needs to know what his/her employees' needs are in order to choose the most appropriate leadership style.

T   F   10. Formation of departmental task groups is a formal technique for increasing employee participation.

Alternate/Multiple Choice

11.   Motivation level is generated:

    a. by an effective supervisor.
    b. within the individual.

12.   Which of the following factors is more likely to influence a supervisor's choice of leadership style?

    a. the prevailing organizational climate
    b. the level of employee problem-solving skills

13.   Employee work committees would most likely be formed under which type of leadership style?

    a. democratic
    b. bureaucratic

14. Which of the following was one of the three most important factors affecting motivational level, according to employees who were recently surveyed?

    a. salary increases
    b. the possibility of promotion
    c. opportunities for cross-training
    d. help with personal problems

15. The classical or traditional approach to management is:

    a. laissez-faire.
    b. autocratic.
    c. bureaucratic.
    d. democratic.

Chapter Outline

Benefits of Conflict
Sources of Conflict
Types of Personal Conflict
    Conflict Within an Individual
    Conflict Between Individuals
Managing Personal Conflict
    Outcomes
    Management Styles
    Turning Styles into Strategies
Tips for Negotiating Personal Conflicts
    Mediating Conflict Between
      Employees
    Resolving Supervisor/Employee
      Conflict
    Accepting Criticism from Your Boss

Learning Objectives

1. Explain benefits of conflict.

2. List and briefly describe sources of conflict within an organization.

3. Identify two types of personal conflict.

4. Describe three outcomes of personal conflict.

5. Describe five typical styles of managing conflict.

6. Explain what supervisors should do before they meet with employees in conflict.

7. Identify six steps supervisors should follow during a meeting with employees in conflict.

8. Describe special problems supervisors have when resolving supervisor/employee conflicts.

9. Explain how supervisors should accept criticism from their boss.

11

Managing Conflict

CONFLICT CAN BE AS SIMPLE as a difference of opinion or as complex as a lengthy battle over matters of significant importance. A conflict can be caused by an event or a clash of personalities. Conflict may also occur when people hold opposing views about a situation and how to handle it. Left alone, conflict may cause serious problems that prevent your department from achieving its goals. Properly managed, however, some types of conflict can be constructive.

This chapter does not deal with employee outbursts caused by pressure from stress or "the heat of the moment." Such outbursts, while potentially disruptive in the short term, do not typically require significant supervisory efforts to resolve. Outbursts usually subside quickly and are generally much easier to manage than more significant conflict-related problems.

This chapter first looks at the possible benefits of conflict to hospitality operations. Next, common sources of conflict and types of conflict that supervisors must manage are discussed. Later sections examine negotiating techniques that supervisors may adopt when resolving personal conflict between employees, between themselves and employees, or between themselves and their bosses.

Benefits of Conflict

It's a fact of life that all hospitality operations are likely to have conflict. A traditional management view holds that conflict should be avoided because it disrupts an organization and prevents optimal performance. Another, more accurate view is that conflict is not only unavoidable, it's often beneficial. For example, during budget planning sessions, department managers compete for the limited resources of the operation. Their conflicting views on how resources should be allocated leads to an analysis of the goals and strategies of the whole organization. At the end of a budget planning session with a healthy degree of conflict, everyone should have a better idea of where the organization is going and how it's going to get there. This beneficial outcome would not happen without conflict. However, a key element in successful conflict management is being aware of the feelings held by everyone involved in the conflict. At some point in resolving the conflict, these feelings must be understood and addressed.

A certain amount of conflict is necessary for good work performance. When there is a low level of conflict and performance levels are low, the organization stagnates (see Exhibit 11.1). On the other hand, when there are high levels of conflict and performance, chaos is a potential result. As Exhibit 11.1 suggests, there is an optimal relationship between conflict and performance. However, there is no magic formula for identifying this relationship. As a supervisor, you must walk a

Exhibit 11.1 Conflict and Performance

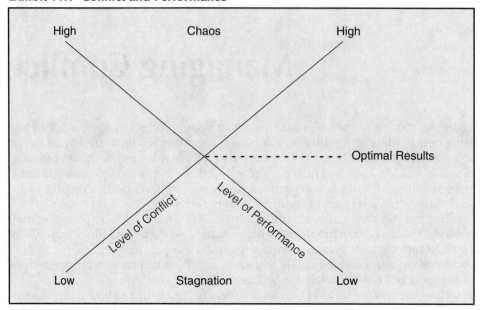

fine line. Your task is to foster honest and objective opposition that will help the department, yet prevent the kind of conflict that leads to disorganization and un-motivated employees. You will be better able to carry out this task if you understand sources of conflict within hospitality operations.

Sources of Conflict

There are numerous sources of conflict within an organization. Many arise from situations or personalities unique to that organization. However, there are sources of conflict common to most hospitality operations, including:

- Limited resources

- Different goals

- Work relationships

- Individual differences

- Organizational problems

- Communication problems

Exhibit 11.2 lists these typical sources of conflict. As the exhibit suggests, a supervisor's ability to manage conflict often determines whether the goals of the department are attained through cooperation, or the department is blocked from reaching goals because of conflict.

Exhibit 11.2 Supervisors and Conflict

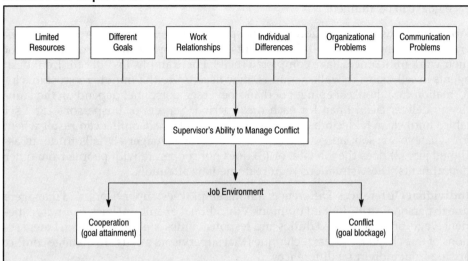

Limited Resources. Resources are limited in every hospitality operation. No department has all of the people, time, money, equipment, and space that it wants. Often, a department can obtain resources only at the expense of another department. For example, if two departments within an organization need a computer and there is only enough money in the budget for one, one department will have to do without. This creates the possibility of conflict. However, as pointed out earlier, this type of conflict might prove beneficial. Limited resources (only enough money in the budget for one computer) force each department manager to justify the request for the computer in relation to the overall goals of the organization. The manager who persuades upper management that the best interests of the organization are served by having the computer in his/her department usually gets the computer.

Different Goals. Departments and individuals in the same hospitality operation can have different goals. Conflict can result about who is right and what strategies to pursue.

For example, a hotel sales department may want to increase the hotel's food and beverage revenues by adding more items to the menu. However, this may conflict with the food and beverage department's goal of keeping food costs down. Similarly, the general manager's goal of providing exceptionally friendly service to guests as they check in may conflict with the front office manager's goal of decreasing average check-in time.

Supervisors are often caught in the middle of these types of conflicts. For example, your boss, the food and beverage director, may ask you to minimize labor costs by scheduling fewer food servers, while the marketing director, who is interested in increasing sales, wants more food servers scheduled so that guests receive fast service and lots of attention. You can only follow your boss's direction and hope that upper management comes to an agreement about the extent to which each goal can be attained.

Work Relationships. The success of a hospitality operation depends on close cooperation from members of all departments. Often, people can't do some or any of their work until others have completed theirs. For example, in order for front desk agents to sell rooms to walk-in guests, they need up-to-the-minute room-status information from housekeeping. Food and beverage personnel depend on the laundry to deliver clean linen for each meal period. Servers or buspersons can't set tables until clean tablecloths and napkins are available. Conflict can result when, for whatever reason, an employee, supervisor, or manager (1) fails to do an assigned job, (2) does the job late, or (3) does not cooperate with people from other departments. These situations require immediate attention.

Individual Differences. Differences among employees, supervisors, and managers due to personal attitudes and opinions, educational or cultural backgrounds, experience, age, or work-related duties and responsibilities can cause conflict. Later sections of this chapter address techniques that supervisors can use to manage conflict arising from individual differences.

Organizational Problems. Organizational problems can be sources of conflict, as when one department believes its efforts are more important than those of other departments. Other potential sources of organizational conflict include overlapping job responsibilities and vague job descriptions. Employees, supervisors, and managers can experience conflicting emotions if their duties and responsibilities are not clearly defined. When the extent of a supervisor's authority is not clear, for example, conflicts can arise within the supervisor, between the supervisor and employees, and between the supervisor and his/her boss.

Communication Problems. Communication problems are at the root of most conflicts. Effective communication about the organization's resources, goals, work relationships, individual differences, and organizational problems can go a long way toward increasing cooperation within the organization and avoiding the type of conflict that blocks goal achievement.

Types of Personal Conflict

Conflict can take many forms. The types of conflict that supervisors are most often called on to manage are personal conflicts that occur within their department or work area. There are two types of personal conflict: conflict within an individual, and conflict between two or more individuals.

Conflict Within an Individual

Anyone within an organization can experience mixed feelings about some of the organization's goals, certain individuals, job tasks and procedures, and the gap between personal and organizational goals. Individuals may deal with internal conflict by becoming quietly frustrated or physically expressing their concerns—throwing or kicking a piece of equipment, for example. They may also withdraw from the internal conflict by daydreaming or pretending they are not angry or upset. These reactions can affect work performance.

When internal conflict occurs within one of your employees, you must first become aware of the conflict and then deal with it through communication, training, coaching, performance reviews, and other techniques discussed in this book.

Of course, conflict can also occur within supervisors. A new supervisor may present a good example of how conflict may arise within an individual, especially when the supervisor has been promoted from the ranks of the employees whom he/she must now supervise. The promotion places the supervisor in a new leadership role. With this role comes the need to enforce the property's policies and procedures. As the new supervisor manages employees who formerly were peers, an internal conflict about where friendships end and professional relationships begin is bound to arise. The future success of a new supervisor may depend on how well he/she handles this unavoidable internal conflict.

Conflict Between Individuals

Conflict can occur between individuals at any organizational level. When two or more of your employees disagree over a situation, event, or "personality problem," you may have to serve as a mediator—an objective third party—to help the employees resolve their conflict.

Because of your role as a linking pin between higher and lower levels within the organization, conflict can occur between you and your employees—for example, when you must enforce unpopular rules and policies or when you must implement changes. Conflict can also occur between you and your boss as you attempt to represent the best interests of your employees to upper management.

Techniques for resolving personal conflicts through negotiation are examined later in the chapter. The following section focuses on general strategies that supervisors can use to manage personal conflict.

Managing Personal Conflict ———————————————

In order to effectively manage personal conflict, a supervisor should analyze each situation in terms of its possible outcomes, and understand how his/her management style can affect those outcomes. Finally, the supervisor should develop an appropriate strategy for either reducing or resolving the conflict.

Outcomes

Three possible outcomes of a personal conflict are lose-lose, win-lose, and win-win.

In a **lose-lose** outcome, no one involved in the conflict satisfies all or even most of his/her needs. Typically, the basic reasons for the conflict remain and conflict may recur.

In a **win-lose** outcome, one party's needs or concerns are satisfied while those of the other party or parties are not. Since this type of outcome typically fails to resolve all of the problems that created the conflict, future conflict may arise over the same or similar problems. Therefore, a win-lose outcome may reduce the conflict temporarily for the "winning" party, but it may not resolve the conflict.

In a **win-win** outcome, the needs of all parties are satisfied in some way and the conflict is resolved. To reach this outcome, those in conflict must understand each other's needs, confront the issues, and work together to objectively resolve the situation so that everyone benefits. Only with a win-win outcome is a conflict truly resolved for the long term.

As a supervisor you can determine which outcome is best for each conflict and try to steer the parties toward that outcome. For example, if your goal is to temporarily reduce conflict, you may adopt a strategy appropriate to a win-lose or lose-lose outcome. If your goal is to fully resolve the conflict, you must be prepared to spend the time and effort required to create a win-win outcome.

Management Styles

Many supervisors make the mistake of adopting a single style or approach to managing all personal conflicts. This can be disastrous, because a particular style of responding to conflict may itself determine the kind of outcome it produces. Therefore, supervisors who consistently manage conflict with the same approach often find themselves facing the same type of outcome—lose-lose, win-lose, or win-win—no matter what the conflict is or what outcome is most appropriate.

A supervisor's style of managing conflict varies in relation to his/her levels of assertiveness and cooperation. Five typical styles of managing conflict are:

- Compromise

- Avoidance

- Accommodation

- Competition

- Mutual Problem-Solving

The following sections examine each style and identify the conflict outcome that each style typically leads to. Exhibit 11.3 diagrams each of these styles in relation to the supervisor's degree of assertiveness and cooperation.

Compromise. A supervisor with moderate levels of both assertiveness and cooperation will likely respond to conflict by seeking a compromise. Generally, a compromise allows each party to partially satisfy some needs and concerns. Depending on how the parties in conflict view the partial solution, a compromise could create a number of different outcomes. For example, a lose-lose outcome results if neither party is satisfied with the partial solution; a win-lose outcome results if one party feels it has won (or lost) at the other's expense; a win-win outcome could result if, over time, the parties in conflict learn to accept the partial solution.

Avoidance. A supervisor with low levels of assertiveness and cooperation will probably avoid conflict. Avoidance behaviors include withdrawing from conflict situations, remaining "neutral," sidestepping the real issues, or constantly postponing a confrontation. Supervisors who ignore problems in the hope that they will go away often see conflict increase. The avoidance style of managing conflict encourages lose-lose outcomes in which the needs of the parties in conflict go unaddressed.

Exhibit 11.3 Approaches to Conflict

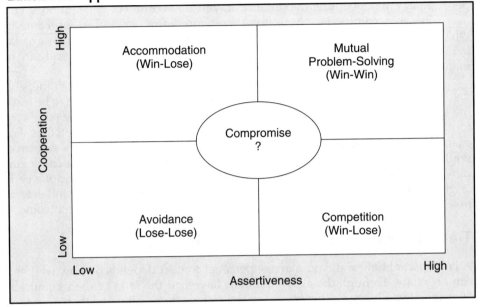

Accommodation. A supervisor with a low level of assertiveness and a high level of cooperation will likely want to accommodate the needs of others, even if it means neglecting his/her own needs. Supervisors who sacrifice their interests inevitably end up on the losing side of win-lose outcomes.

Competition. A supervisor with a high level of assertiveness and a low level of cooperation will likely be competitive in conflict situations. Such a supervisor often attempts to dominate others by using power or authority to ensure that his/her needs are satisfied. Obviously, competitive approaches to conflict usually force win-lose outcomes. When your employees lose all the time, their resentment builds and their performance suffers.

Mutual Problem-Solving. A supervisor with high levels of assertiveness and cooperation will usually resolve conflict by collaborating with others to reach mutually agreed-upon solutions. In this approach to conflict, parties to the conflict acknowledge and accept each other's goals. Honesty and hard negotiating leads to creative solutions that can meet the needs of everyone concerned. This approach encourages win-win outcomes.

Turning Styles into Strategies

Rather than adopting one of these styles for responding to all conflicts, you should develop enough flexibility to use all of these styles, depending on the conflict in question. When seen in this way, styles become strategies—tools with which you can try to direct the parties involved toward the best outcome.

For example, accommodation may be a poor style, but it's not necessarily a poor strategy: it depends on the situation. If you are in conflict with your boss, you may wish to accommodate him/her, thereby avoiding a win-lose outcome in which you will most likely be the loser. While mutual problem-solving may appear to be the most appealing style, you may not have the expertise, time, or desire to manage win-win outcomes for every conflict.

You can use Exhibit 11.3 to analyze the conflict-management style of others involved in the conflict and identify the type of outcome their styles seem to be leading toward. This analysis alerts you to behavioral changes that may be necessary for those involved in the conflict if the conflict is to have a desirable outcome. For example, a conflict may involve two employees, one of whom is very assertive, while the other is non-assertive. If on this particular occasion the assertive employee is (to simplify the example) "wrong" and the non-assertive employee is "right," you should encourage the non-assertive employee to speak up and defend his/her viewpoint if you want the conflict to move toward the desired outcome.

Tips for Negotiating Personal Conflicts

A large part of how well you manage personal conflict depends on how well you can negotiate. Through the ages diplomats have had the fates of their countries, even their lives, hinge on the words they used, how they said them, their approach to their audience—in short, on how well they negotiated. Whether you lead a country, a business, or a bridge club, you must be good at negotiating. As a leader in your department, you must perfect your negotiating skills in order to become the best supervisor you can be.

Most negotiation takes place at a meeting of some kind. The meeting can be very informal—in a hallway, for example—or very formal—a closed-door meeting in your boss's office. As a supervisor, you should carefully choose where you meet your employees, because location affects the meeting's tone and how your employees respond to you.

The best place to meet depends on the nature of the conflict. Deal with a serious conflict between you and your employees in your office with the door closed. If you do not have an office, choose a private area with a formal feel to it—a small conference room, for example, as opposed to a location like the employee break room. Some supervisors borrow their boss's office for very serious meetings. If the conflict is less serious, or if the employees involved will be too intimidated in a formal setting, choose appropriate informal locations. As mentioned, with minor conflicts sometimes a five-minute hallway meeting wherever the employee or employees happen to be is appropriate. Sometimes supervisors choose to hold meetings off the property in order to encourage frank discussion.

Mediating Conflict Between Employees

Conflict between employees occurs more often than most supervisors would like. Despite the fact that dealing with personalities and emotions can be difficult, it has to be done. Dealing with employee conflict is one of a supervisor's most important contributions to the efficiency of his/her department.

Some supervisors prefer to meet with the contending employees individually before meeting with all of them. This strategy is appropriate when the conflict is complicated or serious in nature. On rare occasions two or more employees can't talk about the conflict in the same room without arguing or getting upset. If this is the case, it's best to talk to each employee alone. Minor conflicts usually can be resolved when all parties meet together.

Once you have decided on the site and have chosen a time for the meeting, there are certain things you should do before, during, and after your meeting with your employees.

Before the Meeting. Perhaps the most important thing to avoid before the meeting is jumping to conclusions. Despite what you may feel about the participants or the conflict (as far as you understand it at that point), you must try to keep an open mind.

For some conflicts, you may want to get a version of the conflict from third parties. Ask other department employees who have remained neutral what the conflict is all about and whether it's affecting their work.

If the conflict is serious, you should prepare yourself to hear negative, unpleasant, critical, and perhaps confused talk from your employees. They may be very emotional, and there are bound to be different accounts and interpretations of the events or situations that led to the conflict.

During the Meeting. A meeting to discuss a conflict can become disorderly and lead almost anywhere if you let it. Tips to keep in mind during the meeting are:

- Arrange for someone to handle your phone calls during the meeting.

- Prevent people outside the meeting from interrupting unless it's absolutely necessary.

- Have your desk neat and free of distractions.

- Keep focused during the meeting. Don't keep looking at your watch or rummaging through desk drawers.

- Maintain eye contact.

- Avoid taking notes, especially if employees don't know why you're taking them.

- Investigate the issues thoroughly.

There are six steps you should follow to keep the discussion organized and under control:

- Set the tone.

- Get the feelings.

- Get the facts.

- Ask for help.

- Get a commitment.

- Follow up.

Set the tone. First, you should greet the employees cordially and try to establish an open and non-threatening tone for the meeting. This can be done by the words you choose and the way you say them as you open the floor for discussion. You can begin by saying something like: "Over the last few days I couldn't help but notice that something seems to be different with you two. It seems to be affecting your work. Has anything happened that you want to talk about?" This or a similar approach is better than a more abrupt statement such as "You guys have got a problem and we're going to get to the bottom of it right now." Such statements put employees on guard and make a productive meeting difficult.

Get the feelings. After setting the tone, focus on discovering the employees' feelings. Often what you'll get from the employees at first is a rush of words as they release emotions that have been held in check, perhaps for a long time. Don't interrupt or seek clarification at this time—it's very important to allow the employees to vent their frustration. By allowing the employees to "talk out" their feelings, you are helping to defuse the conflict and enabling them to gain control of their emotions. Once the person has talked it out, you should summarize the feelings expressed and re-state them for clarification.

Sometimes you have the opposite problem—employees who will sit silently even after you have asked them how they feel about the situation. This is not surprising, since many people have difficulty talking about their feelings. You must try to make it easier for these employees to express themselves. If you know something about the conflict, you can try paraphrasing what you think each employee is feeling. This sometimes encourages the employees to start talking. You must be careful with this technique, however; you are trying to discover their feelings, not feed their feelings.

Lastly, it's very important that you don't become emotional yourself. Only when *you* remain under control can you help your employees work things out effectively.

Get the facts. Once employees have talked their feelings through, you can move on to investigating the facts. Listen patiently to what the employees have to say, even if you think it may be wrong or irrelevant. You can keep employees talking without agreeing with them by nodding or occasionally saying "I see" or "Uh-huh." Even now, listen for the feelings the employees are expressing as well as the content of their message.

Keep your questions to a minimum during the fact-finding stage. You can review and clarify the facts after they are all out "on the table." Don't say, "That's not right," "I can't believe that's true," and similar statements because they tend to make employees stop talking.

Listen for what isn't said—missing pertinent points, for example—or quick agreements that seem evasive. These can be clues to a fact an employee wishes to hide. Watch for non-verbal communication as well. Are the employees sending you mixed messages? Do the postures, gestures, and facial expressions agree with the words being said?

If the fact-finding discussion gets bogged down in an argument, there are several strategies you can use to move the discussion to a more productive level:

Before asking for the facts of a conflict, a supervisor should let employees talk out their feelings.

- Try to depersonalize the conflict. Talk about it as if it could have happened to anyone. Talking about the conflict in a less personal way can reduce tension.

- Ask the employees to put aside their feelings for the moment and pretend they are third parties trying to discover the factors that contributed to the conflict.

- Look for ways to expand the employees' awareness of how they can meet their needs.

- Ask each employee to guess how the other employee may have seen the situation that led up to the conflict. This may reveal information gaps or incorrect assumptions about where the other person was coming from. Often, personal conflicts are partly or entirely based on these misunderstandings.

Save most of your comments until you have all the facts. Make sure you can accurately describe the situation as each employee sees it before you make any evaluations of your own. When you speak to the employees, choose your words and tone of voice with care. Ask yourself if you would talk to your boss or to a peer in the same way. Avoid phrases reminiscent of a parent-child discussion such as "You should have known better," or "If you had only listened to me." Treat employees like responsible adults and most will respond in kind.

Ask for help. At this point, too often supervisors tell employees what they should do to solve the conflict. It's better to encourage them to work out their own solution. There is a simple truth that many supervisors tend to forget: employees are ultimately responsible for dealing with their conflicts; they must work harder than you do to resolve them.

Asking the employees for help invites participation and commitment. It also helps build the employees' self-esteem. The employees will be more willing to solve the conflict, especially if you use the ideas they suggest.

You can ask for help either directly or indirectly. A direct approach can be as simple as "If you were me, what would you do about this situation?" Indirect ways include asking open-ended questions that invite the employees to identify causes and offer solutions. However, this approach is most effective when the employee understands all sides of the issue.

As mentioned earlier in the chapter, for some conflicts you may have a desired outcome in mind. Generally, it's best to gently steer employees toward that outcome rather than impose it on them. If the employees come up with a different solution to the conflict, it's often best to go with it. They are more likely to follow their own plan because they have more ownership of the solution and therefore more to lose if the solution doesn't work.

Get a commitment. After all of you have agreed on what to do, get the employees to commit themselves to performing their part of the solution. Usually this is done verbally. You may want to help the employees put their plan in writing. The plan should indicate what's to be done, who does it, how it's to be done, when, and with what help (if any). If it's a serious conflict, it may be appropriate to have the employees sign the plan they've created.

Follow up. If necessary, schedule a follow-up meeting to check whether the employees' solution is being implemented and is working. Let the employees know that you won't accept excuses from employees who fail to do their part. Tell employees that if their plan doesn't work, you have your own plan ready. (This may be the one you had in mind before the employees came up with their own.) Let the employees know about your plan and under what conditions you will implement it.

After the Meeting. After the meeting, take some time—immediately afterwards if possible—to analyze what happened by asking yourself questions such as:

- What did I do that worked?

- What did I do that didn't work?

- What strategy or tactic was most successful?

- What concessions did each employee make and when?

- Did I make any concessions and when?

- What are the consequences of these concessions?

- What information came from the meeting that will be of long-term benefit?

- What would I do differently next time?

Resolving Supervisor/Employee Conflict

Resolving a conflict between you and an employee is difficult because you must step back from your own feelings and try to see yourself objectively. Many of the techniques you apply to conflicts between two or more employees apply to a conflict between yourself and an employee (or group of employees). The trick is to think of yourself as just another party to the conflict, while retaining your roles as supervisor and mediator.

For some conflicts, supervisors choose to meet an employee at a neutral location outside the department or completely off-site—at a local coffee shop, for example. Moving the meeting to a place where the employee may feel more comfortable helps to somewhat equalize the power relationship between you.

Before the Meeting. Before meeting with the employee with whom you are in conflict, you must get control of your emotions. Never attempt to resolve a conflict when you are angry or upset. Put some distance between your reaction to the situation and the meeting you eventually schedule. However, don't delay too long. In many cases, a long delay can build the conflict.

Try to analyze the situation unemotionally. Focus on the facts, not your reaction to them. Look for ways in which you may have exaggerated aspects of the situation.

During the Meeting. Do not open the meeting by reminding the employee of organizational plans or upcoming work duties or meetings. This underscores your position of authority and may intimidate some employees into not talking honestly. Stick to the purpose of the meeting.

Many of the same things discussed for resolving conflict between employees apply here as well. Greet the employee cordially and begin the discussion in a non-threatening way. Try to establish a relaxed and open tone with your introductory remarks. Then ask the employee how he/she feels about the situation. Just letting employees know that their feelings are important to you can help them let go of some of their anger or tension. Don't interrupt or ask too many questions—just let the employee get the feelings out.

After you have acknowledged the employee's feelings, ask the employee to explain the conflict as he/she sees it. The more experience supervisors gain at resolving personal conflicts, the more they realize how true the old saying is, "There are two sides to every story." Even if you were present when whatever prompted the conflict took place, the employee's version of the situation is often very different and may cause you to reassess your own interpretation of what happened.

After you have heard the employee out—without interrupting, of course—tell your side of the story. Even as you tell your side, aim for reconciliation. If appropriate, identify how you may have contributed to the problem.

Because you are not only the supervisor trying to resolve the conflict but one of the people involved in the conflict, you are under a lot of stress. Therefore, you may have a tendency to overreact to being interrupted or misunderstood. Having someone interrupt or say "I don't understand your point" tends to make people irritated or defensive even in non-stressful situations.

If the employee does not understand what you've said, re-state your position in a different way. Talk slowly and pause more often to ask (in a non-offensive way) if the employee understands you so far.

If the employee interrupts you, stay calm. Rather than saying, "Can't you let me finish?" or "You're not listening to a thing I say," try to be diplomatic. Say something like "I understand your comment, but I think as we go on we'll communicate better if we each allow the other person to finish speaking before we respond" or

"This may be difficult for you, but I don't think you'll understand my side of the situation unless I can finish my train of thought."

Sometimes the conflict is resolved after both of you have given your interpretation of the situation. One or both of you may have lacked a vital piece of information or misunderstood something. If the conflict is not resolved so easily, you must work it out with the employee. Ask the employee for his/her ideas. Put in writing what each of you agrees to do. Get a commitment from the employee to follow the plan, and promise to do your part as well.

If the seriousness of the conflict warrants it, establish a date for a follow-up meeting to monitor your progress.

After the Meeting. Just as you would after a meeting concerning conflict between employees, take some time after this meeting to analyze what happened. Are you happy with the outcome? Were you competitive, forcing the employee to be on the losing side of a win-lose outcome? Did you accommodate too much, because you don't like conflict or wanted the employee to like you? Did you compromise—settle for part of what you wanted? If so, do you feel good about that? Or did you achieve a win-win outcome? Analyzing the outcome you achieved and how you reached that outcome will help you with future negotiations.

If the employee does not follow through on his/her part of the plan, some sort of disciplinary action may be called for. Or, if the conflict is serious, you may want to ask a third party to act as mediator at another meeting between you and the employee. The mediator may be another supervisor, your boss, or some other manager. A mediator not involved with the conflict brings a fresh, objective viewpoint to the situation and may be very helpful in sorting out what happened and what action(s) should be taken.

Accepting Criticism from Your Boss

There are many possibilities for personal conflict with your boss. Sometimes your boss's deadlines seem unreasonable, for example. Or some of his/her rules may seem unnecessary. But, because of your organizational relationship to your boss, most situations that hold a possibility for personal conflict are "resolved" because you accommodate your boss rather than try to negotiate with him/her. This avoids personal conflict, though sometimes at the price of internal conflict within yourself.

Many supervisors see criticism from their bosses as a form of personal conflict. Most bosses do not wish their comments to be perceived in this way, but criticism from your boss can lead to internal or personal conflict if you are not careful. Everything depends on how you perceive your boss's criticism.

Never take criticism from your boss as a personal attack. If you perceive criticism as a personal attack, you will become anxious, defensive, and too emotionally involved to see the real points behind the criticism. Everyone makes mistakes. Criticism from your boss generally identifies a mistake you have made. The criticism usually tries to get you to adopt new behaviors or strategies that will prevent you from making the mistake again.

You don't have control over where your boss will meet with you to comment on your performance—your boss does. Where he/she chooses to hold the meeting conveys a message, just as you convey a message to your employees through where you meet with them. The meeting site provides you with a clue as to how serious the criticism of your performance will be.

Before the Meeting. Avoid jumping to conclusions before you meet with your boss. The criticism may not be as serious as you fear. If you are nervous, ask yourself, "Realistically, what's the worst that can happen? How likely is it? How can I deal with that outcome?"

If your boss has given you an idea of what the meeting will be about, think about the problem or behavior that will be discussed. How has it affected your productivity? What steps can you take to rectify the situation?

Above all, tell yourself that you are not going to get upset or angry. As mentioned earlier, most bosses criticize to help people, not hurt them. Take the perspective that the purpose of the criticism is to help you solve problems and grow professionally. A confrontation will only corner you or your boss into rigid positions that make communication difficult.

During the Meeting. During the meeting, make sure your boss knows you are actively listening to the criticism. Don't fidget in your chair, look out the window, or fantasize about getting demoted or fired. Remain calm and concentrate on the discussion.

Communicate to your boss that you appreciate the effort to help you to improve your performance. Keep your head up. Maintain a comfortable amount of eye contact. Ask questions to clarify issues and paraphrase some of your boss's points. This indicates to your boss that you are receiving the message.

It's not a good idea to change the subject or the mood of the discussion. Changing the subject is a defensive or evasive tactic. Never joke about issues that are raised in the discussion. This also indicates defensiveness and may lead your boss to think that you really don't care about resolving the situation.

After you have heard your boss out—without interrupting—take responsibility for the problem. Concentrate on the present and offer positive solutions. Bringing up past experiences or offering excuses only focuses on things that cannot be changed now.

At this point your boss may tell you his/her plan for correcting the situation. If you think the plan will work, agree to it unless you have serious objections. Diplomatically raise any serious objections you have and give reasons for each one. If your boss does not outline a plan, offer one of your own. This demonstrates that you took the criticism seriously and have the initiative to correct matters on your own.

With some problems, it's obvious that you can take certain immediate steps to quickly solve them; other more serious or complicated problems may take time. In these cases, it's usually a good idea to ask your boss for a timetable. Find out how much time is appropriate for resolving the problem, and strive to meet or beat the deadline.

After the Meeting. After the meeting, take a moment to analyze what happened. Do you feel good about the discussion? Why or why not? Did your boss seem to be steering the situation toward a specific outcome—lose-lose, win-lose, or win-win?

Did you learn something new about your boss's management style that will help you in the future?

Most important, do everything you can to make the solution to the problem work. If necessary, request a follow-up meeting with your boss to make sure the problem is corrected to his/her satisfaction.

Key Terms

accommodation	lose-lose
avoidance	mutual problem-solving
competition	win-lose
compromise	win-win

Discussion Questions

1. What are some benefits of conflict?

2. What are some sources of conflict within a hospitality organization?

3. Personal conflict can be categorized as what two types?

4. What is a win-lose outcome?

5. What are some behaviors common to the avoidance style of managing conflict?

6. What should a supervisor do before holding a meeting with employees who are in conflict?

7. What steps should be taken during a meeting with employees in conflict?

8. Why is it not a good strategy to tell employees how to solve their conflict?

9. What are some special issues supervisors have to deal with in resolving supervisor/employee conflict?

10. How can supervisors cope positively with criticism from their boss?

REVIEW QUIZ

When you feel you have covered all of the material in this chapter, answer these questions. Choose the *best* answer. Check your answers with the correct ones found on the Review Quiz Answer Key at the end of this book.

True (T) or False (F)

T F 1. Conflict is not only unavoidable, it is often beneficial.

T F 2. For optimum work performance, all signs of conflict must be eliminated.

T F 3. Hospitality employees are always able to perform their own jobs and duties regardless of what happens in other departments.

T F 4. Some supervisors will actually accommodate the needs of others at the expense of neglecting their own needs.

T F 5. In a well-controlled conflict discussion, it is very important *not* to allow the employees to vent their frustrations.

T F 6. Supervisors are ultimately responsible for dealing with the conflicts of their employees and applying the solutions.

T F 7. In a meeting scheduled to resolve a supervisor/employee conflict, the supervisor should begin the meeting by reminding the employee of organizational goals and plans. That helps set a positive tone.

T F 8. Many supervisors see criticism from their bosses as a personal attack.

T F 9. A supervisor can defuse a boss/supervisor criticism meeting by getting angry. Then the boss isn't sure any more whether he/she is right.

T F 10. After accepting criticism from the boss, the supervisor should take responsibility for the problem and offer solutions.

Alternate/Multiple Choice

11. When the various levels of management are in conflict over the goals of the hospitality operation, supervisors can only:

   a. try to keep up with the latest directive.
   b. follow the boss's direction.

12. A conflict in which *no* participant satisfies all or even most of his/her needs is called:

   a. win-lose.
   b. lose-lose.

13. In a fact-finding discussion, when supervisors speak to employees, phrases like, "You should have known better," are:

   a. appropriate.
   b. inappropriate.

14. Which of the following is *not* one of the numerous sources of conflict within an organization?

    a. limited resources
    b. different goals
    c. work relationships
    d. individual similarities

15. One way in which the supervisor can keep a conflict meeting focused and under control is to:

    a. keep an eye on his/her watch so the meeting won't drag.
    b. have his/her desk neat and free of distractions.
    c. secretly take notes.
    d. avoid looking at the conflicting parties directly.

Part IV

Improving Your Effectiveness as a Supervisor

Chapter Outline

Myths Concerning Time Management
Time Analysis
    Time Robbers
Time Management Tools
    To-Do Lists
    Weekly Planning Guides
    Calendars
Delegation
    Barriers to Delegation
    Steps in Effective Delegation

Learning Objectives

1. Identify common myths of time management.

2. Explain daily time logs and their benefits.

3. Define time robbers, and list examples.

4. Distinguish high-priority interruptions from low-priority interruptions, and summarize strategies for dealing with the latter.

5. Describe the importance of to-do lists.

6. Identify strategies to help supervisors stick with priorities.

7. Describe the importance of weekly planning guides and calendars.

8. Define delegation, and explain why it is important.

9. Describe common barriers to delegation.

10. List seven steps for effective delegation.

12

Time Management

TIME IS ONE OF THE SCARCEST and most precious resources available to a supervisor. Few supervisors have all the time they need to do the work that they should. There are only 24 hours in a day, and no sophisticated management procedures or technological innovations can change that. That limitation makes it imperative that supervisors effectively manage what time they have.

While the work you do is important, you must also have adequate time for your family, personal chores, professional growth, and, of course, some leisure. Supervisors who manage their time wisely lead well-rounded lives. Those who cannot often become workaholics—working during time they should spend on other activities. If you can learn to manage your time well, you'll accomplish more personally as well as professionally, and, at the same time, experience less stress and feel better about yourself.

Myths Concerning Time Management

Some supervisors think that, while the concept of time management is good, they can't manage their time because of the nature of a supervisor's job. Let's look at some of the excuses supervisors often give for not managing their time:

- *"My job is to deal with people, problems, and emergencies that don't lend themselves to specific schedules."* This is true some of the time. There are days when supervisors are confronted with "a million things to do at the same time"—many of which cannot be planned. However, there are also slower, less-demanding days or times during a busy day when time can be planned. Furthermore, some time-consuming problems and emergencies can be avoided if supervisors practice time management.

- *"I can't delegate because no one else can do the work."* Unfortunately, this observation is often true. A primary reason is that the supervisor has not taken the time to train and develop his/her employees so that they can take on additional responsibilities. Supervisors who believe this time management myth are actually saying that they have not given priority to helping their employees grow on the job. (We'll discuss delegation in more detail later in the chapter.)

- *"Time management doesn't work for big projects."* It takes months to plan a budget or to make arrangements for significant events. However, most time-consuming projects can be broken down into small, manageable parts that can be worked on over a period of days. Some supervisors allocate a specific time period each day to work on long-term projects.

- *"I don't need a formal schedule to manage my time."* This may be true for a few supervisors. But most supervisors with many things to do are not able to do and remember everything without some type of written schedule.

- *"Frequent interruptions make time management impossible."* If you have tried to practice time management principles before and have been thrown off schedule by unplanned interruptions, you may believe this myth. There are many practical ways to manage interruptions. These will be discussed in this chapter.

Time Analysis

The first step in learning how to manage time is analyzing how you spend it now. Using a **daily time log** can help (see Exhibit 12.1). Choose a day and record your activities every half hour. Be honest—no one but you will see the log. If an employee or visitor stopped by and the two of you chatted about non-work-related subjects, write that down. Make explanatory notes on each activity. For example, if a task took longer than usual, write down the reason(s).

At the end of the day, note whether this day was typical, busier than usual, or less busy. Add up the time you spent on each major activity and note these totals along with other comments at the bottom of the daily log. Use the back of the sheet if necessary.

For best results, you should record your activities each day during a typical week. At the end of the week, take time to analyze the information you gathered. Did any patterns or tendencies emerge? What were your biggest time wasters, and what can you do to solve them? Are you delegating enough? Who, or what, accounted for most of your interruptions, and how can you control or eliminate these interruptions?

Other questions you may ask yourself include:

- Which part of each day was most productive? least productive? Why?

- What percentage of your week was spent on productive activities? Are you surprised by this figure?

- Did you work on jobs you enjoy at the expense of higher-priority tasks? How often?

- Are there any tasks you consistently avoided?

- How many of your activities were inappropriate or otherwise did not contribute to achieving one of your objectives?

- Where are your best opportunities for increasing your efficiency?

Again, be honest when you analyze your daily time logs. Only you will know the results. You can't solve your time problems until you identify them.

Time Robbers

Chances are good that you discovered several "time robbers" as you created and analyzed your daily time log. A **time robber** is something that requires time but does not contribute to reaching the organization's objectives. Time robbers can be

Exhibit 12.1 Sample Daily Time Log

DAILY TIME LOG	
Day of Week: M T W T F	Date:
Time Activity	Comments
7:00	
7:30	
8:00	
8:30	
9:00	
9:30	
10:00	
10:30	
11:00	
11:30	
12:00	
12:30	
1:00	
1:30	
2:00	
2:30	
3:00	
3:30	
4:00	
4:30	
5:00	
5:30	

Was this day: _____ Typical?   Comments: _____

_____ More busy?   _____

_____ Less busy?   _____

divided into two categories: those you generate, or those that others generate. Obviously, you have the most control over the time robbers you create yourself. Most supervisors have a long list of self-created time robbers, including: procrastination, attempting too much, never saying no, disorganized work station areas (including desk and files), lack of planning, no objectives, not setting job priorities, not working on the high-priority jobs first, unrealistic time estimates, and so on.

Time robbers that others create include interruptions, meetings, requests for help, crises, mistakes by others, unclear directions, lack of information, waiting for others (employees, your boss, meeting attendees, etc.), and junk mail. Supervisors have a harder time controlling or eliminating these time robbers, but there are strategies that can help. Since supervisors often cite interruptions as the time robber they have the least control over, let's talk about interruptions in more detail.

Interruptions. Interruptions include telephone calls, unexpected visitors, unscheduled meetings, emergencies, and even self-imposed unplanned activities. When you analyzed your daily time logs you probably were not surprised to learn that a significant percentage of your time is spent on interruptions, many of which appear to be unavoidable. In fact, some interruptions are very important. Wise supervisors do not try to avoid interruptions, but, rather, try to more effectively manage them.

Before you can start managing your interruptions you must first categorize them as high-priority interruptions or low-priority interruptions. An example of a high-priority interruption is an unscheduled meeting with your boss. With a high-priority interruption, you should usually drop what you're doing and attend to it. Fortunately, high-priority interruptions do not occur very often.

Most interruptions—such as personal phone calls and other supervisors stopping to chat—can be considered low-priority. A good way to manage low-priority interruptions is to set aside a block of time each day that's most convenient for you to deal with them and postpone them until then. If your employees tend to drop by many times a day, perhaps one short meeting can be an acceptable substitute. You can let other drop-in visitors know that you have set aside a time of day for them to stop by—1:00 P.M. to 1:30 P.M., for example. If drop-in visitors come at other times, you can say things like, "I'm sorry, I have a deadline I'm trying to meet. Can you stop by at one o'clock?" or "Can we talk about this some other time?"

Shifting all or at least most low-priority interruptions to a specific time that's convenient for you can free a lot of your time and lower your frustration level.

Time Management Tools

Time management tools include **to-do lists, weekly planning guides,** and calendars. Using these tools may seem awkward at first. With practice, however, it gets easier and you'll find shortcuts that work for you. You'll discover that planning your time can help you avoid crises, get the most important things done first, and still allow time for other activities that are important to you and your organization.

To-Do Lists

Many supervisors find to-do lists valuable for keeping track of jobs and details that they might otherwise forget. You can use pocket-size notebooks, legal pads, and pre-printed forms. There is no set way to keep a to-do list. Use the format that you're most comfortable with.

Some supervisors write their to-do lists at the beginning of the day, some at the end (for the next day). Some do this planning on their own time. You'll regain the time it takes to write a to-do list (probably 10 to 20 minutes), and then some, as you make efficient use of time throughout the day because you're so organized.

When you write your to-do list each day, put down all the tasks you can think of. Don't worry about which tasks are most important. When the list is complete, look it over and decide what to do first, second, third, etc. Consider deadlines, work flow, number of employees, and other variables. Cross off items that do not have to be done that day.

Avoid the mistake of writing a list so long that you get discouraged before you begin. It takes practice to write a realistic list that includes only those items that truly must be done that day. Another mistake is to be too general. Instead of a vague statement like "Get organized," write "Properly file all the papers cluttering my desk."

After you have written a to-do list and have assigned priorities, ask yourself, "What do I have to do myself, and what can I delegate?" Write the names of the people who will do the jobs beside the jobs that can be delegated.

If you haven't used a to-do list in the past, you may find it will take a while to get comfortable with making one out and scheduling your day accordingly. Don't give up! Supervisors have many demands on their time. Your boss and other people often assign new tasks which might cause you to rearrange your priorities. Don't fight it—rearranging priorities is part of your job. Your to-do list helps you stay flexible so you can rearrange your priorities without getting lost and forgetting your own plans. Once you've completed the newly assigned tasks, you can return to your list and pick up where you left off. You'll be better organized, you'll get more done, and you'll feel more in control.

Sticking with Priorities. It's one thing to write a to-do list; it's another to follow it. When it's time to do the work, make sure you do the high-priority items first. What if your most important task will take all day? Then you must make a decision: Can I afford to let everything else go today to complete this task, or can I divide this big project into smaller pieces that can be done over several days?

Doing the most important jobs first is simple to say but sometimes hard to do. You can come up with lots of excuses for not sticking with your priorities. Supervisors can feel overwhelmed at times by all the activities, tasks, and deadlines they face at one time. Yet it's precisely at the point that you feel overwhelmed that you must set and follow priorities in order to stay in control and effectively supervise.

You must determine priorities for your employees as well as yourself. One of the most important responsibilities you have is to create a smooth work flow for your staff. If you continually pull your employees from one project to the next to meet last-minute deadlines, you may meet the deadlines—for a while, anyway— but you may also create a sense of frustration and resentment that will be counterproductive over the long run.

Chances are greater that you can avoid reshuffling your priorities and pulling employees from project to project if you set your priorities with the help of your boss. Meet with him/her occasionally to outline the work priorities as you see them and explain what you've done so far. Point out significant obstacles or problems. Then ask questions. "Do you have any advice on how to solve this problem?" or "Given this situation, which project should be done first?" are questions that can

Exhibit 12.2 Sample Weekly Planning Guide

				WEEKLY PLANNING GUIDE		Week of: _____
	Priorities			Schedule		
Day/Date	Activities	Projects	People	Morning	Afternoon	Evening
Monday _____	Inspect Kitchen	Work on Special Function	Meet with F&B Director	6:00	12:00	6:00 Plan Special Function
				7:00	1:00	7:00
			Meet with Ron— employee review	8:00 To-do list	2:00 Meeting— F&B Director	8:00
				9:00 Inspect kitchen	3:00	9:00
				10:00 Meeting with Ron	4:00	10:00
				11:00	5:00	11:00
Tuesday_____	Safety Committee Meeting	Complete work on Special Function	George—Sales Rep.	6:00	12:00	6:00
				7:00	1:00	7:00
				8:00 To-do list	2:00 George	8:00
				9:00	3:00	9:00
				10:00	4:00	10:00

save you lots of time. If you have fully explained the situation and all the steps you've taken so far, your boss will be more able to help you with problems and share his/her ideas.

If you consistently have trouble setting priorities or getting things done, sit down with your boss to review your responsibilities. An informal discussion may be all that's necessary. However, sometimes it pays to go over your job description with your boss, especially if your organization's job descriptions are out-of-date documents buried in a policy or employee handbook. You may find that your boss's ideas about your job responsibilities are different from your ideas. Resolving any such differences or misunderstandings can eliminate a lot of problems and inefficiencies.

Weekly Planning Guides

In addition to daily to-do lists, weekly planning guides can help you manage your time. You can use these guides to help you allocate time for the most important activities, projects, and people you must attend to during the week. An example of a weekly planning guide is shown in Exhibit 12.2. Modify this form to meet your specific needs, or create your own guide.

Set up a specific time each week to fill out your weekly planning guide. It should only take a few minutes. As the week progresses, you'll probably have to update the guide. You may need to shift priorities, add new tasks, and reschedule activities. Still, using the guide will help you keep on track.

Calendars

Many supervisors use a calendar to write down important dates, meeting times, and activities throughout the current month and year. Calendars can help remind you of the big picture and the long-term commitments that you must not forget. You should look at the calendar each day before you make out your to-do list. Inform your employees of upcoming deadlines affecting them as soon as possible.

Delegation

Throughout the chapter we've mentioned **delegation.** Delegation involves assigning your employees to do tasks for which you are still accountable. The concept is very much in line with a basic definition of management: "Getting work done right through other people."

Why is delegation important? First, it's one of the best ways supervisors can save time for themselves and their organization. Second, it's important because you can't do everything. This seems obvious, but many supervisors try to do just that, because "these jobs are too important to assign to someone else," "it has to be done right," or other reasons. As a supervisor you must remember that a major part of your job is to manage the work of others, not do the work of others.

Delegation is also important to your staff. If you're willing to delegate, it shows that you trust and respect your employees. They can take greater pride in their work, because they've been given a decision-making role. This increases their participation, involvement, and commitment. When you delegate, you give your employees the opportunity to develop both personally and professionally. If you delegate a task you must also delegate the authority to get the task done.

Are you a good delegator? There are many quizzes or checklists that supervisors can use to help them find out. The sample shown in Exhibit 12.3 is typical. The more times you answer "yes" to the questions in Exhibit 12.3, the more you need to learn to delegate.

Barriers to Delegation

Some supervisors are reluctant to delegate because they do not trust their employees or have confidence in their abilities. Other supervisors shy away from the risk involved. They believe an employee's failure reflects badly on the supervisor and shows that he/she is unable to delegate authority effectively. Still others know that an employee can do a good job, but they are reluctant to share the credit with an employee for a job well done. Other reasons that supervisors may be uncomfortable with delegating include:

- Lack of experience
- Lack of organizational skills

Exhibit 12.3 Sample Delegation Guide

---

1. Do you take work home regularly?
2. Do you work longer hours than your employees?
3. Are you unable to keep on top of priorities?
4. Do you rush to meet deadlines?
5. Are you still handling activities and problems you had before your last promotion?
6. Do you spend time on routine details that others could handle?
7. Do you spend time doing for others what they could be doing for themselves?
8. Are you constantly interrupted with questions or requests about ongoing projects or assignments?
9. Do you like to be personally involved with every project?
10. When you return after a vacation or some other absence from the office, is your in-basket too full?

- Insecurity

- Fear of being disliked by employees

- Perfectionism

- Reluctance to spend the time it takes to train employees

- Failure to establish effective control or follow-up procedures

Your staff may be another barrier to delegation. Employees may not want the freedom and authority involved in delegation. They may fear criticism or failure. They may lack self-confidence. They may feel that they won't be rewarded for a job well done, but they will be punished if the job is not done right. Or, in the past, they may have been rewarded for asking their supervisor how to do everything and for strictly following orders.

The reluctance of many employees to be placed in what they perceive to be an uncertain situation is an often-overlooked barrier to delegation. Generally speaking, there are three levels of delegation, and, unless you make it clear which level an employee is operating on, the employee may resist your efforts to delegate. The three levels are:

- *Level 1:* Full authority is given to the employee to take whatever actions are necessary to carry out the assignment, without consulting or reporting to you.

- *Level 2:* Full authority is given to the employee to take whatever actions are necessary to carry out the assignment, but you must be informed of the actions taken.

- *Level 3:* Authority is limited. The employee must present his/her recommendations to you, and cannot take action until you make a decision.

If your own boss is sometimes unclear about what level of authority you have when he/she delegates a task to you, you'll have an idea of how uncomfortable your employees may be when you're unclear with them. The best way to delegate is to tell employees up front exactly how much authority they have to carry out the task.

Lastly, the **fallacy of omnipotence**—otherwise known as the "I can do it better myself" fallacy—is often found among new supervisors and is perhaps the greatest obstacle to delegation. That new supervisors feel this way is understandable. Their determination, sense of responsibility, and ability to "get the job done" is often why they were made supervisors in the first place. As a new supervisor, you may feel that you were promoted to your position because no one else can do a task quite like you can. That reasoning leads you to want to do everything yourself. The problem with such reasoning is that every time you complete a task rather than assigning it to an employee and providing any necessary coaching, you're ensuring that you'll have to do the job yourself the next time it comes up. You haven't taught anyone else how.

Even if you can do a better job, is the quality of your work so much better than your employees' that it's better for the organization that you do the work—rather than spend the time planning, delegating, supervising, coaching, and training? These are tasks your employees can't do, and you must do. Supervisors who trust their employees and take the time to train and build a good staff typically outperform and out-last those supervisors who burn themselves out trying to do it all.

Steps in Effective Delegation

There are many ways to delegate effectively. Each supervisor develops his/her own particular style. However, there are seven general steps that supervisors should take when delegating work to others.

Think the Project Through. Think the project through before you assign it to an employee. What materials or other resources are needed? What are the results you want? What options can you give the employee? The more options you give, the more the employee acquires a sense of responsibility and ownership of the task and its solution.

Set a Deadline. If it's up to you to set a deadline for the project, be realistic. Don't set a target date that can't possibly be met just to impress your boss. The boss won't be impressed when you miss it. Develop a reputation for getting things done on time, but don't pad your schedules with extra time so that you always meet your deadlines. You'll be building wasted time into the schedules and sooner or later your boss will catch on. If you consistently establish realistic deadlines and meet most of them, your boss will probably be more than willing to negotiate when a job takes more time than you allotted for it.

Many supervisors ask the employee who is performing the work to help set the deadline for its completion. Including the employee in this decision-making process is recommended whenever possible.

If your boss sets the deadline, you must do everything you can to meet it. If possible, negotiate with your boss if you feel you haven't been given reasonable time to get the project done. Keep in mind, however, that your boss may have had the deadline handed down to him/her from higher-level managers.

Choose an Employee. Consider your employees' abilities and work loads, jobs that are coming up in the near future, the importance of the project, and other variables before choosing an employee. Make sure the employee you have in mind has the time and skills to get the job done.

Meet with the Employee. Fully explain the project and its importance to the employee and inform him/her of the deadline. Occasionally you may need to adjust the deadline because of your discussion with the employee. As mentioned previously, you may not even set a deadline until this point, when you can ask the employee to help set it. Tell the employee what level of authority he/she has to get the job done. Point out any possible obstacles you foresee, and suggest possible ways to overcome the obstacles. Encourage the employee to ask questions and listen to his/her ideas on how to approach the task. End the meeting only when both of you agree on how the project should be tackled. Last but not least, express your confidence that the employee can get the job done. Also, remind the employee that you are available if questions or problems arise.

Monitor Progress. Don't constantly look over the employee's shoulder. On the other hand, don't wait until just before the deadline to check his/her progress. Despite your best efforts, sometimes employees misunderstand what is expected of them. See how things are going early and help the employee correct any start-up problems. Be friendly and helpful, not judgmental. Check on the employee from time to time as the project moves forward.

Provide Assistance if Necessary. If an employee gets stuck or goes off in a wrong direction, give him/her just enough help to get going again. Only on the most unusual or difficult task should you provide more help. Don't be condescending or sarcastic, and don't take over the project.

Praise the Employee. Throughout the project, be generous with your praise. This will help build the employee's self-confidence. When the project is finished, thank the employee and make sure he/she receives recognition for the work. Nothing is more discouraging to an employee than having a supervisor take all the credit for an accomplishment.

Key Terms

daily time log	time robbers
delegation	to-do lists
fallacy of omnipotence	weekly planning guides

Discussion Questions

1. What are some of the myths of time management?
2. What is the first step in learning how to manage your time?

3. Into which two categories do time robbers fall?

4. How can you control interruptions?

5. How are to-do lists used by supervisors?

6. Why should you go over your job description with your boss?

7. How can supervisors use weekly planning guides and calendars?

8. Why is delegation important?

9. What are some barriers to delegation?

10. What are seven steps in effective delegation?

REVIEW QUIZ

When you feel you have covered all of the material in this chapter, answer these questions. Choose the *best* answer. Check your answers with the correct ones found on the Review Quiz Answer Key at the end of this book.

True (T) or False (F)

T   F   1. Some time-consuming problems and emergencies can be avoided if supervisors practice time management.

T   F   2. Most supervisors are able to do and remember everything they need to without any type of written schedule.

T   F   3. Your daily time log should include your biggest time wasters.

T   F   4. Deadlines need not be considered on a supervisor's to-do list.

T   F   5. At the point that you feel overwhelmed, you must forget priorities in order to stay in control and effectively supervise.

T   F   6. Delegation of authority involves risk, and some supervisors are afraid of taking risks.

T   F   7. Unless you make it clear which level of delegation an employee is operating on, you may discover a reluctance on the part of many employees to have powers delegated to them.

T   F   8. The fewer options you give an employee to help him/her complete a delegated task, the more he/she has a sense of responsibility and ownership of the task and its solution.

T   F   9. It's a good idea to set a deadline for a project that your employees can't possibly meet to make your people work harder and to impress the boss.

T   F   10. Supervisors should pad their schedules with extra time so that they can always meet their deadlines.

Alternate/Multiple Choice

11. A personal phone call is an example of a:

    a. high-priority interruption.
    b. low-priority interruption.

12. To-do lists should be:

    a. general.
    b. specific.

13. Chances are greater that you can avoid reshuffling your priorities and pulling employees from project to project if you set your priorities:

    a. with the help of your boss.
    b. with the help of your employees.

14.   The text suggests that planning guides be written:

    a. daily.
    b. weekly.
    c. monthly.
    d. yearly.

15.   Supervisors use calendars to record important dates, meeting times, and activities throughout the current month and year. Calendars can also help remind you of:

    a. the big picture.
    b. long-term commitments.
    c. both of the above are correct.
    d. none of the above are correct.

Chapter Outline

The Forces of Stability and Change
    External Forces of Change
    Internal Forces of Change
A Model for Change
    Unfreeze the Existing Situation
    Work Toward the Desired Change
    Refreeze the Revised Situation
Overcoming Resistance to Change
    Analyze Change from the Employees'
       View
    Establish Trust
    Involve Employees
The Supervisor as Change Agent
    Assess Employee Response to Change
    Plan the Implementation of Change
    Evaluate the Change

Learning Objectives

1. Explain how change can affect a single department or an entire organization.

2. Identify stabilizing forces that create continuity within a hospitality organization.

3. Distinguish external forces of change from internal forces of change.

4. Identify changes that affect the structure of an organization.

5. Explain how a model for change can guide supervisors in planning and implementing change.

6. Identify ways in which supervisors may benefit from employees' resistance to change.

7. Explain how supervisors can analyze change from the employees' perspective.

8. Identify actions supervisors can take to overcome employees' resistance to change.

9. Explain why indicators of effective change are essential to the evaluation of the change process.

13

Managing Change

Y ESTERDAY'S SOLUTIONS may not solve today's problems. In the fast-paced world of hospitality, the needs, wants, and expectations of our guests change. Effective supervisors recognize this, are challenged by opportunities to evolve with these changes, and, in the process, help the organization to better attain its goals.

Today's solutions may not solve tomorrow's problems. Applying existing procedures to new situations cannot replace the need to be innovative and to think carefully about the future and how it may be quite different from the present. Supervisors who respond positively to the need for change will be recognized as valuable contributors within their organizations and may be considered first when promotional opportunities arise. Conversely, those who resist purposeful change will be viewed as unable to contribute to the continuing growth and success of the company. In most cases, this will lead management to overlook these individuals when filling positions which require increased responsibility.

Change occurs when there is a variation, alteration, or revision in the way things are done. When change occurs, it usually affects an initial area in the organization and a specific group of employees. For example, the impact of a new equipment item, such as a tilting skillet in the kitchen, may have little effect on other areas of the organization. Yet, within the kitchen, cooks may need to change their methods for preparing certain items, and cooks or stewards will need to learn how to clean and maintain the new equipment.

Any change which, on the surface, seems to affect only one aspect of a single department may in fact affect the entire organization. Normally, the greater the amount of change that is planned, the greater the likelihood that other—or all—aspects of the organization will be affected. For example, consider the implications of change when a new marketing strategy is implemented at a hotel. Top-level executives may decide to attract a new market segment, or to increase business from a particular market segment, such as from corporate travelers. In this instance, it is very likely that the change in marketing strategy will create the need for change in virtually every department within the hotel. Appropriate managers and supervisors may need to adjust performance and productivity standards, upgrade amenities, provide express check-in and check-out service, speed the delivery of room service orders, and address many other concerns.

This chapter begins by identifying the types of forces that create change within the hospitality work environment. Next, a model for analyzing the process of change is examined. Later sections of the chapter focus on how you can succeed in the role of **change agent** and effectively plan, implement, and evaluate changes within the work place.

259

The Forces of Stability and Change

In hospitality operations the forces of stability and change operate at the same time. Every operation needs some form of continuity. In order to plan effectively, you must be able to assume that some conditions affecting how work is done today will persist in time and affect the way work is done tomorrow.

There are many elements of stability within the work environment, such as the physical facility, the available equipment, and the basic needs of the guests. These elements generally do not change quickly. In addition, the relationships established among departments and among employees within departments serve as **stabilizing forces** providing consistency in day-to-day activities. Also, the tendency of staff members at all organizational levels to resist change can serve as a stabilizing force. In opposition to these stabilizing forces are the external and internal forces which drive change within an organization.

External Forces of Change

External forces of change arise from changing social, economic, political, and legal conditions. The changing wants and needs of guests form the most important external force affecting hospitality operations. Many of the changes in guest behavior reflect wider societal changes. For example, a health-conscious public may demand more nutritional meals in restaurants or fitness facilities in hotels. Also, a public concern about drunk drivers and the number of alcohol-related highway deaths may motivate guests to frequent hospitality operations that provide a varied non-alcoholic beverage service.

The shrinking labor market serves as another example of how external social change may drive changes within a hospitality organization. As it becomes more and more difficult to find new employees, managers and supervisors may need to implement changes within the operation to minimize turnover. Political and economic changes, such as an increase in minimum wage, may require managers and supervisors to find more innovative ways to reduce labor requirements in order to control rising labor costs. Changes in the political and legal climate may also drive change within an operation. For example, an increased focus on workers' rights and a resultant increase in the number of lawsuits brought against employers for wrongful dismissal may require an organization to improve the processes for selecting, hiring, and evaluating employees.

Internal Forces of Change

Internal forces of change are also at work within an organization. These forces are closer to the day-to-day operation of the business and are usually more in the realm of management's control than are external forces.

The following sections briefly examine change as it relates to three aspects of hospitality businesses: employees, technology, and organizational structure. These three aspects are so closely related that a change in one aspect may affect the others.

Employees and Change. One of your most important responsibilities as a supervisor is to constantly seek ways to improve the job performance of employees.

Improving job performance often means changing the behavior or attitudes of employees. It is frequently easier, quicker, and more effective to improve employees' job performance by focusing your efforts on changing their behavior rather than on changing their attitudes. Attitudes are difficult to define. Behavior, on the other hand, is observable and measurable.

Supervisors train, coach, and evaluate performance as a means of changing the behavior of individual employees. Team-building activities and group training programs are techniques which supervisors can use to try to change employees' behavior when working with groups. Supervisors can use these same techniques to try to change employee attitudes. However, keep in mind that the process of changing employee attitudes will be difficult at best, even when experienced supervisors apply these techniques.

Technology and Change. New technology often creates the need for change within an organization. At times, change is forced upon an organization. These days, for example, a hotel usually needs a modern, computerized reservations system in order to be competitive. On occasion, the organization itself may desire technological change. For example, a food and beverage department may choose to implement a computerized beverage system for added control in bar areas. Introducing new technology will require changes in the skills employees need to function effectively and, in some cases, will create a need to restructure certain aspects of the organization.

Organizational Structure and Change. There are many ways by which change can affect the structure of an organization. For example, the owners or high-level executives of a hospitality business may wish to decentralize operations. Decentralizing would mean establishing smaller, self-contained organizational units with increased decision-making power. As a supervisor, you might welcome such a change because it may offer increased opportunities to motivate employees in smaller work units and enable you to more carefully structure both the work unit and the employees' tasks. Changes in organizational structure also occur when top-level managers revise the chain of command, thereby increasing (or decreasing) areas of responsibility for departments or positions. Organizational changes such as these may result in revised job descriptions for the affected positions. Also, as new employees enter the organization and assume leadership positions, they are likely to use their influence to initiate changes.

Another structural approach to change focuses on improving the work flow within the organization. This is usually done to increase employee productivity. Think about how changes in the work flow between stewarding, the kitchen, and banquets (service and setup) could improve the management of banquet activities. Given a limited amount of cross-training, tasks could be reassigned based on the volume of business and the number of employees at hand on any given day. For example, tasks currently performed by banquet setup or service employees, such as requisitioning china and silver or preparing table setups (placing water, butter, salt, pepper, etc.), could be reassigned to stewards. Tasks usually assigned to kitchen staff, such as plating meals or re-supplying hot boxes, could also be reassigned to stewards. Or, tasks currently assigned to stewards, such as setting up

Exhibit 13.1 A Model for Change

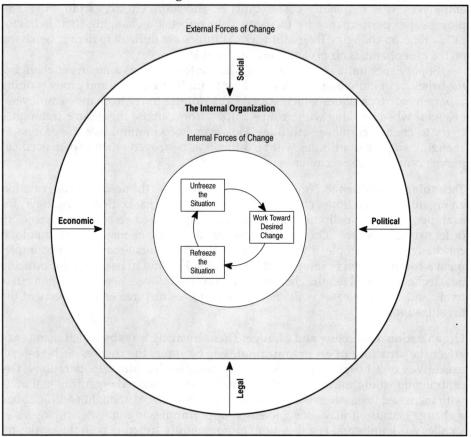

and organizing break-down tables in banquet corridors, could be reassigned to banquet setup crews. Under certain conditions, any of these changes could potentially improve overall productivity by enabling the staff that's already available to assist in the completion of the necessary tasks.

A Model for Change

Many years ago Kurt Lewin proposed a framework within which the process of change could be studied.[1] He and others believed that three procedures were necessary for change to occur: first, the existing situation must be *unfrozen;* next, the change agent (the supervisor) must work toward the desired change; then, the revised situation must be *refrozen.* Exhibit 13.1 diagrams this model for change as it operates under the pressures exerted by external and internal forces of change.

While it simplifies the discussion of change to suggest that the process is composed of three distinct parts, you should remember that change is a continuous process without an obvious beginning or end. Change occurs at more than one point in the organization at the same time. The following sections examine each of the steps within the model for change.

Unfreeze the Existing Situation

Unfreezing the existing situation applies to those planning change (change agents, such as the supervisor) as well as to those who will ultimately be affected by the change. To develop strategies by which to unfreeze the situation, those who are planning change must analyze the driving and restraining forces at work in the existing situation. For example, consider high turnover within a department. There may be a variety of forces driving the high turnover, such as the following:

- Employees may not feel comfortable about their jobs because the training given them has been inadequate.

- Wages may not be competitive within the area, motivating employees to seek jobs at other properties.

- Employees may feel that opportunities for advancement are too limited, or even nonexistent.

If left uncontrolled, these driving forces could result in even higher turnover. On the other hand, restraining forces that could be keeping the existing turnover from becoming even higher might include: pleasant working conditions and environment, fair management practices, reliable equipment, recognition for work done well, etc.

By unfreezing the existing situation, those planning change in this particular situation can develop strategies that will decrease the impact of any single driving force, or that will increase the impact of any single restraining force. The key in planning for change is to recognize that any existing situation is the result of a variety of forces, any one of which can be worked on to unfreeze the situation.

After those planning change have unfrozen the situation for the purpose of developing strategies, the change agents must consider ways to unfreeze the situation for those who will ultimately be affected by the change. The first step in this process should be to generate a need for change in the minds of affected staff members. As the change agent, you must show employees why *they* should be dissatisfied with the current situation. A need for change might be developed by explaining reasons for the change, by increasing pressure for change (with rewards or punishments), or by taking action to reduce employee resistance to change. A later section in this chapter examines how supervisors can prepare themselves as change agents by analyzing change from the point of view of employees affected by a proposed change. By anticipating the advantages and disadvantages of change from the perspective of employees, a supervisor can develop strategies to unfreeze the situation for employees and lead them toward the desired change in behavior.

Work Toward the Desired Change

The process of working toward the desired change generally requires that you attempt to modify employee behavior and, at the same time, analyze affected policies and train staff in improved job methods and operating techniques. These tasks are easier when you have the respect of your employees. Also, it is better to work first with those employees who are highly respected by their peers or are informal group leaders in the department.

If employees are placed in job situations in which they confront new problems (or old problems which must be resolved with new methods), the process of change might, by necessity, be easier. For example, an employee who does not want to use a new piece of equipment will likely have to use it when the older equipment is no longer available. In this instance, the employee has only two options—continue to "fight" the equipment or adapt by learning how, and for what, to use it.

Refreeze the Revised Situation

After the desired change is implemented, stabilizing forces tend to create a new status quo. This is called the refreezing process.[2] New relationships are established, and the new behavior, procedures and policies become part of the day-to-day activities. However, over time the current job situation (which continues to be influenced by the organizational structure, existing work procedures, and currently employed staff members) will be affected by external and internal forces which may initiate further changes in the job situation. The change process will evolve once again. This process will yield a revised job situation which will itself, over time, be influenced by external and internal forces stimulating change. In this respect, then, the process of change is cyclical and ongoing.

Overcoming Resistance to Change

Change is often difficult to implement because people who feel comfortable with what they are doing typically want to maintain established routines. Employees are no exception; most have a natural tendency to resist changes required by revised work procedures. As a supervisor, you must understand why employees might resist specific changes so that you can develop strategies to overcome their resistance.

Some employees may resist change simply because it is inconvenient to learn new procedures and assume extra duties. An effective strategy in this case is to conduct appropriate training sessions. At the very least, you should explain new procedures and other work requirements to employees. In addition, if the training is conducted with informational and persuasive techniques designed to reduce **resistance to change**, the training sessions can be even more valuable.

Other employees respond to change with feelings of uncertainty and anxiety. They may feel threatened. These fears can create an emotional resistance to change. Some employees may even feel anxious about "good news," such as promotions or transfers. An effective strategy for these situations is to communicate with employees and explain the "who, what, where, when, and why" behind the proposed change. Employees may just be resisting change because they fear the unknown. You can reduce or eliminate this fear simply by providing appropriate information to those both directly and indirectly involved in the change.

Change can disrupt professional and personal relationships. Employees relate with other staff members and work groups on the job; they know about status, leaders and followers, task specialists, and other aspects of their current work groups. As changes occur on the job, patterns of personal and professional relationships may be disrupted. These and related social dimensions of change will influence the employees' ability to accept change. In this type of situation, persuasive leadership techniques may be helpful. During an individual counseling session you may discover the reasons for an employee's resistance. Then, you can identify what the problems are with the employee's reasoning, supply the proper information, and explain why the change will be beneficial to him/her. Using this approach with informal group leaders might make them "salespersons" for the proposed change.

Before discussing other strategies you can use to overcome resistance to change, it is important to stress some positive aspects of the employee tendency to resist change. As a supervisor, you should look for ways in which employees' resistance to change can work for you, not against you.

Earlier, this chapter identified resistance to change as a stabilizing force within an organization. Almost everyone within an organization will resist change when reasons for the change are not clearly explained. Without an accompanying explanation, a proposed change often seems pointless, as merely "change for the sake of change." Because employee resistance to change creates the need for an explanation, you can identify poorly thought-out changes early and thus avoid trouble. Also, impulsive decisions made by those in higher positions of authority can be evaluated and revised.

Your role as a supervisor is to anticipate the types of resistance employees may have and prepare reasonable explanations for the proposed change. By anticipating employee resistance, you may be able to identify specific areas in which change could, in fact, create problems, and you may be able to take corrective action before serious problems arise. This is one of the ways you can make employee resistance to change work for you, not against you. Resistance forces you to justify a proposed change, and can help you to refine aspects of a change which you and others may have overlooked.

Anticipating resistance to change begins with knowing your employees and using this knowledge to modify your leadership styles to meet the needs of the situation. Try to look at the situation from the employees' perspective. How would you feel if you were an employee? What could make you feel differently about the need for change?

For example, in some instances, change can have an economic impact on employees. Employees may be greatly concerned about their job security regardless of whether this is a real threat. You must anticipate the economic implications of proposed changes and inform employees about them. If employees realize there are no economic disadvantages to the change and, in fact, there are advantages for them, they will be more receptive to it. You should practice your skills of thinking about change—and how to discuss it—from the employees' perspective. This will help identify major issues to discuss and resolve with employees. The need to explain, defend, and justify reasons for changes—from the employees' perspective when possible—is critical to the process of successfully planning and implementing change. The following sections present strategies supervisors can use to overcome employees' resistance to change.

Analyze Change from the Employees' View

In order to implement change effectively, supervisors need to analyze change from the perspective of employees. This is accomplished by identifying, from the employees' viewpoint, the advantages and disadvantages of the proposed change.

For example, consider the following situation. The front office manager wants to change the way reservations are handled. Currently, employees manually record reservations on cards and, later, enter data from the cards into the front office computer system. A number of problems have surfaced in relation to these procedures. For example, when cards are misplaced, reservations do not get into the computer system. Also, data correctly recorded manually are, at times, incorrectly entered into the computer system. The manager now wants to do away with the written cards and enter reservations directly into the computer system.

The supervisor responsible for implementing this change should begin by analyzing how employees might view the change. This analysis often takes the form of identifying some of the advantages and disadvantages of change for the affected employees. For example, reservations staff might view the situation in the following way:

Advantages

1. The front office manager will like me more if I cooperate.

2. My work might be easier.

3. The way it's done now is cumbersome and time-consuming.

4. Now I won't get into trouble because a reservation didn't get into the system soon enough.

Disadvantages

1. I won't get more pay.

2. I'll have to make an effort to learn the new procedures.

3. There's no guarantee that the new method will be better for me in any way.

4. I'm concerned that I won't be able to enter the reservations fast enough to keep up with the calls.

Behavioral change is likely if the advantages outweigh disadvantages. If, on the other hand, the disadvantages of change seem more powerful than the advantages, behavioral change is less likely. If the change does, in fact, benefit the employees, a new status quo will result from the new procedures. However, if employees judge the implemented change to be disadvantageous for them, they will resist it and the supervisor can expect a very awkward transitional period.

Establish Trust

Employees who do not trust or respect their supervisors are likely to resist change. Past experiences influence reactions to present or future expectations. Perhaps changes have not been effective in the past: "Here comes another change, I wonder how long it will last" may be a common thought. If there have been problems with changes before—ideas did not work out, unexpected results occurred, employees were hurt by changes in unexpected ways, etc.—it will be difficult to convince employees that new changes will be beneficial. Clearly, the supervisor who emphasizes one thing today and another thing tomorrow is likely to be confronted with employees who will resist change.

Some changes, however, are not initiated by the supervisor but are mandated by top management. Emphasis in the operation may change. Areas of concern today—about which changes might be proposed—may take a back seat to other priorities tomorrow. Employees recognize this and may attempt to resist change with the thought that the emphasis on the issue might "go away." You should recognize, however, that continual change, regardless of necessity, can frustrate employees.

In some cases your use of authority may be helpful—or all that is necessary—to implement change effectively. If you have strong position authority, supervise in very structured situations, and have poor relationships with employees, the use of authority may be one of the few tools you have available. At the very least, you must be certain that you have the authority to make decisions and to implement changes.

The supervisor with a history of problems in implementing change will most likely need to gain the support of informal group leaders or upper management levels as change is implemented. New supervisors will do well to delay changes, if possible, to allow them to observe: (a) existing employee relationships, (b) factors influencing the way work is being done, and (c) exactly how standard operating procedures are carried out. New supervisors will need time to generate and carefully evaluate alternative plans and procedures.

Perhaps the most important factor in implementing change successfully is for you to develop and maintain an atmosphere of trust and respect in all of your interactions with employees. Employees are more likely to respond favorably to changes when they trust you; that is, when they agree with your stated reasons for the change and when they also concur with your assessment of the benefits they will gain from the change. You cannot, however, develop an atmosphere of trust simply for the purpose of implementing change. A history of honesty, fairness, and concern for employees influences the development of a positive attitude toward you; as this occurs, the relationship will carry over in the acceptance of change.

Involve Employees

It is important for individual employees to become involved in the change process. Involvement begins when changes are first considered (employees may have ideas about alternatives), continues to the actual decision-making process (employee input is important), and concludes with the employee's involvement in the trial, implementation, modification, and evaluation processes.

Make employees aware of a problem and give them an opportunity to generate ideas for change. To the extent that you can use employee input to develop and select alternatives, your work in the implementation phase will be easier (since resistance to change is likely to be lower).

Employees who are involved in the decision-making process leading to change will more likely accept change than those who are "kept in the dark." Some employees, probably not all, will want to become involved in the process. To the extent possible, these employees should become partners with you as you implement changes.

Involving both formal and informal employee groups in the decision-making process can also be useful. Some supervisors find the technique of "buzz sessions" helpful. For example, you can explain the problem to a group and ask for potential solutions. You can then discuss advantages and disadvantages. The results may be usable new ideas which you can consider as you make decisions. Since employees have been involved in the process, they will view the decision and the subsequent change as "our" ideas, not "the supervisor's" ideas.

The Supervisor as Change Agent

Supervisors serve as change agents when they assume responsibility for helping to create changes in an employee's behavior or within the organization itself. Serving as a change agent is an integral part of a supervisor's job. You must constantly be alert to problems, remain open to new ideas, and support changes which those at higher organizational levels impose. This section reviews material presented earlier in this chapter and focuses it on the supervisor's role as the agent of change.

Assess Employee Response to Change

Exhibit 13.2 reviews factors and implications that help supervisors to determine how employees may respond to change. When a change is proposed, employees typically evaluate the situation in relation to:

- The extent to which they trust the supervisor

- Their experiences with change in the work environment

- Implications of the change, given available information

- The extent to which they have been asked for input to the change decision

Based upon these and related factors, employees might judge the impact of the change to be destructive, threatening, uncertain, good, or very positive:

- When employees judge the impact of change as destructive or threatening, the supervisor can expect them to oppose and resist change.

- When employees are uncertain about the impact of change, the best the supervisor can expect is that they will tolerate the change.

Exhibit 13.2 Employee Response to Change

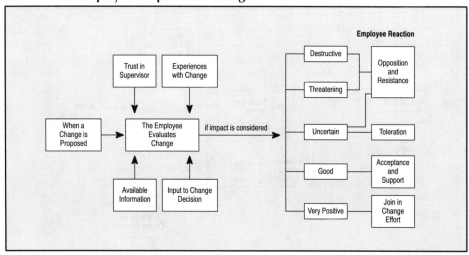

- When employees judge change as good, the supervisor can expect acceptance and support.
- When employees feel very positive about a proposed change, the supervisor can expect them to actively join in the change effort.

Plan the Implementation of Change

Exhibit 13.3 reviews helpful procedures for supervisors to follow when implementing change. As shown in the exhibit, you will need to implement change when (a) you determine its necessity after careful study, or (b) upper management requires change. For change to occur, you must first help employees reject the current situation. Do this by practicing techniques designed to overcome resistance to change and, at the same time, by creating (from the employees' perspective) a need for change.

Second, you must lead the employees through a transition to the desired change. Do this by working with informal group leaders, seeking input from employees, and providing the necessary training and equipment. Likewise, there is a need at this point to assess the impact of the change on the total organization. If you can successfully undertake this procedure, you can gain employee and organizational acceptance of the new situation. You must then reinforce revised procedures, evaluate activities, and, in the process, the changes now become the "way things are done."

Evaluate the Change

Supervisors often find it difficult to evaluate changes which have been implemented in the work environment because the necessary information is either unavailable or

Exhibit 13.3 Steps in the Process of Change

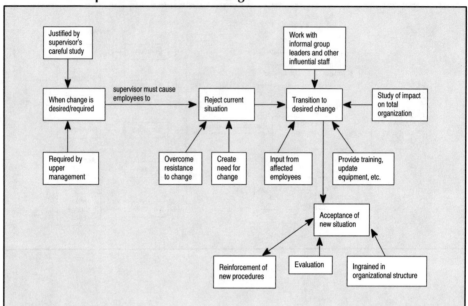

inaccurate. In many cases, these difficulties arise because the expected results of the change were never stated in measurable terms.

For example, if changes are implemented to "increase productivity," the supervisor must determine how much productivity must increase in order for the change to be effective. In situations where objective measurement is not possible, you can, at least, be alert to the possibility that further change may become necessary. If differences between what is observed and what is expected are significant, it is possible that the change has not been successful because it did not accomplish what was expected.

The importance of stating objectives, or **indicators of effective change**, cannot be overemphasized. Without such indicators, the supervisor has no target or benchmark by which to measure the effectiveness of change. Other aspects of evaluating change include:

- Determining whether any additional changes are necessary

- Assessing whether the change has created any spin-off problems

- Analyzing the procedures by which changes have been made

By evaluating all of these aspects of change, supervisors may be able to refine and simplify tasks when change is again necessary. Exhibit 13.4 reviews many of the factors that must be incorporated into the process by which change is effectively managed.

Exhibit 13.4 Supervisor's Checklist for Implementing Change

		Yes	No
1.	Is change necessary?	☐	☐
2.	Do you completely understand—from your perspective as a supervisor—why the change is necessary—and what exactly it is supposed to do?	☐	☐
3.	Do you think about possible reasons why employees might resist the change—and develop effective counter arguments for these reasons?	☐	☐
4.	Do you use an individual counseling technique to discuss the change and its implications with each affected employee?	☐	☐
5.	Do you use a persuasive technique to discover employee perceptions of disadvantages—and to counter these with information which will help employees see advantages to the change?	☐	☐
6.	Do you involve group leaders—both formal and informal—and request their help in gaining acceptance to change?	☐	☐
7.	Do you use a trial approach (test the proposed change and then modify it as necessary) rather than implement it on an "all or nothing" basis?	☐	☐
8.	Do you make sure that affected employees know what must be done differently before changes are implemented?	☐	☐
9.	Do you provide carefully designed training experiences before changes are implemented?	☐	☐
10.	Do you carefully supervise employees during the awkward transitional period when changes are being implemented?	☐	☐
11.	Do you develop indicators of effective change that measurably describe what the situation should be after the changes are made?	☐	☐
12.	Do you evaluate the results of the change based upon the extent to which indicators of effective change are seen in the network situation?	☐	☐
13.	Do you try to recognize any benefits that may result from employee resistance to change?	☐	☐
14.	Do you know how to generate a need for change?	☐	☐
15.	Do you have the respect of the employees who must change?	☐	☐
16.	Do you have a good track record for implementing change with few surprises for employees?	☐	☐
17.	Do you know what other changes are occurring in the organization at this time?	☐	☐
18.	Do you know the impact of the proposed change on other departments?	☐	☐

(continued)

Exhibit 13.4 *(continued)*

	Yes	No
19. Do you have necessary training programs already planned and in place?	☐	☐
20. Do you know whether existing work flows will be improved as a result of the change?	☐	☐
21. Do you know whether the situation requiring change is of continuing importance to the organization?	☐	☐
22. Are all employees permitted, to the extent possible, to participate in all activities relating to change?	☐	☐
23. Do you know what you can and should do to increase pressure for change?	☐	☐
24. Do you have all the information you need to make the change?	☐	☐

Endnotes

1. Kurt Lewin, *Frontiers in Group Dynamics: Human Relations Concept, Method, and Reality in Social Science,* vol. 1, no. 1, 1947, pp. 5–41.

2. Lewin, *Frontiers in Group Dynamics,* pp. 5–41.

Key Terms

change agent
external forces of change
indicators of effective change
internal forces of change
resistance to change
stabilizing forces

Discussion Questions

1. In what ways can an entire organization be affected by changes implemented by a single department?

2. What role do stabilizing forces play in the operation of hospitality businesses?

3. How do external forces of change differ from internal forces of change?

4. How can change affect the structure of an organization?

5. How can supervisors use a model for change to guide their efforts as change agents?

6. How can supervisors develop strategies for implementing change by analyzing driving and restraining forces?

7. In what ways do supervisors benefit from employees' resistance to change?

8. Why should supervisors analyze change from the employees' perspective?

9. Why should supervisors involve employees in the change process?

10. Why are indicators of effective change essential to the evaluation of changes which have been implemented?

REVIEW QUIZ

When you feel you have covered all of the material in this chapter, answer these questions. Choose the *best* answer. Check your answers with the correct ones found on the Review Quiz Answer Key at the end of this book.

True (T) or False (F)

T F 1. It is likely that all aspects of an organization will be affected if the amount of change that is planned is great.

T F 2. In hospitality operations the forces of stability and change operate at different times.

T F 3. Available equipment, physical facilities, and basic needs of guests are examples of elements of stability within the work environment that change quickly.

T F 4. The changing wants and needs of guests are the most important external force affecting hospitality operations.

T F 5. Organizational changes have little or no impact on job descriptions.

T F 6. The process of changing employees' attitudes toward change is easier for experienced supervisors.

T F 7. Change occurs at more than one point in an organization at the same time.

T F 8. A positive attitude toward the supervisor based on a history of fairness and concern for employees will most likely carry over in the acceptance of change.

T F 9. Individual employees should be involved in the change process from beginning to end.

T F 10. All employees are likely to want to become involved in the decision-making process of change.

Alternate/Multiple Choice

11. Increased or decreased areas of responsibility for departments or positions may occur when:

   a. the needs of guests change.
   b. top-level managers revise the chain of command.

12. In the _____ process of change, new relationships may be established, and the new attitudes, procedures, and policies become part of the day-to-day activities.

   a. "refreezing"
   b. "working toward the desired change"

13. In order to implement change effectively, supervisors need to identify the advantages and disadvantages of the proposed change from the view of:

   a. upper management.
   b. the employees.

14. Which procedure is necessary before change will occur?

  a. The existing situation must be unfrozen.
  b. The change agent must work toward the desired change.
  c. The revised situation must be refrozen.
  d. All of the above.

15. The process of working toward the desired change generally requires:

  a. placing employees in different jobs.
  b. modifying the behavior of employees.
  c. controlling turnover.
  d. introducing new technology.

Chapter Outline

Supervisory Certification
Management Development Programs
    Program Steps
Career Ladder Programs
    Not Everyone Takes the Same Path
    Implementing a Professional
        Development Program
Professional Development in Action
    Steps in Planning Your Future
Special Concerns in Career Management
    Decisions
Networking: Associations Help You Learn
Hospitality Trends and Supervisors
    Tomorrow's Work Force
    The Changing Needs of Guests
    Quality Concerns
    Supervisory Techniques
Conclusion

Learning Objectives

1. Identify steps you can take toward your professional development, and explain what effect future trends may have on the hospitality industry and your career.

Note: This chapter is presented to help you in your career planning and to give you an idea of how future trends may affect the hospitality industry. The test materials for the course include no questions on this chapter.

14

Professional Development and Future Trends

SUPERVISORS IN THE HOSPITALITY INDUSTRY must have the knowledge, skills, and common sense to consistently make good decisions about many problems. One of these problems relates to your own professional and personal development. Many think that careers are shaped on the basis of good or bad luck. They do not realize that, just as a map points out the path from one destination to another, a planned career management program will help people get from where they are to where they want to go.

People often delay their career planning. However, in both your private and professional life you must set priorities and do the most important things first. Set aside time today to consider your career goals and alternatives to reach them.

Organizations should create ways for employees to attain goals that are important to both the operation and the individual. Managers must think about what is best not only for the property but for employees when staffing and personnel decisions are made. Employees' abilities and needs must match the jobs to be done. Likewise, employees' concerns about their future with the organization also must be considered. Therefore, both the employees and the organization must be involved in career planning. Employees must continually consider their strengths, weaknesses, needs, and interests in terms of their jobs. At the same time, organizations must offer opportunities for employees to grow on the job.

Organizations can develop career development programs to help employees grow and attain personal and professional goals while on the job. Programs can range from a policy of promoting from within to planned training and development experiences that help the employee climb the organizational ladder. We'll look at many aspects of career development programs in this chapter.

Supervisory Certification

The Educational Institute of the American Hotel & Motel Association awards professional certification and recognition to hospitality supervisors, industry executives, and allied industry professionals who demonstrate an exceptionally high level of expertise, competence, and experience. Certification recognizes your commitment to professionalism and indicates a mastery of both operational and management skills. The Institute's certification and recognition programs elevate the professionalism and image of both the individual recipient and the industry as a whole.

The Certified Hospitality Supervisor (CHS) program offers recognition to those special individuals who have long-term career potential within the hospitality industry. It is the only professional certification program exclusively for hospitality supervisors that is acknowledged worldwide and sanctioned by the American Hotel & Motel Association. The program is open to *anyone* in a supervisory position within a hospitality organization. Supervisors in every department may qualify.

When you earn the Certified Hospitality Supervisor designation, it means that you have displayed the commitment and talent needed for a management career in the hospitality industry. The Certified Hospitality Supervisor stands out from others as an individual who has combined learning and experience to reach a higher level of professionalism. Becoming a Certified Hospitality Supervisor provides you with the opportunity to sharpen your on-the-job skills and may lay the groundwork for further career advancement.

To become a Certified Hospitality Supervisor, you must pass the special CHS certification test. This test consists of questions designed to measure your managerial knowledge. Many of the questions are based on actual decisions that supervisors have to make on a daily basis.

In order to take the CHS test, you must qualify for application to the CHS program. Successfully completing the Educational Institute's Hospitality Supervision course (251) *and* Hospitality Human Resources Management course (356) will qualify you to apply to the CHS program and take the exam. Certification is awarded upon successful completion of the exam and a minimum of three months of supervisory experience in a hospitality setting. For more information about the CHS program, contact the Certification Department at (517) 353-5500, or write to the following address:

> The Educational Institute
> Certification Department
> P.O. Box 1240
> East Lansing, MI 48826 USA

Management Development Programs

Supervisors are more likely to participate in than to actually plan the management development programs used by their organizations. However, some background knowledge about the steps required to plan these efforts can lead to an appreciation of the important role they play in helping an organization develop its managers.

Program Steps

The following four steps briefly review general procedures for planning and implementing an ongoing management development program.

Step 1: Analyze the Organization's Needs. Top managers must forecast business growth and then study the organizational structure to assess how many new supervisors and managers will be needed in the future. Current and accurate job descriptions and specifications for all management positions are needed for this assessment.

Step 2: Assess Managers' Abilities. An inventory of existing management talent must be taken to determine if the organization currently employs individuals who can, with training and management development, perform all tasks identified to be important now and in the future.

Step 3: Plan Individualized Career Development Programs. Based on the analysis in Step 2, programs that meet the needs of individual staff members should be developed and implemented. This step will be explained later in our discussion of career ladder programs.

Step 4: Use a Variety of Management Development Programs. Special training programs can be developed by the organization. It can encourage staff members (through financial assistance) to attend seminars, professional association meetings, and other educational activities.

Employee development programs geared specifically to the hospitality industry are offered through the Educational Institute of the American Hotel & Motel Association. A non-profit educational foundation, the Institute develops courses, seminars, and certification programs for the professional and personal development of individuals in the hospitality industry and those wishing to enter the field.

Job skills also can be learned and improved through planned work experiences. In the context of management development programs, however, work experience programs must be more structured than typical training programs. Although the hospitality industry lends itself to management development opportunities, the success of these programs depends on the planning efforts given them. Examples of programs that can be planned to provide career broadening experiences include the following:

- Use of understudies

- Job rotation

- Job enlargement

- Coaching

- Learner-controlled instruction (LCI)

- Mentor programs

Use of Understudies. Understudies are employees who eventually will assume the positions for which they are being trained. For example, the rooms department manager might select a promising supervisor to help work on a special project which has been assigned to the department. This supervisor then might assume some increased duties when the rooms manager is absent from the job. "Assistant department head" and "administrative assistant" are examples of titles sometimes given to understudies.

Job Rotation. Transferring promising employees to other jobs is another example of professional development through on-the-job experiences. However, these employees should be used for more than vacation relief or emergency purposes. Job rotation must be a planned program in which knowledge and skills are learned as employees perform important tasks in other positions.

Job Enlargement. Job enlargement means redesigning existing jobs to include new tasks. This prepares employees for the possibility of advancement after the new competencies have been acquired and successfully demonstrated.

Coaching. Supervisors can learn about their shortcomings, discuss how problems can be resolved, and can be given a formal evaluation of their work performance when coaching activities are undertaken by their boss.

Learner-Controlled Instruction (LCI). Learner-controlled instruction (LCI) combines formal training with learning gained through experience. LCI includes a list of job-related competencies that must be mastered. The management trainee, progressing at his/her own pace, acquires skills and knowledge with the help of experienced staff members. This approach can be applied to management development programs. The property's needs can be translated into tasks structured into LCI programs that can be learned by management trainees.

Mentor Programs. Mentor programs involve a professional relationship between a senior manager and, perhaps, a supervisor who is interested in learning from the higher-level manager. Typically, the senior manager recognizes the potential of the supervisor. The supervisor, in turn, recognizes that the senior manager would be an excellent source of support and guidance.

Mentor programs can be formal or informal, with relationships between senior managers and trainees lasting for varying periods. The trainees benefit in any good mentor program. Information learned from a mentor can relate to work procedures, internal politics, and ideas about one's future and how to attain career goals. The mentors also benefit from the program because they gain able assistants.

Mentors can have a significant long-term influence on the careers of young associates. However, the relationship will dissolve as the trainee eventually moves beyond the direct responsibility of the mentor. Although professional differences can cause stresses in the relationship, the immediate advantages to the mentor, trainee, and organization point to an increased use of this professional development program.

Career Ladder Programs

A career ladder is a road map that indicates possible career progression courses through the organization. It is a tool to help *all* employees logically plan career advancement strategies. Career ladders can be used by individuals planning their own careers and by managers helping their employees with career development decisions. While it is unlikely that employees will advance in exactly the way outlined in a long-term plan, the career ladder can still be an effective decision-making and analysis tool. Exhibits 14.1 and 14.2 are examples of career ladder guides.

There are many potential advantages to a career ladder:

- When used with planned training programs, a career ladder helps reduce employee turnover and increase productivity.

- It proves management's commitment to training and promoting staff; it is an integral part of an employee morale-building program.

- It assists in cross-training and the planning of job enlargement, job enrichment, job rotation, or related programs.

- Career ladders help tell others (such as those considering careers in the lodging industry) what our business is all about, how they might fit into it now, and how they might advance within it throughout their careers.

- Career ladders are valuable when revising organization charts, job descriptions, and job specifications.

- Career ladders help top managers assess the long-range personnel needs of the operation.

- Used as an integral part of an orientation program, career ladders reinforce employment decisions made by new staff.

Not Everyone Takes the Same Path

Not only do organization structures differ among properties, which means career ladders differ as well, career ladders can also differ within a single organization. Consider, for example, the influence of factors such as:

- Interests of individual employees

- Needs of the organization at different points in time

- Fortunate or unfortunate events (from the employee's perspective) that alter one's career goals and plans

- Changes in business demands

- Type of property (for example, full service versus limited facility)

These and other elements mean that career plans frequently have to be altered. At the same time, these factors should not reduce your efforts to move your career forward. Do employees typically follow career ladder plans to the letter? It depends. Some properties allow only minimal deviation from their career ladders, while others permit considerable latitude, and still others have no formal career ladders.

Implementing a Professional Development Program

As a supervisor, you are not only concerned with your own career advancement, you also play an important role in helping your employees advance. If your

Exhibit 14.1 Sample Career Ladder: Rooms Division

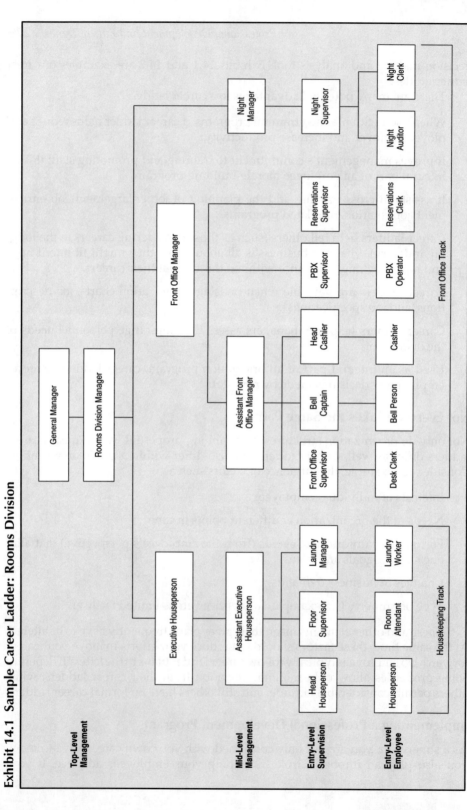

Exhibit 14.2 Sample Career Ladder: Food and Beverage

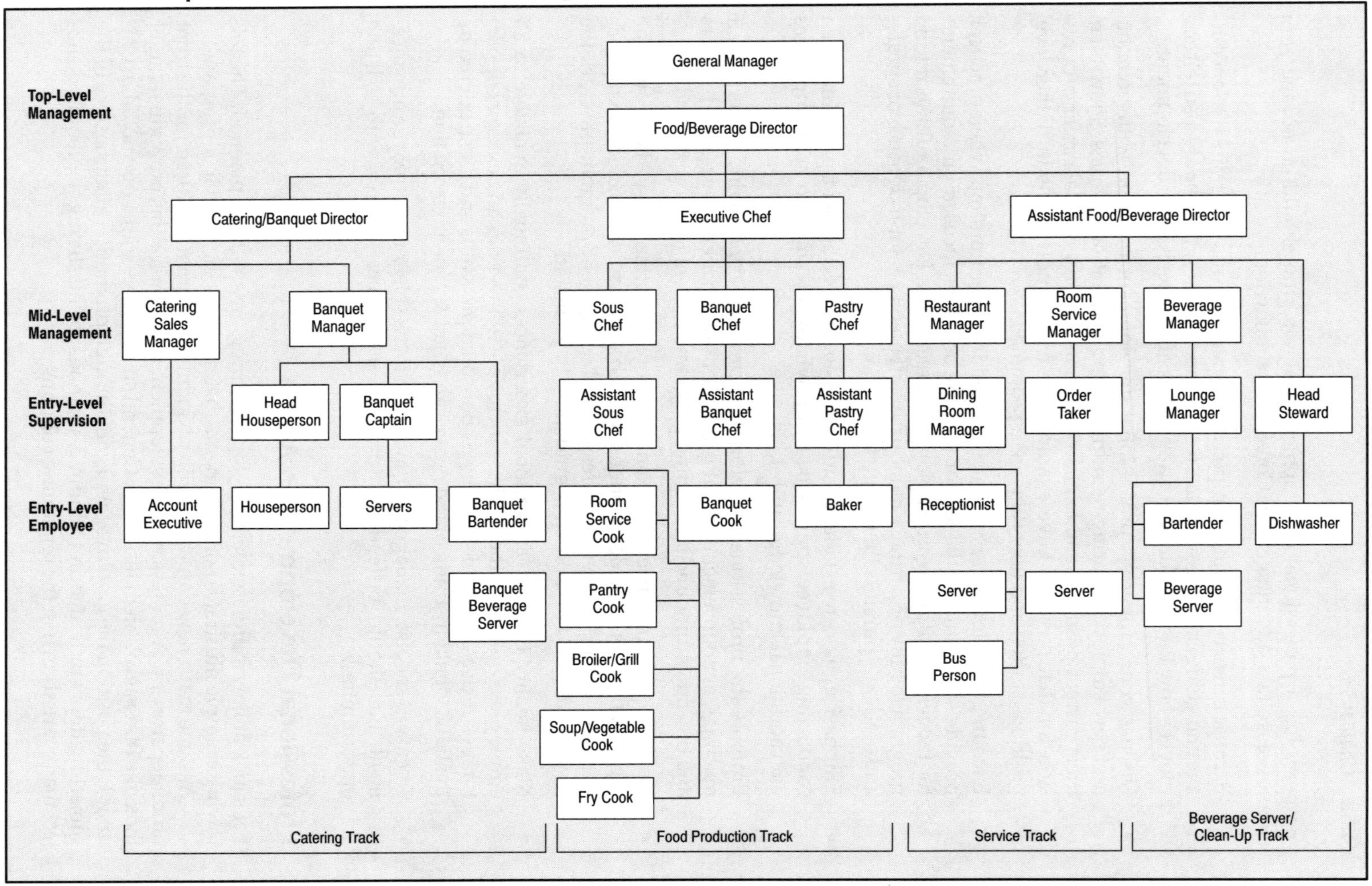

property has a professional development program, you should encourage your employees to take advantage of it. Consider the following:

- Because career counseling is important, supervisors must be trained to encourage and guide employees toward future opportunities. You should also tell employees how their performance appraisals affect their career development.

- Discuss your property's professional development program with potential and new employees during recruitment and orientation sessions. Show them their current positions and explain the organization's normal career progression for that position. Give examples of where individuals in higher-level positions started and how they were promoted.

- Encourage employees to become involved in career training. When practical, provide some time on the job for training activities focused on requirements for the next position in an employee's career track. Develop a tuition refund program to fully or partially reimburse staff members for independent studies and academic pursuits that relate to their jobs.

- Emphasize the career ladder and professional development program when conducting employee appraisals. Learn what you can do to help employees gain additional knowledge and skills.

- Promote the professional development program continually. General staff meetings, announcements about promotions of other employees, and posters and brochures announcing training programs present ideal opportunities.

- Keep the program current by examining it on a routine basis. Also review the organization chart, job descriptions, and job specifications, making changes as required. Ensure that your professional development program provides the most current and best possible guidelines to your staff.

- Make quality training/educational experiences continually available to all employees who desire them. These include staff meetings and external opportunities such as association/college-sponsored programs and those offered by the Educational Institute of the American Hotel & Motel Association.

- To ensure success, management must not focus solely on employee advancement, but should instead try to match employees' desires with existing opportunities.

Professional Development in Action

Let's look at how a professional development program might be planned. The following example illustrates some elements that might be included in a program.

Assume that a new employee with no lodging experience is hired for the front office department. A professional development program for this individual might look like the example in Exhibit 14.3. General subject matter areas are noted in Column 1; the position the employee will gain through promotion after mastery of the subject matter is indicated in Column 2; methods for mastering the required subject matter are shown in the remaining columns.

Exhibit 14.3 Professional Development Program for Entry-Level Front Desk Employees

General Subject-Matter Areas (What Employees Must Know) (1)	Position Title (2)	Property Orientation Program	Training Alternatives			
			On-Job Training	Ongoing Staff Meetings	Educational Institute Course	. Other (college courses, seminar meetings, readings)
1. General Property Information	Trainee	X	X	X		
2. Specific Property Procedures (Front Desk)		X	X	X		
3. Front Office Procedures	Front Desk Agent		X	X	X	
4. Housekeeping Operations					X	
5. Convention Management	Front Desk Supervisor				X	
6. Hotel Sales Promotion					X	
7. Hospitality Law	Asst. Front Office Mgr.				X	
8. Introduction to Hospitality Industry		X	X	X	X	
9. Hospitality Supervision	Front Office Manager		X	X	X	
10. Hospitality Human Resources Management			X	X	X	
11. Hospitality Industry Training			X	X	X	
12. Managerial Accounting for the Hospitality Industry			X	X	X	

As you can see, general and specific property information will be provided to the trainee during times of orientation, on-the-job training, and staff meetings. Next, the trainee must learn general front office procedures before becoming eligible for promotion to front desk agent. The trainee can learn these procedures from both internal and external programs. After learning about housekeeping operations and convention management, the employee might be eligible for promotion to front desk supervisor. Two additional subject matter areas (hotel/motel sales promotion and hospitality law) are prerequisites for possible promotion to assistant front office manager. By mastering additional information and skills, the staff member can continue to advance up the career ladder as vacancies and other opportunities arise.

Steps in Planning Your Future

This chapter has focused on ways that the organization can plan and implement management development programs for employees. It is also important, however, for you to learn specific procedures that are helpful in planning for your own career. Exhibit 14.4 outlines important steps in making decisions about a career.

Exhibit 14.4 The Career Management Process

> **Step 1. What Do I Want to Do?**
>   1. What do you like to do?
>   2. What can you do well?
>
> **Step 2. Discover Opportunities**
>   1. Analyze personality
>   2. Consider important positions
>
> **Step 3. Select Career Goals**
>   1. Consider long/short range
>   2. Review alternatives in light of goals
>
> **Step 4. Choose Your Plan**
>   1. Assess potential
>   2. Analyze advantages, disadvantages
>
> **Step 5. Select the Organization**
>   1. Sell yourself
>   2. Make job decision
>
> **Step 6. Perform Well on First Job**
>   1. Don't get "comfortable"
>   2. Learn as much as possible
>
> **Step 7. Monitor Progress**
>   1. Maintain "options"
>   2. Continually reassess career options
>
> **Step 8. Plan New Experiences**
>   1. Examine possibilities within the organization
>   2. Leave the organization if—and when—necessary

Step 1: "What Do I Want to Do?" The first thing you should do is decide what kind of work appeals to you. Consider your aptitudes, the things you do well, and your interests. You are more likely to want to do things that interest you and at which you are currently successful. Consideration of your likes, dislikes, strengths, and weaknesses provides insights into what you like to do and can do well. Exhibit 14.5 is a checklist of personal inventory questions that may help you better understand yourself as you address these important questions.

Thinking about how you got to your present position can be helpful. If you are currently working in the hospitality industry, how did you get your first job? What are the factors that led you to consider professional opportunities in the industry? If you are not in the hospitality industry now, why are you considering it as a career? Why is it more attractive to you than other industries?

Step 2: Discover Opportunities. Once you have a general idea about what you want to do, think of ways you can do the type of work you enjoy. Consult your supervisors, teachers, counselors, and human resources (personnel) representatives. Students in schools visited by company recruiters should discuss industry-wide employment alternatives as well as the recruiter's specific company.

Exhibit 14.5 Checklist of Personal Inventory Questions

1. Do I know my strengths?   Yes _____   No _____
2. Do I know my weaknesses?   Yes _____   No _____
3. Am I involved in a program to improve my deficiencies?   Yes _____   No _____
4. Am I in good physical and mental health?   Yes _____   No _____
5. Do I follow a planned program to enhance my health
    and well-being?   Yes _____   No _____
6. Am I willing to relocate?   Yes _____   No _____
7. Will I work long hours?   Yes _____   No _____
8. Will I work nights, weekends, and holidays?   Yes _____   No _____
9. Do I like to work with people?   Yes _____   No _____
10. Am I willing to start at or near the bottom of an
    organization and work my way up?   Yes _____   No _____
11. Do I like responsibility?   Yes _____   No _____
12. Can I handle responsibility?   Yes _____   No _____
13. Am I dependable?   Yes _____   No _____
14. Can I make mature decisions?   Yes _____   No _____
15. Can I follow orders?   Yes _____   No _____
16. Can I work as a member of a team?   Yes _____   No _____
17. Do I like close supervision?   Yes _____   No _____
18. Do I like working with details?   Yes _____   No _____
19. Am I comfortable working in a job that has many routines?   Yes _____   No _____
20. Can I manage other people?   Yes _____   No _____
21. Do I like to follow through on my work from beginning
    to end?   Yes _____   No _____
22. Do I like to make decisions and solve problems?   Yes _____   No _____
23. Do I like to work with people rather than with things?   Yes _____   No _____
24. Do I get along well with people?   Yes _____   No _____
25. Can I work well under pressure?   Yes _____   No _____
26. Can I do hard work?   Yes _____   No _____
27. Do I like to seek creative ways to do things when
    there are no set procedures?   Yes _____   No _____
28. Do principles in the "art and science" of management
    interest me?   Yes _____   No _____
29. Would I like to be a professional manager?   Yes _____   No _____
30. Do I like to study people?   Yes _____   No _____
31. Do I learn from my past mistakes?   Yes _____   No _____
32. Do I believe that the guest is always right?   Yes _____   No _____
33. Do I recognize that there is always a better way?   Yes _____   No _____
34. Do I think it is fun to learn?   Yes _____   No _____
35. Am I a creative and inventive person when it comes
    to making decisions?   Yes _____   No _____

Read trade publications for employment listings. Participate in career days. Talk with employees in other departments, your boss, and anyone else who can give you information.

Step 3: Select Career Goals. After you have an idea about what you want to do and have learned about available opportunities, you should select career goals. Making a career decision is not an exact science. The kind of self-analysis and information exploration just described will help reduce the possibility of errors.

The process of making career decisions is ongoing. People change and so do their interests and opportunities. Also, as the work environment changes, new career opportunities develop.

There is no way to gain perfect insight into career management decisions. Tests for aptitude, interests, skills, and knowledge can be helpful. Yet, they will not provide the answer to a career choice. Therefore, be flexible about your career management decisions.

Delaying career management decisions is not wise. Wanting to "think about it for a year or two" is usually procrastination rather than an earnest attempt to make a better decision.

When selecting career goals, you must honestly attempt to match the findings of Steps 1 and 2 with a realistic appraisal of what you should try to accomplish. Remember, realistically there are only so many hotels where you may be employed. Develop a strategy that takes into consideration:

- Where you are now
- Where you want to be in one year, five years, and ten years
- What intermediate steps you can take to make your goals possible

When attempting to select career goals, a "balance sheet approach" might be used. With this approach, you study the advantages and disadvantages of reaching each goal. For example, one goal might require that you either continue your education, relocate to another part of the country, or accept a lower-paying job in a different career field. These undesirable aspects should be weighed against how important the goal in question is to your career plan.

Step 4: Choose Your Plan. After your career goals are determined, you should decide what plan you will use to attain them. Perhaps now you are in the right organization and on the first rung of your career ladder. On the other hand, you may realize that your current job does not have the growth potential you need. Or you may be in school and considering vocational opportunities after graduation. In any event, the process for making this first career decision (staying, moving on, entering an organization) is basically the same. Consider your short- and long-range career goals and decide how your career can be advanced. Your assessment of the situation will depend on the information you have gathered and how you analyze the advantages and disadvantages of attaining a goal for each alternative.

Step 5: Select the Organization. As a result of the analysis process, select the organization that you believe will best help you reach your goals. First, you have to discover what qualities the organization expects of employees in the position you're after. Then you must convince recruiters that you possess those qualities. A good resume and a command of job interview skills will be helpful. Knowledge about the company and yourself can also help you to obtain the job of your choice.

The availability and type of management development programs offered by the company are important factors when making a job selection decision. A company with formal programs may be a better choice than an organization with no clearly defined career development program.

After interviewing with and studying as many organizations as possible, you will have to make a job decision. Your decision should be the one that seems the most likely to keep you on the track of reaching your career management goals.

Step 6: Perform Well on First Job. Once hired, you must perform well on the job. Constantly evaluate how your new experiences and job information can benefit you and the company. Don't become comfortable with doing your work routinely. Contribute ideas whenever possible; ask your supervisor how you can improve; study and learn job-related information on your own.

If you perform well, you are likely to be recognized as a candidate for promotion. Remember, the most certain way to get a promotion is to always be the best you can be at the job you are currently performing.

Step 7: Monitor Progress. Ensure that your work meets your boss's standards and expectations. At least once a month, ask your boss how well you are performing the important tasks of your job. At the same time, make certain you are reaching your career goals. Consider whether you want to continue with or change your career goals. Examine your current situation and, if you are not comfortable with it, continue the process of finding and evaluating alternatives that are compatible with your career plans.

Step 8: Plan New Experiences. You will want to plan new experiences. Examine career development possibilities in your current organization. Consider other alternatives if they have potential benefits.

Special Concerns in Career Management Decisions

Remember these points as you plan your career:

- Set realistic goals.

- Some jobs do not offer significant challenges for you, but they might be necessary steps to the top. While working in entry-level positions, it's more productive to learn all you can about the organization and its procedures rather than resent how the organization is wasting your talents.

- Attempt to find challenges in your present job. Think about ways to make the job better.

- Recognize that experiences in your first jobs may not be similar to those in subsequent jobs. Often, you must defer attainment of ego and status needs during your first job experiences.

- It is unlikely that all the supervision principles discussed in this book will be practiced where you work. At times, your supervisor will do things that seem incorrect. Work is not always done "by the book."

The most important point to remember is that you can directly influence your future. The person who can meet the needs of our changing industry will likely be well-prepared to reach his/her goals. Remember, if you don't know where your career is heading, you will never get where you want to go.

Networking: Associations Help You Learn

One of the best opportunities for professional education and training in the lodging industry is the American Hotel & Motel Association (AH&MA) and its non-profit subsidiary, the Educational Institute of the American Hotel & Motel Association.

The AH&MA is a federation of more than 9,000 hotels, motels, inns, resorts, and other lodging properties that offers many benefits and services to its members. A variety of committees address specialized concerns such as technology, tourism, human resources, and food and beverage management.

Professional associations are active in many areas and provide good opportunities for interacting with others with common problems and interests. Associations provide legislative, professional, social, and other benefits to their members. Many professionals believe in the need to give something back to their industries in return for the help they received when they were moving up their career ladders. Working with associations at the state and national levels provides opportunities for you to grow professionally while making practical contributions to the industry.

Hospitality Trends and Supervisors

Everywhere you look these days there are people talking about what the world will be like in the future. Futurists specialize in communicating what our future holds. Environmentalists tell us about the worsening condition of our planet and what that means for our children and their children. Economists speak about the consequences of a world economy. Politicians tell us what we ought to do with our money, our lives, and our votes. Finally, educators tell us what they think we need to know in order to be successful in the future.

Some of these messages are encouraging. For example, a worldwide economy provides many exciting opportunities. We can look forward to an improved quality of life—many of us can expect to have an increased amount of free time. And there will be wonderful new technologies to aid us in every aspect of our work and personal lives.

The purpose of this section is to give you a glimpse of your future as a supervisor in the hospitality industry. The section begins with a discussion of trends that are dramatically altering the work force you will be supervising in the year 2000 and beyond. It also discusses the changing needs of guests, quality concerns, and new supervisory techniques.

Tomorrow's Work Force

Workforce 2000, a 1988 report on the future work force of the United States, paints a challenging picture for U.S. employers. According to the report, four key trends will shape the work force in the last years of the twentieth century:

- The American economy should grow at a relatively healthy pace, boosted by a rebound in U.S. exports, renewed productivity growth, and a strong world economy.

- Despite its international comeback, U.S. manufacturing will claim a much smaller share of the economy in the year 2000 than it does today. Service industries will create most of the new jobs and most of the new wealth during the next several years.

- The work force will grow slowly and be more culturally diversified. In addition, there will be more older and more female workers.

- The new jobs in the service industry will demand much higher skill levels than today's jobs. Very few new jobs will be created for those who cannot read, follow directions, and use mathematics. Ironically, the demographic trends in the work force coupled with the higher skill requirements of the economy will lead to both higher and lower unemployment. There will be higher unemployment rates among people with few skills, and low or no unemployment among educated and/or skilled workers.

These trends create a number of challenges for supervisors in the hospitality industry. You must improve productivity by increasing worker speed and output in the future. At the same time, you must find strategies to maintain the energies of an aging work force. As the average age of American workers climbs toward 40, you must make sure that your employees do not lose their adaptability and willingness to learn new skills.

Another major challenge confronting the hospitality industry is how to reconcile the conflicting needs of women, work, and families. Almost two-thirds of the new entrants into the work force between now and the year 2000 will be women; 61 percent of all women of working age are expected to have jobs by the year 2000. This presents a significant challenge to organizations, because most current policies and procedures covering pay, fringe benefits, time away from work, pensions, welfare, and other issues were designed for a society in which men worked and women stayed at home.

In the years ahead, non-traditional employees will make up a larger-than-ever share of new entrants into the labor force. The rapid pace of technological change in the hospitality industry and the industry's ever-rising skill requirements make the task of fully utilizing these workers particularly urgent between now and 2000. The challenge for employers will be to educate and train those groups who lack the skills necessary to perform in the workplace of the future.

Immigrants will represent the largest share of the increase in the population and the work force since the end of World War I. Even with the Immigration Reform and Control Act of 1986, approximately 600,000 legal and illegal immigrants are expected to enter the United States annually through the balance of the century.

Two-thirds of this number will enter the work force. Again, many of these immigrants will need special education and training.

It's clear that the hospitality industry and you as a supervisor must develop better strategies for attracting, hiring, training, motivating, and keeping people in order to cope with the changing demographic and employment environment. There will be many opportunities for those supervisors who can adjust and meet the challenges presented by the changing work force.[1]

The Changing Needs of Guests

Tomorrow's guests will demand more than guests do today. In addition to greater income and education levels, six other changes are forecast for the life-style of our future guests:

- With increased amounts of leisure time and more income to spend on non-essential items, people will be traveling more than ever before.

- Population diversity is growing and there will be an increased acceptance of cultural differences in our society.

- People will have increasing expectations for success, especially economic success.

- People will expect higher levels of medical care. There will be an increase in preventive medicine, and "wellness" movements will emphasize life-styles focusing on exercise, nutrition, and health maintenance.

- Consumers will become smarter buyers because of the continued growth of the consumerism movement.

- Family trends will include a decline in birthrates, decrease in the divorce rate, and growth in leisure-time and "do-it-yourself" activities. There will be an increase in single heads of households (the "new poor") and in the elderly population.

Each of the preceding trends suggests a potential increase in the use of products and services offered by the hospitality industry. The successful hospitality organizations of the future will be those that recognize and use their opportunities to consistently deliver the products and services desired by society.

Quality Concerns

The present emphasis on quality will continue and probably increase in the future. This will have a direct impact on you, since supervisors help to define quality and ensure that it's consistently delivered.

While the term "quality assurance" is frequently used in our industry, there are few hospitality organizations with long-term quality assurance programs. Sometimes these programs are poorly conceived or implemented or do not have top management support. Others that start well may end abruptly because of a change in management, or simply because managers lose interest. Regardless of whether they have a formal quality assurance program in place, tomorrow's hospitality operations must emphasize quality. Producing quality products and services depends as much on philosophy or attitude as it does on procedures. One of the ways supervisors will meet quality goals is to allow their employees to plan and implement ways to do jobs better.

Supervisory Techniques

Future industry changes will affect supervisory styles and techniques. This section presents ideas that today's experts have about how your role as a supervisor is likely to change.

The Supervisor as Planner and Strategist. Planning will become more important in the increasingly competitive hospitality industry for managers at all levels, including supervisors. Supervisors will have to do more planning than ever before to control labor and other costs. And they will no longer be planning only day-to-day activities. They will increasingly be asked to contribute to their organization's long-range, business, financial, and marketing plans.

Empowerment. The term "empowerment" relates to the delegation of decision-making authority to the level within the organization at which the particular decision must be made. Because situations constantly change and the needs of guests change, it's unlikely that standard operating procedures will cover every situation. As a result, more hospitality operations are allowing employees greater freedom to determine what's best in certain situations. Supervisors who have informed their employees about the organization's mission and objectives and who have trained them well to provide good service are likely to have employees who can be empowered to make more decisions on their own.

Managing Up. The new work force will want to be self-directed. This means more than just having a say in matters that affect them. Employees will want the freedom to plan and perform significant parts of their jobs. And they will want to be rewarded based on how well they do this work.

"Managing up" will be a critical skill for you to develop in the future. Just as your boss will empower you with broader authority and responsibility, you must learn how to empower your employees. Your challenge will be to perform assignments efficiently and on schedule without constantly turning to your boss with questions about issues that you are empowered to resolve. In turn, you must trust the judgment of your employees and encourage them not to check with you about every little detail. Dictatorial supervisors will have decreasing roles in tomorrow's hospitality organizations.

Organizational Structures. Hospitality organizations are likely to become "flatter." This means that many traditional middle-management positions will be eliminated. As these positions are eliminated, supervisors and employees will assume greater responsibilities. Supervisors will make more decisions and be more instrumental in their organization's success or failure.

Organizational structures will change in another way. In the past, most organizations seldom changed except to become bureaucratic in nature. Their structures became rigid and in many cases they were unable to respond to new opportunities and problems. Increasingly, bureaucratic structures will be replaced by teams, business planning units, quality circles, or other groups of employees. These employee groups will form to work on specific issues and then disband when the issues are resolved. They can benefit the organization by providing quick, flexible assistance with no long-term, unproductive consequences. This group structuring will likely appeal to employees because it will offer them fast-paced work on specialized problems, giving their jobs more variety and interest.

Technology and Robotics. Will future technology and robotics replace the need for people in the hospitality industry? Most authorities think not. To date, computerization has helped the industry in those areas that require the fewest people to begin with. For example, front office, accounting, and purchasing departments have been computerized. However, the two most labor-intensive departments—food and beverage, and housekeeping—have not been greatly affected by computers. It's likely that we will be well into the next century before technology eliminates any significant number of positions in these departments.

The "high tech—high touch" concept has real meaning in our industry. Simply stated, many people believe that as technology decreases the amount of human interaction, the quality of person-to-person contact becomes more important than ever before. For example, although some properties have automated check-in machines, a front desk agent is still available. Some properties offer in-room check out but, again, front desk personnel are also available. Today's guests—and probably tomorrow's as well—believe that service is provided by people, not machines. As a result, the ability to deliver the "high touch" aspects of service will remain an important part of the way hospitality operations provide service.

Legal Issues. Tomorrow's supervisors will be confronted with even more legal challenges than their counterparts are today. Employees will increasingly use legal means when they believe they have been wronged. A variety of laws and regulations dealing with compensation, discrimination, safety, and other important matters establish limits within which supervisors must manage. Through education and training, supervisors will have to become more aware of how their organization's and their own personal liability are affected by their actions.

Conclusion

There is no question that the hospitality industry is changing. The wants and needs of consumers are changing, and these dictate what the commercial segment of the industry must do. Not-for-profit institutional food service operations are also changing. These operations are recognizing that keeping costs down requires the effective use of basic management principles.

Growth in the industry will create many unfilled positions. This will make organizations compete with each other for personnel. There will be increasing pressure to meet employees' needs on the job in order to retain them. The entry-level employees that supervisors will manage in the future probably will come to their jobs with higher expectations about the quality of their life at work. Supervisors will have to practice the best principles of management, human relations, and motivation to meet those expectations.

New technology will solve many of today's problems. Additional, better types of equipment, systems, and facilities will be available. Therefore, the supervisor of tomorrow must know and practice effective people-related skills while simultaneously learning how to manage new technologies. If a supervisor's job is difficult today, it will be even more so in the future. The principles of supervision discussed in this book must form the foundation on which new skills—some of which may not even be known today—can be built.

We hope that you are excited about the future of the hospitality industry and will want to become—or remain—a part of it. Don't be intimidated by the amount of knowledge, skills, and abilities that you will need in the future. Rather, take advantage of all the opportunities the hospitality industry has in store for you. In the process you will grow personally and professionally and be more than ready to meet tomorrow's challenges.

Endnotes

1. Many of the statistics cited in this section are found in *Workforce 2000: Work and Workers for the 21st Century, Executive Summary* (Indianapolis, Ind.: Hudson Institute, Inc., 1988).

Glossary

A

ABSOLUTE STANDARDS METHOD

An evaluation method in which the evaluator assesses each employee's work performance without regard to other employees. Generally, there are three popular approaches: the critical incidents approach, the weighted checklist approach, and the forced choice approach.

ACCOMMODATION

A conflict-management style usually practiced by supervisors with a low level of assertiveness and a high level of cooperation. This style typically leads to win-lose outcomes. Supervisors with this style accommodate the needs of others even if it means neglecting their own needs. Those who sacrifice their interests inevitably end up on the losing side of win-lose outcomes.

ACTIVE VOICE

In the active voice, the subject of the sentence does the acting. The active voice is usually stronger because it is more direct and uses fewer words than the passive voice. See Passive Voice.

AGENDA

A meeting plan listing when and where the meeting will take place, as well as the meeting's objectives and time limits for discussions.

ALTERNATIVE SCHEDULING

Scheduling staff to work hours different from the typical 9:00 A.M. to 5:00 P.M. workday. Variations include part-time and flexible hours, compressed work schedules, and job sharing.

ARBITRATION

A method of settling a dispute between managers and union representatives in which the parties sit down with an unbiased third party—an arbitrator—who reviews the dispute and makes whatever decisions he/she feels are necessary to resolve it. The parties involved must abide by those decisions.

AUTOCRATIC LEADERSHIP

A leadership style in which the supervisor retains as much power and decision-making authority as possible.

AVOIDANCE

A conflict-management style usually practiced by supervisors with low levels of assertiveness and cooperation. This style typically leads to lose-lose outcomes.

Avoidance behaviors include withdrawing, remaining "neutral," sidestepping, or postponing a confrontation.

B

BENCHMARK
A standard against which progress is measured or evaluated; a point of reference from which progress is measured or evaluated.

BONA FIDE OCCUPATIONAL QUALIFICATIONS (BFOQ)
A provision of the Civil Rights Act that allows an employer to hire people based on the need for a specific age, sex, religion, or national origin for the performance of a job.

BONDING
A type of insurance which will reimburse the company for thefts incurred by employees who misuse company funds.

BUREAUCRATIC LEADERSHIP
A leadership style in which the supervisor "manages by the book" and enforces rules, policies, regulations, and standard operating procedures.

C

CALL-BACK LIST
A list a supervisor keeps that includes the names of all talented internal and external applicants who are interested in positions in the supervisor's department. The list may contain names of former employees who may be willing to help out on a temporary basis.

CHANGE AGENT
A person responsible for planning, implementing, and evaluating changes within the work environment.

CLIQUE
A potentially harmful type of informal group, consisting of two or more members who place the group's goals ahead of the organization's goals.

CLOSED (DIRECT) QUESTIONS
Questions calling for very brief responses, usually requiring yes or no answers. Used to verify facts or cover a lot of ground quickly.

COMMAND GROUP
The most common type of formal work group, typically consisting of a manager, supervisors, and employees.

COMPARATIVE PERFORMANCE REVIEW METHODS

Performance review methods which involve comparing employees to each other. There are four types of comparative methods: the simple ranking approach, the alternative ranking approach, the paired comparison approach, and the forced distribution approach.

COMPETITION

A conflict-management style usually practiced by supervisors with a high level of assertiveness and a low level of cooperation. This style typically leads to win-lose outcomes. A supervisor with this style often attempts to dominate others by using authority to ensure that his/her needs are satisfied.

COMPRESSED SCHEDULES

Alternative work schedules which allow employees to work the equivalent of a standard workweek in less than the usual five days. A typical adaptation is a workweek consisting of four ten-hour days.

COMPROMISE

A conflict-management style usually practiced by supervisors with moderate levels of both assertiveness and cooperation. This style can lead to win-win, win-lose, or lose-lose outcomes, depending on how the parties in conflict view the compromise. Supervisors with this style respond to conflict by trying to meet some of the needs of everyone involved.

CONCEPTUAL SKILLS

One of the three critical supervisory skills. Conceptual skills are the intellectual skills supervisors need to perform their jobs well, including the ability to visualize problems, think of solutions, and make decisions.

CONTROLLING

The supervisory task of measuring actual results against expected results. Controlling also refers to safeguarding the operation's property and income.

COORDINATING

The supervisory task of assigning work and organizing people and resources to achieve the operation's objectives.

COUNSELING

A problem-solving technique which uses a one-on-one process to help employees solve their own problems. Job-related counseling concentrates on the employee's attitudes toward the job and the work environment. Non-job-related counseling involves personal problems not directly connected to work.

CROSS-TRAINING

A form of training in which employees are taught additional skills to fill the requirements of more than one position.

D

DAILY TIME LOG
A standard form used for keeping track of a supervisor's activities during the day.

DELEGATION
The supervisory task of assigning authority to employees to perform tasks or make decisions for which the supervisor is still accountable.

DEMOCRATIC LEADERSHIP
A leadership style in which the supervisor involves employees as much as possible in aspects of the job that affect them.

DIRECTING
The supervisory task of managing, scheduling, and disciplining employees. Directing includes such things as training and motivating employees.

DISCIPLINE
In a positive sense, discipline consists of those activities that correct, strengthen, and improve employee performance. Discipline may involve minor, on-the-job corrections, or may be built into a formal program with increasingly serious steps.

DISCRIMINATION
The practice of treating someone differently—usually wrongly—based on a factor such as the individual's race or nationality.

DOWNWARD COMMUNICATION
The passage of information from an organization's higher levels to its lower levels.

E

EMPATHY
The ability to see circumstances from the other's viewpoint or to understand the other's feelings.

ETHICS
Principles or standards about what is "right" and "wrong."

EVALUATING
The supervisory task of: (1) reviewing the operation's progress toward organizational goals, and (2) measuring employee performance against the organization's standards.

EXIT INTERVIEW
A meeting between an employee who's leaving the organization and an organization supervisor or manager (usually not the employee's immediate supervisor).

The meeting is held to discuss aspects of the job, the company, and the employee's reason for leaving.

EXTERNAL FORCES OF CHANGE
Social, economic, political, and legal conditions that drive change within an organization.

F

FALLACY OF OMNIPOTENCE
Also known as the "I can do it better myself" fallacy, this fallacy is often found among new supervisors. It is a supervisor's feeling that "No one else can do the job as well as I can." It is perhaps the greatest obstacle to delegation.

FEEDBACK
The reaction of a listener or reader to the verbal and non-verbal communication of a speaker or writer. Feedback may evaluate something the speaker/writer said or did, and may provide corrective information.

FIXED STAFF POSITIONS
Positions which must be filled regardless of the volume of business.

FLEX-TIME
A system of scheduling work hours that allows employees to vary their times of starting and ending work. There is usually a period of time during each shift (core time) when all employees must be present.

FORMAL AUTHORITY
The authority that comes with the position a person holds in the organization.

FORMAL COACHING
Coaching that is usually conducted privately, away from the work station. It focuses on knowledge, skills, or attitudes that negatively affect a large part of the employee's job performance. A formal coaching session may also be referred to as a performance improvement session.

FOUR-STEP TRAINING METHOD
An on-the-job training method based on the buddy system. The trainer works with the employee on a one-to-one basis, conducting training at the work station(s) the employee will use on the job. The four steps are: Prepare to train, conduct the training, coach trial performances, and follow through.

G

GENERAL PROPERTY ORIENTATION
Also known as new employee orientation, this type of orientation teaches new employees about the organization and its mission, policies, and procedures, using

videotapes, slides, and speakers. New employees also learn about fringe benefits and guest relations, and receive personnel forms and tours of the property.

GRAPEVINE

A term used to denote the means by which information passes between informal groups in an organization.

GROUP TRAINING

A training method used to provide the same skills or information to many employees at once. May include lectures, demonstration, role playing, conferences, or case studies.

H

HEIMLICH MANEUVER

A first aid technique that forces air through a choking person's lungs to dislodge an obstruction in the windpipe.

HUMAN RELATIONS SKILLS

One of the three critical supervisory skills. Human relations skills include all those abilities necessary to deal effectively with employees on a personal level (communication, leadership, understanding of how people work in groups, and so on).

HUMAN RESOURCES DEPARTMENT

Also known as personnel department, this department helps you define, identify, and recruit the type of employee your department needs, among other tasks. Human resources staff members are involved in virtually all aspects of every employee's work history with an organization.

I

INDEPENDENT LEARNING COURSES

A training method in which students read and study materials alone, usually on their own time. Students complete exams and submit them, to the organization offering the course, for feedback and credit.

INDICATORS OF EFFECTIVE CHANGE

Measurable, expected results that are used to evaluate the effectiveness of implemented changes in the work environment.

INFORMAL AUTHORITY

The power someone has because of his/her abilities, charisma, or other personal traits. Also referred to as personal authority.

INFORMAL COACHING

A type of coaching that is usually conducted at the employee's actual work station. It occurs in the course of normal day-to-day operations. It often is conducted to improve a skill, communicate a single piece of knowledge, or adjust an inappropriate behavior.

INTERNAL FORCES OF CHANGE
Conditions within a hospitality operation that drive change within the organization.

INTERNAL RECRUITING
A method organizations use to fill jobs quickly with applicants from within the organization.

INTERNSHIP PROGRAMS
Arrangements between a school and an employer which allow students to obtain actual work experience, often while earning school credit.

INVERTED PYRAMID
A style of writing which newspaper reporters and writers use. It involves putting the most important information at the beginning of a written piece, and leaving less important detail for the final paragraphs. Reporters write with the knowledge that readers may skip closing paragraphs, or that editors may delete them entirely to fit available space.

J

JOB BREAKDOWN
A set of written details describing how to perform each task of a job.

JOB DESCRIPTION
A written description used to define a job and its requirements.

JOB LIST
A list of tasks which an employee in a certain position must perform.

JOB SHARING
An alternative work schedule which allows two or more part-time employees to assume the responsibilities of one full-time job. The participants may be responsible for all duties of the job, or they may divide duties between them.

JOB SPECIFICATION
A selection tool which lists the personal qualities employees need to perform a job adequately.

L

LABOR UNION
An organization of workers formed for the purpose of advancing its members' interests in respect to wages, benefits, and working conditions.

LAISSEZ-FAIRE LEADERSHIP

A leadership style in which the supervisor maintains a hands-off policy and delegates to employees as much discretion and decision-making authority as possible.

LATERAL COMMUNICATION

The passage of information between peers, or members of the same level.

LATERAL TRANSFER

The transfer of a current employee from one section or department to another at the same level of responsibility.

LEAD TIME

The amount of time required to hire the best possible applicant for a position.

LEADERSHIP

The ability to attain objectives by working with and through people. A leader creates conditions that motivate employees by establishing goals and influencing employees to attain those goals.

LINE DEPARTMENT

A department which directly provides services or products to guests. Also called operating department.

LOSE-LOSE

An outcome of conflict in which no one involved satisfies all or even most of his/her needs. With a lose-lose outcome, the basic reasons for the conflict remain and conflict may recur.

M

MANAGEMENT

The process of using resources to attain organizational objectives.

MANAGEMENT BY OBJECTIVES (MBO) PERFORMANCE REVIEW METHOD

A method in which the evaluator works with the employee to determine a set of goals and how the employee will reach the goals. They then work together to establish evaluation procedures. Procedures in an MBO plan consist of four steps.

MEDIATION

A method of resolving disputes between managers and union representatives in which the disputing parties sit down with an unbiased third party—a mediator—who reviews the dispute and gives advice on how to resolve it. The mediator's advice does not have to be taken.

MEETING MINUTES

A record of the participants, events, and actions of a meeting.

MIRRORING

Exactly repeating a speaker's key words to show the speaker how a key word or phrase sounds. It indicates the listener's interest in the speaker's words and desire to understand them. Mirroring helps both you and the speaker determine the importance of any words the speaker uses. Also called re-stating.

MUTUAL PROBLEM-SOLVING

A conflict-management style usually practiced by supervisors with high levels of assertiveness and cooperation. This style typically leads to win-win outcomes. Supervisors with this style resolve conflict by accepting the needs of others and negotiating solutions that meet all or almost all of the needs of everyone involved.

N

NETWORKING

The use of personal contacts, such as friends, peers at other properties, business associates, vendors, service personnel, and others, to help locate potential applicants for job openings.

NON-PROGRAMMED DECISION-MAKING METHODS

Decision-making methods used for non-routine decisions or problems that call for the use of reasoning, judgment, creativity, intuition, and past experiences.

NON-VERBAL COMMUNICATION (BODY LANGUAGE)

The gestures and body movements a person uses, including facial expression, eye contact or movement, and posture. Our body language may contradict our words or reveal information we don't intend to reveal. We can hear certain types of non-verbal communication, such as laughter, weeping, whistling, or tone of voice.

O

OCCUPATIONAL SAFETY AND HEALTH ADMINISTRATION (OSHA)

A federal agency responsible for developing and managing regulations and standards for employee safety and health in the workplace.

ON-THE-JOB TRAINING (OJT)

Training in which trainees learn job procedures while watching, talking with, and helping an experienced employee. The four-step training method is a popular OJT method.

OPEN-ENDED (INDIRECT) QUESTIONS

Questions that permit the applicant to respond in a free, unstructured way. Such questions are broad and ask for responses of more than just a few words.

ORGANIZING

The supervisory activity that attempts to best assemble and use limited human and other resources to attain organizational objectives. It involves establishing the flow of authority and communication among people.

OUTLINE

A list of significant points someone makes before starting to write a memo, letter, or report. It helps the writer to organize his/her thoughts before actually starting to write.

P

PARAPHRASING

Using your own words to re-state what a speaker is saying, or to reflect the content of the sender's message as well as the feeling behind the content. Paraphrasing helps to clarify what the speaker is saying. It also helps the speaker, because a paraphrase reveals how the speaker's message sounds to others.

PASSIVE VOICE

Verbs in the passive voice are easy to identify. The main verb is always in the past tense, such as *made, found,* or *decided.* A form of *be* always appears before the past tense, as in *will be made, was found, has been decided.* Passive verbs may be colorless because their subjects are acted upon; they do not act themselves. Even though the passive voice is grammatically correct, it is usually weaker. Furthermore, the passive voice often uses too many words, and it may sound bureaucratic or self-important. See Active Voice.

PERFORMANCE EVALUATION

A periodic evaluation of an employee by a supervisor or manager. The supervisor/manager and employee together evaluate job performance and discuss steps the employee can take to improve job skills and performance.

PERFORMANCE IMPROVEMENT PLAN

During or following performance evaluations, the evaluator and employee prepare practical, time-oriented, and specific actions and approaches the employee will take to improve job performance.

PERFORMANCE STANDARD

A required level of performance that establishes the quality of work that must be done.

PERSONNEL FILE

A file of an employee's records used in making employment-related decisions, usually kept for all employees in a central location, such as the human resources department.

PLANNING

The supervisory task of creating objectives and action plans to reach those objectives. Planning should be done before other supervisory tasks.

POSITIVE REINFORCEMENT

Rewards in the form of praise, compensation, or other incentives. Positive reinforcement can be a powerful tool in an ongoing positive discipline program. It tends to increase the likelihood of acceptable behavior and decrease the likelihood of unacceptable behavior. In order for positive reinforcement to work, the reward being offered must be timely, frequent, and meaningful to the affected employee.

PRODUCTIVITY STANDARD

An acceptable amount of work that must be done within a specific time frame according to an established performance standard.

PROGRAMMED DECISION-MAKING METHOD

Decision-making that relies on procedure manuals, staffing guides, job descriptions, and so on to handle routine problems.

PROGRESSIVE DISCIPLINE PROGRAMS

Discipline programs that involve several steps as follows: (1) an oral warning; (2) an oral warning, possibly followed up by a written, filed warning; (3) an official written reprimand placed in the employee's file; (4) a suspension of a few hours or several days without pay; (5) a disciplinary transfer or demotion; (6) a "one last chance" step immediately before termination; and, finally, (7) termination of employment.

R

RECRUITMENT

The process by which qualified applicants are sought and screened to fill currently or soon-to-be vacant positions. The process involves announcing or advertising job vacancies and evaluating applicants to determine whom to hire.

RESISTANCE TO CHANGE

The tendency of individuals to maintain established routines.

RISK MANAGEMENT

Programs designed to discover and remedy risky situations at a property (unsecured stair rails, flammable materials, etc.) and to prevent accidents. Risk management involves more than purchasing insurance.

RUMOR MILL

A term used to describe how informal groups may generate and communicate unconfirmed information in an organization.

S

SELF-DISCLOSURE STATEMENTS
Statements you can use to show a speaker how you feel about what he/she said. When you report experiences or feelings similar to the speaker's, it shows that the speaker is not the only one to think or feel a certain way.

SELF-ESTEEM
Confident, positive feelings about oneself; self-respect.

SEXUAL HARASSMENT
Conduct that is (1) sexual in nature, and (2) unwelcome. Sexual harassment may be physical, verbal (including suggestive comments), or visual (for example, displaying pornographic photographs).

SPECIFIC JOB ORIENTATION
Orientation that teaches the new employee how to do the specific job for which he/she was hired. The employee also learns how the job relates to other jobs and how to use applicable equipment. The employee may receive a job description, an organization chart, and a performance evaluation form.

SPECIFIC QUESTIONS
Questions that begin with words like *who, what, where, when, why, which.* They seek additional information about unclear statements or ask for specific details when the speaker has provided only general information.

STABILIZING FORCES
Conditions that create continuity within an organization and work in opposition to external and internal forces of change.

STAFF DEPARTMENT
A department that provides support and advice to line or operating departments. It doesn't directly provide services or products to guests.

STAFFING
The supervisory activity of recruiting and hiring employees.

STAFFING GUIDE
A system used to establish the number of workers needed.

SUBSTANCE ABUSE
The consumption of drugs (including alcohol) to the point where an individual's health and personal and professional life are negatively affected.

SUMMARIZING STATEMENTS
Statements that condense parts of what the speaker said and stress important points. Use them to focus attention on a certain topic, to show that you agree on

specific points, to guide the speaker to another part of the subject, and to reach agreement on specific points in order to end the conversation.

SUPERVISOR

Someone who manages entry-level or other employees who do not have supervisory responsibilities.

T

TASK GROUP

A type of formal work group, created to carry out non-routine tasks in an organization. Sometimes made up of supervisors and employees working together.

TECHNICAL SKILLS

One of the three critical supervisory skills. These skills form the basic work behaviors of any job. For example, technical skills required of a food server are basic math, good eye-hand coordination, balance, strong communications, etc.

TERMINATION

An ending of a worker's employment.

TIME ROBBERS

People or activities that require time but do not contribute to reaching the organization's objectives. Time robbers can be divided into two categories: those the supervisor generates or those that others generate.

TITLE VII

A section in the amended Civil Rights Act of 1964 that guarantees the right of an individual to work in an environment free from discrimination based on race, sex, religion, or national origin. Title VII also deals with some aspects of employee selection.

TO-DO LISTS

Lists supervisors may create each day to help them determine and set priorities for tasks that must be done. To-do lists can be kept in pocket-size notebooks, legal pads, on pre-printed forms, or in other formats.

TOPIC SENTENCE

A sentence—or main point—that shows what a paragraph is about. Using the topic sentence as a guideline, the writer logically develops the rest of the paragraph.

TRAINING

A process that provide employees with the knowledge or experience necessary to perform tasks required of their positions.

TURNOVER

The rate at which an organization or work unit loses employees.

U

UPWARD COMMUNICATION
The passage of information from an organization's lower levels to its higher levels.

V

VARIABLE STAFF POSITIONS
Positions which are filled in relation to changes in business volume.

W

WEEKLY PLANNING GUIDES
Guides supervisors use to help them allocate time for the most important activities, projects, and persons they must attend to during the week. Guides can be pre-printed forms, or a supervisor can create them to meet his/her unique needs.

WIN-LOSE
An outcome of conflict in which one party's needs are satisfied while those of the other party or parties are not. A win-lose outcome typically fails to address all of the problems that created the conflict, so future conflict may arise over the same or similar problems.

WIN-WIN
An outcome of conflict in which the needs of all parties are satisfied and the conflict is resolved. To reach a win-win outcome, those in conflict must acknowledge each other's needs and work together to resolve the situation so that everyone benefits.

Index

HOSPITALITY SUPERVISION

REVIEW QUIZ ANSWER KEY

The numbers in parentheses refer to the page(s) where the answer may be found.

Chapter 1	Chapter 2	Chapter 3	Chapter 4
1. T (5)	1. T (23)	1. T (60)	1. F (81–82)
2. T (7)	2. F (29)	2. T (61)	2. T (88)
3. T (6)	3. F (31)	3. F (63)	3. T (88)
4. F (11, 12)	4. F (33)	4. T (63)	4. F (92)
5. T (13)	5. T (36)	5. T (64)	5. F (93)
6. F (14)	6. T (37)	6. T (68)	6. F (94)
7. T (15)	7. F (40)	7. F (71)	7. T (97)
8. F (16)	8. T (47)	8. F (71, 73)	8. F (94–95)
9. F (16–17)	9. F (50)	9. F (75)	9. F (101)
10. F (16)	10. F (54)	10. F (76–77)	10. F (103)
11. a (5)	11. a (31)	11. a (61)	11. b (93)
12. b (5)	12. b (47–48)	12. a (63)	12. b (94)
13. a (6–7)	13. b (28)	13. b (70)	13. b (94)
14. c (11)	14. c (29)	14. d (63)	14. c (81–82)
15. c (15)	15. b (32)	15. c (70)	15. b (90-91)

Chapter 5	Chapter 6	Chapter 7	Chapter 8
1. F (110)	1. T (134)	1. F (155)	1. T (171)
2. F (110)	2. T (134)	2. T (156)	2. T (172)
3. T (114)	3. T (134)	3. F (160)	3. F (172)
4. F (120)	4. T (135)	4. F (160–161)	4. F (174)
5. F (122)	5. T (135)	5. F (162)	5. T (175–176)
6. T (124)	6. F (136)	6. F (163)	6. F (176)
7. T (126)	7. F (138)	7. F (163)	7. F (179)
8. T (126)	8. T (141)	8. T (164)	8. T (183)
9. F (129)	9. T (146)	9. F (164)	9. T (184)
10. F (129)	10. F (148)	10. T (165–166)	10. F (187)
11. a (113)	11. b (138)	11. a (156)	11. b (175)
12. a (120)	12. b (142)	12. b (156)	12. b (181)
13. a (125)	13. b (145)	13. b (164)	13. a (188–189)
14. a (113)	14. b (149)	14. a (158)	14. c (172)
15. c (129)	15. c (150)	15. b (166)	15. a (177)

Chapter 9	Chapter 10	Chapter 11	Chapter 12
1. T (194)	1. F (215)	1. T (229)	1. T (247)
2. Г (195)	2. T (215)	2. F (229)	2. F (248)
3. F (198)	3. F (216)	3. F (232)	3. T (248)
4. F (198)	4. T (218)	4. T (235)	4. F (251)
5. F (200)	5. F (218)	5. F (238)	5. F (251)
6. F (200)	6. T (219)	6. F (239)	6. T (253)
7. T (200–201)	7. F (222)	7. F (241)	7. T (254)
8. T (203)	8. F (222)	8. T (242)	8. F (255)
9. F (208)	9. T (223)	9. F (243)	9. F (255)
10. F (210)	10. T (225)	10. T (243)	10. F (255)
11. a (195)	11. b (215)	11. b (231–232)	11. b (250)
12. a (204)	12. a (223–224)	12. b (233)	12. b (251)
13. b (211)	13. a (224–225)	13. b (239)	13. a (251)
14. c (193)	14. d (216)	14. d (230)	14. b (252)
15. d (199)	15. b (221)	15. b (237)	15. c (253)

Chapter
13

1. T (259)
2. F (260)
3. F (260)
4. T (260)
5. F (261)
6. F (261)
7. T (262–263)
8. T (267)
9. T (267–268)
10. F (268)
11. b (261)
12. a (264)
13. b (266)
14. d (262)
15. b (263–264)